The UK Social Policy Process

**Catherine Bochel and
Hugh M. Bochel**

First published 2004 by
PALGRAVE MACMILLAN
Houndmills, Basingstoke, Hampshire RG21 6XS and
175 Fifth Avenue, New York, N.Y. 10010
Companies and representatives throughout the world

PALGRAVE MACMILLAN is the global academic imprint of the Palgrave
Macmillan division of St. Martin's Press, LLC and of Palgrave Macmillan Ltd.
Macmillan® is a registered trademark in the United States, United Kingdom
and other countries. Palgrave is a registered trademark in the European
Union and other countries.

ISBN 0–333–75340–2 hardback
ISBN 0–333–75341–0 paperback

This book is printed on paper suitable for recycling and made from fully
managed and sustained forest sources.

A catalogue record for this book is available from the British Library.

Library of Congress Cataloging-in-Publication Data
Bochel, Catherine.
  The UK social policy process / Catherine Bochel and Hugh M. Bochel.
    p.   cm.
  Includes bibliographical references and index.
  ISBN 0–333–75340–2 (cloth)
  1. Great Britain—Social policy—1979– 2. Great Britain—Politics and
government—1945– 3. Policy sciences. I. Bochel, Hugh M. II. Title.

  HN385.5B56 2003
  361.6′1′0941—dc22   2003059511

10   9   8   7   6   5   4   3   2   1
13 12 11 10 09 08 07 06 05 04

Printed and bound in Great Britain by
Creative Print & Design (Wales), Ebbw Vale

THE UK SOCIAL POLICY PROCESS

Also by Catherine Bochel

The Careers of Councillors

Also by Hugh M. Bochel

Parliament and Welfare Policy
Scotland Decides: The Devolution Issue and the Scottish Referendum
The Careers of Councillors

For Alistair and Isobel

Contents

List of Exhibits, Figures and Tables

Exhibits

Figures

Tables

Preface

This book developed from our teaching and research interests and in particular from concerns about the importance of the policy process in influencing and affecting social policies and their impacts. The book itself arose from a view that whilst there were some good public policy texts and a wide range of journal articles dealing with this topic there was relatively little available which could easily be applied to social policy. What we have sought to do here is to examine some of the main contemporary debates over the policy process and social policy using conceptual frameworks and recent developments in both policies and the policy process. Whilst the range of concepts and influences is, given the subject matter, inevitably disparate, the thread that runs through the work can perhaps be characterised as an examination of the different ways in which power can be and is exercised on social policies throughout the policy process, from formulation through to implementation and evaluation. It is intended to provide theoretical understanding through which the policy process can be better analysed and understood. We hope that this book will therefore be of particular interest to students of social and public policy and to professionals whose work may well reflect many of the influences discussed here.

Although this work is our responsibility we would like to thank the two anonymous reviewers whose constructive observations informed the final shape of the book. We are also grateful to our editors at Palgrave Macmillan: Catherine Gray, both for listening to our idea initially and for her support throughout the project, and Kate Wallis for her enthusiastic encouragement as the writing came to an end. Finally, we must thank our students who have contributed to our thoughts on this work, and in particular those who read and commented on various drafts.

CATHERINE BOCHEL AND HUGH BOCHEL
University of Lincoln

Acknowledgements

The authors and publishers wish to thank the following for permission to reproduce copyright material:

Arnstein, S, 'A Ladder of Citizen Participation', *Journal of the American Institute of Planners*, vol. 35 (1969). Reproduced with permission of the Journal of the American Planning Association.

Crown copyright material is reproduced with the permission of the Controller of HMSO and the Queen's Printer for Scotland.

Flinders, M, 'Mechanisms of Judicial Accountability', *Parliamentary Affairs*, 54/1 (2001) p. 61. Reproduced with permission of Oxford University Press.

Hall, W and Weir, S (1996) *The Untouchables: Power and Accountability in the Quango State*. Reproduced with permission of The Democratic Audit.

Jones, B, Kavanagh, D, Norton, P and Moran, M, *Politics UK* (4th edition). © Pearson Education Limited 2000, reprinted by permission of Pearson Education Limited.

Lindblom, C E, 'The Science of "Muddling Through"', *Public Administration Review*, vol. 19 (1959). Reproduced with permission of Blackwell Publishing.

Pinkerton, J, Higgins, K and Devine, P (2000), *Family Support – Linking Project Evaluation to Policy Analysis*. Reproduced with permission of Dr J R Pinkerton.

Saunders, P, 'Rethinking Local Politics' in M Boddy and C Fudge (eds) *Local Socialism* (1984). Reproduced with permission of Peter Saunders.

Skelcher, C (1998) *The Appointed State*. Reproduced by permission of Open University Press.

Every effort has been made to trace the copyright holders but if any have been inadvertently overlooked the publishers will be pleased to make the necessary arrangement at the first opportunity.

Introduction

One of the key characteristics of the study of social policy is its interdisciplinary nature, drawing upon subjects such as economics, history, sociology and politics. It also embraces a variety of approaches. These include the exploration of social issues, such as the ageing population or community care, or social problems, for instance, crime, poverty and unemployment; the consideration of particular social groups, such as children or homeless people, or those in isolated rural areas; and examination of the main services: education, health care, housing, personal social services and social security. Given the dynamic nature of the subject, these and other methods are constantly developing. Yet the emphasis has, until recently, continued to lie largely in examinations of policies as responses to problems and demands, and the description and evaluation of those policies, rather than through insights that might emerge from wider consideration of the policy process. This book therefore seeks to present the analysis of the policy process as one means of encouraging a broad approach to the subject matter, drawing upon a wide range of concepts and models that can help us to contextualise, understand and explain developments from a perspective that provides, to some extent, an alternative consideration of the exercise of power in contemporary society.

As discussed in greater detail in Chapter 1, some of the mechanisms which the Conservative governments of 1979 to 1997 utilised in their attempts to reform social policy, such as the greater use of competition and the market, including internal markets in welfare services, the increased emphasis on managers as opposed to professionals, and the extension of techniques such as audit and inspection, helped draw attention to the importance of these developments for social policy. Following the election of the Labour government in 1997 a host of new terms, including 'joined-up government', 'partnership', 'evidence-based policy', 'modernisation' and 'democratic renewal' not only became familiar, but continued to direct attention at the importance of the processes of policy making and implementation in social welfare. At the same time, many of the reforms introduced in the early years of the Labour government, such as devolution to Northern Ireland, Scotland and Wales, and the passage of the Human Rights Act, further encouraged analysts to re-examine the policy process and its importance not only for the practice of social policy but also for adding to our understanding of key topics.

Using this book

Each of the chapters in this book provides information that can be used in an examination of the processes of policy formulation, implementation and evaluation as they relate to social policy. Whilst in general the book is designed to be read sequentially, clearly at any one time some chapters will be more relevant than others, depending upon the reader's existing knowledge and their current interests. However, a fundamental point is that there are important inter-relationships between many of the ideas and structures that are contained in the separate chapters. In particular, many of the ideas in the later chapters can be interpreted and better understood by utilising those from earlier chapters. For example, the perspectives on bureaucracies introduced in Chapter 2, and the insights from public choice theories discussed in Chapter 3, might be applied in an analysis of the role and influence of the civil service as discussed in Chapter 4, to some parts of local government in Chapter 5, or to welfare bureaucracies more generally, including large parts of the National Health Service (NHS). Used in this way, the level of knowledge and understanding that can be gained from combining insights from different chapters is thus designed to be greater than the knowledge that arises from treating each chapter on its own.

The book is also designed to be used to help analyse and understand case study material, with the reader applying ideas, concepts and models as appropriate, to develop personal interpretations and understanding of the policy process and social policy. Included amongst the chapters are therefore a number of 'Figures' and 'Exhibits'. The Figures provide a variety of examples of the ideas that can be applied to the policy process and the exercise of power, whilst the Exhibits draw upon real-world examples to illustrate the applicability of certain ideas to contemporary social policy. Following a similar line of reasoning, and emphasising the frequent very real value of consulting original work, the Further Reading suggested at the end of each chapter in a number of instances, together with many of the references, refers readers to the original and sometimes distinctive sources, rather than to the often readable and enlightening secondary analysis of those.

Chapter 1 seeks to provide an underpinning for the remainder of the book. It considers the reasons for exploring the key role of the policy process in social policy, together with the parameters of policy analysis and associated fields such as public administration and public management. It explores the type of developments that occurred under the Conservatives during the 1980s and 1990s, noted briefly above, that helped focus attention not solely on their policies and the outcomes of these but also on the importance of the process in affecting the development of policies. It also outlines the intellectual challenges, perhaps most notably from the 'New Right' and from rational choice theory, which emerged for the traditional approaches during this period, some of which are examined in greater depth in the following chapters.

The book then moves on to a consideration of the key concepts, theories and models that can be used to aid our comprehension of the policy process, including through their application to some of the topics considered in later chapters. Chapter 2 introduces a variety of perspectives that can heighten our understanding, including different interpretations of the ways in which power can be exercised, with the introduction of the three dimensions or faces of power and models of 'rational' and 'incremental' decision making. This chapter also considers analyses of the role of bureaucracies, often of great but underestimated importance in social policy, and the implications of these for our understanding of power, decision making and the use of resources. Chapter 3 maintains the focus on power, examining different theoretical approaches to understanding the distribution of power within society, from those which see power as being widely dispersed to those which see it as being largely exercised by small groups, or elites. Similarly, the lessons that can be learnt from the application of Marxist and public choice analyses are explored in this chapter. These ideas can in turn be used in the consideration of the concerns of the later chapters, with, for example, interpretation from pluralist and Marxist perspectives being used to inform our understanding of the role of elected representative bodies, including parliament and local government, in Chapters 4 and 5, and notions of participation in Chapter 6.

Chapters 4, 5 and 6 are largely concerned with 'structural' features, reflecting to some extent the importance of institutions as noted in Chapter 3, but also drawing upon some of the insights that the earlier discussion provides.

Chapter 4 outlines and analyses some of the key features of central government in the United Kingdom (UK), clearly important in the making of social policy, but also more or less directly responsible for policy implementation in areas such as health, income maintenance and employment, as well as more generally given the greater willingness of the Treasury to intervene in social policy in recent years. It also considers the role of the judiciary, which has been further increased by the passage of the Human Rights Act and the greater willingness to use legal processes as means of challenging the actions of public bodies.

Chapter 5 examines the newer tiers of decision making that are now relevant to social policy, including the European Union and the devolved administrations established in Scotland, Wales and Northern Ireland, each of which has arguably started to exert new pressures on the development of social policies which may, in time, lead to greater diversity within the United Kingdom. Local government is also covered under this chapter, since, despite over twenty years of pressure from central government, it remains a significant player in some areas of welfare provision, particularly social care and education, as well as having a strategic and sometimes still an important providing role with regard to housing. Here the importance of central–local relations is analysed, together with the implications of these for social policy.

The concern of Chapter 6 is an area which has not generally been widely covered in social policy analyses, that of quasi-governmental organisations, or quangos. Particularly from the 1970s bodies such as these have been widely used by successive governments, despite frequent promises by the main political parties when in Opposition to reform or abolish them, and they, or organisations like them, are increasingly playing a significant role in social policy. This chapter considers the reasons for the continued importance of quasi-governmental bodies, despite frequently expressed concerns about them, particularly over the 'democratic deficit', with the use of appointed rather than elected members of local authorities.

In Chapter 7 a central concern of social policy, participation, is examined in relation to the policy process. It considers different approaches to participation and the mechanisms that have been utilised in attempts to realise this as a goal. The role of pressure groups, previously outlined in the discussion of pluralism in Chapter 3, and concepts such as voluntarism and the 'active citizen', are discussed in relation to the social policy goals of governments.

Chapter 8 deals with evaluation, arguably always an important aspect of social policy, even if more often neglected than put into practice, but which has become more central, at least in terms of official rhetoric, under Labour since 1997. The chapter outlines different methods of evaluation and the uses to which evaluation has been put, including the now widespread use of performance indicators and targets. The place of policy transfer in the making of social policy is also discussed here. As throughout the book, connections can be made to other chapters, with, for example, policy transfer sometimes being linked to rational approaches to policy making, outlined in Chapter 2. The book concludes with a brief consideration of some of the lessons for social policy that can be learned from developments since 1979.

As with other perspectives on social policy, an approach grounded in the policy process is ever-changing, as evidenced by much of the discussion in this volume. However, it is perhaps possible to make a broad generalisation that over the past 25 years we have witnessed a move from what might be called the *government* of social policy to a position that is sometimes summarised as the *governance* of social policy. This change in phraseology reflects what has often been seen as a decline in the power of governments over the policy process, with more actors becoming involved, boundaries between public and private spheres becoming blurred and more tiers of government. Instead, it can be argued that we have moved to a more complex situation where it is more difficult for governments to take a top-down approach to policy making and implementation and it is more necessary to recognise the processes of consultation, exchange and the bringing together of resources and interests required for the exercise of power in contemporary society. However, this itself brings further implications for the making and implementation of social policies.

Social Policy and Social Policy Analysis

CHAPTER OVERVIEW

This chapter outlines the development of interest in social policy analysis and the benefits to our understanding that can arise from this approach. In particular, changes that occurred under the Conservatives from 1979 to 1997 are highlighted in order to provide a setting against which developments under Labour since 1997 can be better analysed and understood. The variety of meanings and interpretations of terms such as 'social policy' and 'policy analysis' are outlined as a background to the core of the book, whilst links, overlaps and differences with the analysis of public policy are also examined. A number of intellectual challenges to the subject that have emerged from the 1980s onwards are discussed.

Whilst the contents of this book are wide-ranging, discussing both theoretical perspectives on and real-world examples of social policy, at its heart might be said to lie a consideration of who has power and how it is used and applied in social policy. Arguably it is impossible to take a considered overview of social policy without some consideration of this important question. The key concern of this book is therefore to examine the processes by which social policies are formulated, implemented and evaluated.

The book considers who has power in the making of social policy and the different ways in which power can be exercised. It therefore looks at models of agenda-setting, policy and decision making and at the various actors in the policy process, including politicians, bureaucrats and managers, and at the operation of different levels and forms of government, such as central government, local government and quasi-government. However, it seeks to go beyond a concern with who makes decisions to consider the entire policy process from the formulation of policies to their implementation and evaluation.

Why look at social policy making?

> Social policy uses political power to supersede, supplement or modify operations of the economic system in order to achieve results which the economic system could not achieve on its own. (Marshall, 1975, p. 15)

This quotation gives us a clear direction; it not only serves as a reminder that social policy can have a significant effect on people's lives but also refers explicitly to the use of political power. Recognition of this aspect of social policy implies the need to examine the *policy process* from the point of view of the exercise of power and influence as well as the development of policies. In other words, even if we have a solid grasp of particular social policies and their outcomes, perhaps including their impact upon different social groups or upon society as a whole, we none the less have to recognise and understand the relationship with politics and in particular the exercise of *power*. That power is of central importance to social policy and the provision of welfare is aptly demonstrated by the title that Beveridge himself gave to his autobiography, *Power and Influence* (1953), and his recognition that the theme of the title was 'the chief alternative ways by which things get done in the world of affairs' (p. 3).

From the 1980s the study of social policy has developed rapidly for a variety of reasons. These include what was seen by some as a 'crisis' of the welfare state and the impact of new and different critiques of welfare, such as those from the 'New Right', feminists, black people and disabled people, all of which had important implications not only for the delivery of social policies and welfare but also for the way in which we see the subject. For example, there is now more attention paid to the way in which needs and dependencies are created and reinforced, including by society and social policies. Similarly what Cahill (1994) termed the 'new' areas of social policy, such as food, transport and the environment, have frequently been accorded more attention than was previously the case, and links from these increasingly made to 'old' social policy issues. The rapid expansion of comparative social policy has greatly increased our knowledge of the welfare systems of other countries; Britain is no longer seen as unique in providing comprehensive welfare, and different models of welfare from around the world are now used in social policy. In addition, due in part to the long period of Conservative government from 1979 to 1997, there has also been a major shift in emphasis and awareness away from a concern with state welfare and the welfare state towards looking beyond the state, to the role of individuals, the voluntary sector and the private sector, in the provision of welfare. However, importantly for this book, there are a number of issues around this. For example, whilst the state may traditionally have had little involvement in some areas of welfare provision (such as child care for young children) there may be much to be learnt from examining the reasons for its absence from these areas, and we should also recognise that the state may be as important in its policies and lack of policies as in what it provides. There is, for instance, considerable debate about the extent to which it is possible for the state to regulate and control public services without owning and providing them directly. This book will therefore inevitably have a focus upon government and the state, although it will take account of 'non-state' activities and areas of social policy.

Despite these advances there are arguably a number of weaknesses remaining in much of the academic study of social policy. In particular, for the purposes of this book, the study of social policy tends to have concentrated (albeit for understandable reasons) on deliberate decisions and policies (legislation being an obvious pointer here), and on the impact of social policies. This means that there is a tendency to neglect alternatives that are excluded, deliberately or otherwise, from the policy-making process, and the reasons for such exclusions. Less attention has been given to areas in which the state has shown relatively little interest, such as child care for young children, and to exploring the reasons for the lack of positive policies. Social policy as a subject has therefore tended to neglect consideration of the processes of policy formulation and what the study of these can tell us about the way in which power to influence policies is distributed and exercised. Whilst this is to some extent inevitable, given that individuals can only have a limited breadth of knowledge and expertise, there is room for a greater appreciation of these issues and their implications for the understanding and development of social policy, as illustrated by Exhibit 1.1.

EXHIBIT 1.1   ANALYSING THE POLICY PROCESS: QUALITY ASSURANCE IN HIGHER EDUCATION

Salter and Tapper provide an elegant example of the ability to make links between the role and impact of ideology and the policy process, using what they term the discourse of quality assurance in higher education. They note the transition in higher education since the 1960s, from a position where the autonomy of both institutions and individual academics was seen as the cardinal principle to a situation where the governance of the two main activities of higher education – teaching and research – have been brought significantly closer to control by state bureaucrats and politicians. This, they suggest, has occurred through the development of arguments about the need for public accountability and the imposition of mechanisms of audit for research (the Research Assessment Exercise) and teaching (the Quality Assurance Agency and its work). These can be linked to the growth of a view within governments about the economic ideology of education – that education is an economic resource that should be used to maximise its contribution to the country's economic development. However, they note that during the 1960s and 1970s the Department for Education and Science lacked the bureaucratic power to change the situation, particularly given the 'historically entrenched interest of the academic profession' (p. 70). It was only with the election of the New Right influenced Conservative governments, the development of the new public management and the growth of mass higher education that the discourse shifted to enable an outright challenge to the traditional orthodoxy, at least in part, through support for consumerism, the market and the emergence of an 'audit culture' in higher education. In addition they note a change in power relations with a decrease in power for academics and an increase in power for managers, and for intermediate organisations such as the Quality Assurance Agency.

B Salter and T Tapper, 'The Politics of Governance in Higher Education: The Case of Quality Assurance', *Political Studies*, vol. 48 (2000), pp. 66–87.

What is policy?

But what is policy? There is considerable disagreement on this. It has been described as 'whatever governments choose to do or not to do' (Dye, 1984, p. 1) and as 'a course of action or inaction rather than specific decisions or actions' (Heclo, 1972, p. 85). Hill (1997a) builds upon Easton's (1953, 1965) view that whilst policy may sometimes involve one decision, more often 'it involves either groups of decisions or what may be seen as little more than an orientation' (p. 7) and notes that this leads to an increasingly complex set of implications and understanding of the use of the term 'policy'. Other writers also argue that we need to take much more into account, such as 'non-decisions' or 'the mobilisation of bias', as discussed in Chapter 2.

However, Anderson (1997) prefers a conceptualisation of policy that emphasises actions rather than intentions: 'A relatively stable, purposive course of action followed by an actor or set of actors in dealing with a problem or matter of concern' (p. 9). He argues that this differentiates between decisions, following which there may be no action, and policy. An alternative approach is taken by systems theory (for example, Easton, 1965), which argues that political activity can be analysed in terms of a system containing a number of processes which need to be kept in balance if the system is to survive. According to proponents of this view we need to look at the environment in which the political system operates and which contains a number of other systems, including social systems and ecological systems. At its most basic, there are a range of inputs to the political system which are converted into outputs, including policies, which themselves have an impact upon the wider economic, political and social environment and may again lead, directly or indirectly, to new inputs. Whilst there are a number of strengths and weaknesses with this approach it does suggest that policy analysts do have to consider the social, economic and political contexts within which problems are tackled.

It is certainly true that most of us talk happily about 'policy' and 'policies'. But, reflecting the definitional difficulties discussed above, what do we mean when we use these words? We may be clear about the usage in each particular instance, but can we then be sure that we are using them consistently? For example, Hogwood and Gunn (1984) identify ten uses of the term 'policy', as:

1. A label for a field of activity – this is used, for example, in broad statements about 'economic policy' or 'social policy', as well as to more specific areas such as pensions policy, education policy, transport policy, health policy or housing policy.
2. An expression of general purpose or desired state of affairs – such as the statement in Labour's 1997 election manifesto that 'An explicit objective of a Labour government will be to raise the trend rate of growth by strengthening our wealth-creating base. We will nurture investment in industry, skills, infrastructure and new technologies. And we will attack long-term unemployment, especially among young people. Our goal will be educational and employment opportunities for all' (Labour Party, 1997, p. 11).

3. Specific proposals – in its 1997 manifesto *Because Britain Deserves Better*, Labour undertook to hold referendums for devolution to Scotland and Wales and then to introduce a Scottish Parliament and a Welsh Assembly; other specific proposals may arise out of short-term or *ad hoc* problems or opportunities, such as the hospital bed shortages that frequently occurred in the winter months during the 1990s, with governments feeling obliged to respond in some manner.

4. Decisions of government – these may frequently be more immediate responses to domestic or international challenges or opportunities, such as the Conservative governments' responses to the BSE (bovine spongiform encephalopathy) cattle crisis in the 1990s. In the UK, governments can generally be fairly sure about getting formal ratification through Parliament because of their overall majorities in the House of Commons, and these are widely seen as one form of 'policy'.

5. Formal authorisation, perhaps reflected in a specific piece of legislation – however, the passage of an Act does not ensure that the activities will then take place. For example, the full requirements of the 1986 Disabled Persons' (Services, Consultation and Representation) Act were never implemented, partly as the government had fears about the full costs and implications of the legislation.

6. A programme – a relatively specific sphere of government activity, such as community care in the 1980s and 1990s, or within that the intention to run down long-term psychiatric hospitals, both of which could be referred to as 'policies'.

7. Output – what government delivers – these may be varied in nature, from examples such as payment of social security benefits, through reductions in class sizes to tax cuts or increases.

8. Outcome – what is achieved – here the distinction with outputs may often be hard to make. However, the study of outcomes involves an assessment of whether the policy is achieving its stated aims, as opposed to a focus on what is actually delivered.

9   A theory or model – policies involve assumptions about cause and effect. In 1979, in the new Conservative government's first budget, the then Chancellor of the Exchequer, Geoffrey Howe, argued that 'Public expenditure is at the heart of Britain's present economic difficulties' (HM Treasury, 1979, p. 1), the assumption clearly being that reductions in public expenditure would improve the country's economic performance. On a rather different note, Labour's 1997 manifesto claimed that 'In a global economy the route to growth is stability not inflation. The root causes of inflation and low growth are the same – an economic and industrial base that remains weak... Our goals are low inflation, rising living standards and high and stable levels of employment' (Labour Party, 1997, p. 11). Both of these statements make assumptions that if governments do one thing, then another will happen. Yet in practice the causal relationships are generally more complex than this, and other factors have a major impact on the success or failure of policy.

10. A process – policy making and implementation is a continuous process: it cannot easily be analysed through the examination of specific decisions, and the introduction of one policy may itself have implications for others. Those who study social policy need to be aware of this and to take account of the complex and longitudinal nature of the process.

From this discussion it is clearly the case that the term 'policy' will be utilised differently in different contexts and by different groups of users. Levin (1997) has drawn attention to the differences in the use and definition of 'policy' between politicians, who he suggests generally use the term 'to denote a proposal or set of proposals carrying commitment to future action' (p. 20), and academics who 'set out to *define* "policy" rather than investigate how politicians and officials use the term' (p. 23).

The lesson from all of this is that rather than attempting to single out one true 'definition', we should accept that the term 'policy' will be used in a variety of senses, and that as students of social policy we need to be aware of the possible distinctions and take these into account in our explorations and analyses. Much of the discussion in the remainder of this book will shed light on alternative approaches to the understanding and analysis of policy in its different guises and may itself alter our understanding of the concept.

What is social policy?

What then distinguishes *social* policies from other forms of policy? As with 'policy' there are a variety of definitions. If anything, as the academic subject of social policy has developed and expanded, so attempts to define it have become more difficult. Placing emphasis on its role as an agent of distribution of various desirable factors in society, Alan Walker suggested that social policy might be defined as:

> the rationale underlying the development and use of social institutions and groups which affect the distribution of resources, status and power between different individuals and groups in society. Thus social policy is concerned both with the values and principles which govern distribution as well as their outcome. The task of the social policy analyst is to evaluate the distributional impact of existing policies on social welfare, their implicit and explicit rationales, their impact on social relations and the implications of policy proposals (A Walker, 1983, p. 141).

Social policy has also frequently been defined in relation to the major areas of policy which it is commonly seen as encompassing, perhaps most frequently including education, employment, health, housing, the personal social services and social security. However, as indicated earlier, academics at least are now extending the concept of social policy to 'new' fields such as the environment, food, transport and even arts and cultural policy (for example, Baldock *et al.*, 1999; Cahill, 1994). These and other developments, such as the emphasis on social exclusion and inclusion, mean that an approach grounded in 'areas of policy' becomes more complicated and cumbersome. In addition, issues such as crime and criminal justice have sometimes been treated as part of social policy and at others have largely been excluded from discussions of social policy.

Traditionally much of the social policy literature was concerned primarily with the role of the state, and in particular with its direct provision of welfare, implying a definition of social policy as what the state does in the areas of policy discussed above. Now that there is widespread understanding that a large amount of welfare is provided outside the public sector, social policy is often taken to include not only state provisions and decisions but also those of the informal, voluntary and private sectors.

Criteria have sometimes been suggested which attempt to enable a distinction to be made between social and other forms of policy. For example, it might be said that there is a difference between services delivered on a one-to-one basis, such as a social security payment or a GP (general practitioner) consultation, and the more shared outputs of, say, foreign or cultural policy, and that the former but not the latter would be included in the category of 'social policy'. However, making such distinctions can be tortuous and unprofitable. It may not be advantageous, or even desirable, to attempt to identify where boundaries lie between (traditional) social and other types of policy. Whilst economic policy and social policy are often viewed as very different and are studied separately, there are clearly and inevitably close links between them. During the Thatcher years the primacy of economic policy over and its effects upon social policy were clear. Much of the emphasis was on monetary controls and limiting public expenditure, but this in turn placed welfare services under financial stress; at the same time the rise in unemployment and consequently in the number of benefits claimants created an increased demand for the social security budget that made it hard for the Conservatives to achieve their intended cuts in public expenditure. In contrast, since 1997 Labour have arguably been using economic policy more in conjunction with social policy, reducing unemployment, raising the possibility of full employment, and introducing a measure of redistribution (to some groups) through the tax and benefits systems.

In the light of the above discussion, there is a strong argument for supporting Levin's (1997) observation that rather than concentrating on what he views as the use of rather narrow and ethnocentric academic definitions, it is preferable to focus on:

> the coming into being of policies and measures, which is part of a wider phenomenon, the interaction of government and society. From this standpoint, the definitions and boundaries which academics seek to assign to 'social policy' are irrelevant as well as arbitrary (Levin, 1997, p. 26).

What is policy analysis?

So what is policy analysis? It is arguable that policy analysis can be traced back to the Second World War as governments began to gather increasing amounts of information about economic policy and about defence policy. However, as the state grew in size and responsibilities, governments began to require more information about other areas such as urban planning, transport, health and education. In the 1960s, particularly in the United States, there was the development of a culture which saw the government as a 'problem-solver' and the use of methods of investigation which aimed to look at 'problems' and develop possible options to reduce or solve those problems (see, for example, the discussion of rationalism in Chapter 2). This was linked to some extent to a belief that we could have a 'social science' that was like 'real' science – that knowledge of society could make it better and that decisions could be grounded in 'facts' or 'laws'. Policy analysis therefore began to grow as part of this view of governments as problem-solvers.

At roughly the same time there was also a growth in interest, particularly among political scientists and political sociologists, in the analysis of the policy process – especially in how problems come onto agendas and in how decisions are made. Before then the study of politics had largely been limited to looking at constitutions, such as the different role of presidents and prime ministers, and comparisons of institutions such as the British Parliament and the United States Congress. With the growing attention paid to policy formulation and decision making, ideas such as rational planning and incremental decision making were developed, and people began to study the role and influence of bureaucrats (civil servants), to look at power (how is it exercised and by whom), the setting of agendas, the role of the media and so on. Easton's (1953, 1965) model of the policy process extended the range of interest further by directing analysis towards a consideration of inputs and outputs, and to taking account of the wider environment in which decisions are made.

'Policy analysis' is frequently sub-divided, for example into 'analysis of policy' and 'analysis for policy'. The former is the analysis of policy as an academic discipline, concerned primarily with advancing understanding; the latter is policy analysis as an applied activity concerned mainly with contributing to the solution of social problems. As students of social policy we may be at least in theory primarily concerned with the former; however, in reality the distinction is often blurred, so that, for example, academics may have a role in advising politicians and pressure groups on policy, a function which clearly overlaps the two categories.

Indeed, the position may be still more complicated. Hogwood and Gunn (1984) suggest that there are seven types of policy analysis:

1. Studies of policy content – where analysts seek to describe and explain the genesis and development of particular policies (in the UK much social policy work is of this type – largely descriptive (although often valuable) accounts of policies in areas such as housing, education, health, and so on). The policy analyst usually investigates a number of issues in order to trace how a particular policy emerged, or how it was implemented and what the results were. Such work is often conducted for academic reasons, although in some cases the results may have some direct or indirect impact on policy makers.

2. Studies of policy process – here attention is focused on the stages through which issues pass, and attempts are made to assess the influence of different factors on the development of the issue. Whilst such studies show some

concern with policy content, the emphasis is on uncovering the various influences on policy formulation. They are often concerned with single issues but they may also focus on the policy process within an organisation or on the influences on policy within a particular community or society. This would include case studies of the passage of particular pieces of legislation.

3.   Studies of policy outputs – these seek to explain why variables such as levels of expenditure or service provision vary between areas. They take policies as dependent variables and attempt to understand them in terms of social, economic, technological and other factors. Examples of this approach can be found in the literature which seeks to explain national differences in the development of social welfare policies, and why, for example, disability policy in Britain has developed differently from that in the United States. Research of this type can look at who exercises power, who influences decision making and how, how policy proposals change, and to what extent prevailing values and beliefs limit the range of policy possibilities.

4.   Evaluation studies (sometimes also referred to as impact studies) – for Hogwood and Gunn (1984) this marks the borderline between analysis of policy and analysis for policy. These are concerned to analyse the impact policies have on the population. However, such research can sometimes be of a rather basic and uncritical nature, concentrating on the collection of information rather than any real analysis of the goals and outcomes of the policy. On the other hand it can also be much more important, perhaps highlighting shortcomings with existing policies and providing information on the factors which influence the success and failure of policies, so suggesting a way to 'better' future policies. Even work such as the General Household Survey might fall into this category as it not only provides detailed survey data but can be used to examine the impact of some policies. It is to a sophisticated form of this type of analysis, along with that described under the 'Information for policy making' heading below, that Alan Walker is referring when he says: 'The task of the social policy analyst is to evaluate the distributional impact of existing policies on social welfare, their implicit and explicit rationales, their impact on social relations and the implications of policy proposals' (A Walker, 1983, p. 141).

5.   Information for policy making – data are collected and analysed in order to assist policy makers to reach decisions. This might occur when policy makers are considering the introduction of a new policy, or the revision of existing policies. Information may come from reviews carried out within government as part of a regular monitoring process, or it may be provided by academic policy analysts concerned to apply their knowledge to practical problems. It might involve only the provision of useful information, or it may go on to analyse this and to recommend possible options. However, the emphasis is clearly on the contribution to policy making.

6.   Process advocacy – this is a variant of analysis for policy in which analysts seek to improve the nature of policy-making systems. Process advocacy is manifested in attempts to improve the machinery of government through the reallocation of functions and tasks, and in efforts to enhance the basis for policy choices through the development of planning systems and new

approaches to option appraisal. It generally aims to work towards 'better' policy making, for example through taking a more 'rational' approach (see Chapter 2). The emphasis is likely to be on the efficacy of different approaches, methods and procedures for the making of policy.

7. Policy advocacy – the analyst is involved in pressing specific options and ideas in the policy process, either individually or in association with others, for example through a pressure group. Hogwood and Gunn (1984) note that this can take two principal forms: (*a*) the analyst as a political actor, supporting or lobbying for a particular policy, for example those who work in pressure groups, who examine policies but have particular values which clearly influence the way in which they interpret research; (*b*) the political actor as analyst, who again interprets research from a particular perspective. Both of these roles are clearly controversial as their objectivity as analysts and as consumers of analysis can be questioned, but both also reflect the role of values in social policy and the difficulty of achieving objectivity.

Here we are concerned mainly with the analysis of policy – our concern is primarily with the study of the policy process – but we cannot disregard insights from studies that fall elsewhere in Hogwood and Gunn's categories. For example, studies of policy outputs may well provide insights into process.

Who are policy analysts?

Over the past two decades there has been a growth of employment for 'policy analysts'. The nature of their work varies according to which of Hogwood and Gunn's types of policy analysis they have been recruited to carry out. Some will be working on the provision of information, others on evaluation, and yet others on the study of outputs or outcomes. They can be found in a variety of settings. These include a significant number of academics in universities, researchers and others for independent research institutions and think-tanks, and researchers and policy analysts employed in different tiers of government and in many other public bodies, including quangos. In addition they may also be found in voluntary organisations and pressure groups – which may be seeking to monitor and influence policy, the political parties – and among freelance consultants and lobbyists.

Some of the main areas in which policy analysts are involved, which are closely related to the coverage of this book, include health, transport, the environment, education, housing, economic policy, race and urban planning. They have a number of concerns (Parsons, 1995) including:

- 'problems' and the relationship of public policy to these;
- the content of public policies;
- what decision makers and policy makers do and do not do, and the inputs and processes in a policy area;
- the consequences of policy in terms of outputs and outcomes.

Themes and developments under the Conservatives, 1979 to 1997

This section is not concerned with particular policy developments under the Conservatives, or even with changes in broad policy areas. Rather it attempts to draw out some of the main 'themes' which can be seen as having underpinned or which derive from the Conservatives' years in government. The 1980s and 1990s saw enormous changes in government and social policy, many of which were designed to reduce the role of the state and to give individuals greater power and responsibility over their own lives. Yet, after almost two decades, public and social policy and the public sector remained significant factors in everybody's lives. Privatisation may have been a major feature of the Conservative era, and concerns such as efficiency, value for money, competition and the market may have been far more familiar by the late 1990s than they were in the 1970s, but despite this a vast range of services, benefits and regulations continue to be provided and performed by the public sector.

Nevertheless the degree of change in debates about social policy, its formulation and implementation, should not be understated. These include questions about the distinctions between public and private sectors, for example where the privatised utilities are now in the private sector but remain regulated by independent offices such as the Office of Telecommunications (OFTEL) and Office of Water Services (OFWAT); community care, where in many areas formerly public services such as residential homes or domiciliary care services have been transferred to the private sector, or where the private sector may be involved in NHS provision, such as through the Private Finance Initiative or other forms of collaboration with the public sector; discussion over the differences between 'public administration' and 'public management'; concerns over accountability and control, not only of former public bodies but also quasi-governmental organisations, such as the Housing Corporation, and of 'Next Steps' agencies, including the Benefits Agency or the Child Support Agency; and debates over the role of markets in providing goods and services ranging from public transport to school-age education.

Even under the Labour governments, whilst some of the more conflictual elements of the Conservative years may have been reduced, these issues remain important; and the idea of 'partnership' (whatever that might be taken to mean) between different sectors and organisations is being emphasised across whole areas of public and social policy.

In addition there have been new areas of interest in what were formerly termed public policy and public administration, with the growth in influence of New Right perspectives including theories about rational choice and the growth of bureaucracies (such as the civil service), together with the rise of what some have called a new 'public management' orientation which has affected many organisations involved in the delivery of social policy.

There have also been some more overtly political dimensions to change in public policy and administration, in part due to the arguably more ideological leanings of the Conservative Party from the late 1970s, and in part due to that party's continuous dominance of government from 1979 to 1997. These might include the Conservatives' attachment to the idea of the market and their translation of this into policy through privatisation, and through the introduction of market forces into many of the remaining areas of the public sector. The Conservatives also brought a new perspective to the concern with accountability, arguing that real accountability comes through the power of the consumer to move to another provider, for example through policies such as parental choice of schools, rather than the traditional concern with accountability to the public through their elected representatives in Parliament and in local government. The commitment to controlling and reducing public expenditure, although perhaps more emphasised in rhetoric than achieved in practice, also had a significant impact on social policy, its implementation and its management. And the long period of one-party dominance also raised some perhaps inevitable questions about ethics, accountability and morality, with the rise of non-elected public bodies and the powers of patronage and appointment available to ministers and others.

Finally, despite a significant level of hostility within the Conservative Party to both, the contradictory rises of nationalism (in Scotland, Wales and Northern Ireland) and European integration were emerging as features of the period, although the former only really became a significant influence on policy following Labour's return to power, whilst the importance of the latter was also extended by Labour's acceptance of the social chapter of the Maastricht Treaty (see Chapter 5) and passage of the Human Rights Act (Chapter 4).

Policy, administration and management

There are a number of difficulties in any attempt to define and distinguish clearly between public policy and the administration of those policies. 'Administration' is not necessarily any easier to define than 'public' or 'policy'. Administration was traditionally viewed as the way in which policy was implemented after being made. Indeed the academic subject of social policy arguably had a large part of its origins in what was termed 'social administration', which was concerned primarily with the way in which the welfare state was run or administered. However, Greenwood and Wilson (1989), among others, have argued that such a distinction between policy and administration does not stand up to close scrutiny. They suggest that 'all policy decisions are to some extent predicated upon considerations about implementation' (p. 3). Governments inevitably must consider the means of implementation before establishing policies. At the same time administrative decisions also require implementation and themselves often take the form of a policy decision. Secondly, they point out that it is very simplistic to suggest that politicians determine policy whilst officials implement policy decisions. In contemporary Britain politicians are frequently seen to be involved in the implementation of policies at central and local levels. At the same time it is equally clear that officials can have significant influence on policy, through their expert advice to politicians at the formulation stage and through their ability to influence the implementation of policies.

Whether there is a distinction between 'public administration' and 'public management' is much discussed in many of the books dealing with these subjects.

Similarly, there is considerable debate over whether public administration or public management is distinct from private sector management. One perspective has been to distinguish between 'management' and 'administration'. This view suggests that 'management' refers to a rational approach to organisational decision making which has traditionally been associated with the private sector through attempts to achieve organisational goals with the most efficient use of resources. The term 'public administration' has traditionally been used of the public sector, including welfare provision, with the emphasis on public officials implementing policies which have been determined by political decision makers within a framework of law, with the efficient use of resources often being only of secondary importance.

An alternative view has been that 'management' and 'administration' describe very similar activities, with the former being used in association with the private sector and the latter with the public sector, implying that many of the basic practices and activities are transferable between organisations in different sectors. More recently, and perhaps most importantly for the implementation of social policy, with its often large public sector bureaucracies, some have argued that there has been the emergence of a new 'public management' which differs from both traditional 'public administration' and from private 'management'. This new model is said to combine elements of public administration with the more instrumental approach of business management. Rhodes (1991) cites Hood (1991) as providing five key features of the new public management:

1. A focus on management, not on policy, and on performance appraisal and efficiency;
2. The disaggregation of public bureaucracies into agencies which deal with each other on a user-pay basis;
3. The use of quasi-markets and contracting-out to foster competition;
4. Cost-cutting;
5. A style of management which emphasises output targets, limited-term contracts, monetary incentives and freedom to manage.

These characteristics have been strongly pressed by central government in Britain from the 1980s, as well as by bodies such as the Audit Commission, and have been reflected across welfare providers from the central government departments (such as the former Department of Social Security and agencies such as the Benefits Agency), through the NHS and quangos (such as the Housing Corporation and Scottish Homes) to local government. Clarke, Gewirtz and McLaughlin (2002a) noted that from the 1980s managerialism has also 'tended to subordinate other principles of judgement to the managerial calculus of economy and efficiency' (p. 10) and that this was not only a key feature of the Conservative years but also formed a significant part of New Labour's approach to the welfare state. These developments have in turn served to further blur any distinction between public administration and public management.

Not only has the emergence of the new public management been of significant importance of itself, but Ranson and Stewart (1994) note that the Conservative governments' attempts to rebuild the public sector in the image of the private sector itself contributed to the blurring of the differences between public and private management. However, they point out that there remain significant differences. For example, it can be argued that public organisations are created to serve the needs of society as a whole within a statutory framework which imposes legal obligations and which are concerned to identify needs rather than demand and to serve rather than to accumulate profit. Public administration can also be seen as intrinsically political in nature with an obligation to carry out policy in accordance with the values which determine it. And ultimately, the performance of public services are evaluated through the ballot box, where the representatives of the public interest – such as local government councillors and Members of Parliament (MPs) – can be defeated and replaced. Public organisations are therefore accountable to the electorate in a way in which private organisations are not.

On rather similar lines Farnham and Horton (1996a) suggest that one of the significant differences between public and private sectors lies in the goals and accountabilities of the two sectors. In the public sector politicians are responsible for setting goals; the success or failure of those goals is often not easily reduced to a notion of 'profit' and 'loss', and public sector organisations cannot go bankrupt, as they do not rely on the market for revenue. At the same time it can be argued that the absence of market discipline can lead to waste, inefficiency and a failure to respond to customers' wants, and that management in public bodies can be significantly diluted from that in private organisations.

The goals of public organisations are often complex, vague, conflicting or even unattainable. There are a number of reasons for this, but in part it arises from governments' need to build broad bases of support; the fact that goals can change significantly over time, even within the lifespan of one Parliament; the difficulty of assessing the extent of success or failure to achieve objectives in many areas of public policy; and the potential for governments to present different perspectives on their actions as required during political debate (Pollitt, 1990).

The divisions of responsibilities between public organisations add another level of confusion. For example, responsibility for various major aspects of community care can be located in the Department of Health, the Department for Work and Pensions, and the Office of the Deputy Prime Minister, whilst the Treasury maintains an interest through its overseeing of public expenditure. In addition, policies and goals may be set at one level of government and implemented at another, with education being a fairly obvious example of this (see Chapter 5). The sheer size and complexity of policy implementation can make it impossible for policy makers to exercise full control over those responsible for carrying out a policy.

It can also be argued that the exercise of public power means that it is necessary for public organisations to be held accountable to the public, as providers of goods and services, in relation to the public interest, and in their role as spenders of public money. Whilst the form of public accountability varies widely with the type of agency, its responsibilities and functions, it is an important part of their character.

It is sometimes observed that public organisations are administered whilst private organisations are managed. Farnham and Horton (1996a) suggest that the dominance of an administrative system rather than a management system in the public sector was partly due to the historical emergence and growth of the public services as administrative bodies to support policy makers and legislators. Civil servants in particular did not view themselves as managers but as policy advisers to ministers and as guarding the public interest. On a related but different line, Flynn (1993) argues that the accountability structures in the public sector make managers' jobs different from those in the private sector. The variety of pressures and controls and the complicated interface with the political process create an 'ambiguous accountability' for much of the public sector, with the need for political accountability in terms of following decisions and policies at the same time as being accountable to the users of public services. Flynn sees this as contrasting with the clear ultimate accountability to shareholders in the private sector.

Intellectual challenges

It is not just the mechanisms and processes of social policy making and implementation that have changed. Our interpretation of them has also had to adjust significantly to account for both intellectual challenges, particularly, although not solely, from the New Right and rational choice theory, and the practical outcomes of government policies and practices grounded in at least some parts of these ideas. These include rational choice theory which has had a significant impact upon British politics, public policy and public administration from the 1980s. These ideas were put forward most strongly by the New Right think-tanks such as the Adam Smith Institute, the Institute of Economic Affairs and the Social Affairs Unit. These can be seen as having three main impacts: they have led to new policies and types of policies; they have challenged some of the fundamental assumptions about the form of policies and how they should be administered and delivered; and they have led to major changes in the administration of public policy. However, although often lumped together, New Right ideas and rational choice theory are not identical. One of the key themes from much of this debate was the idea that bureaucrats attempt to maximise their budgets – in other words there is a constant pressure from within many public organisations for growth, and this counteracts some aims such as efficiency (see the discussion in Chapter 2 for greater detail). Perhaps most importantly for the delivery of social policy were the accompanying changes in British government – such as the establishment of 'agencies', quangos, the use of contracting, markets, and so on – that are discussed elsewhere in this book.

From an academic perspective, organisation theory has also affected the way in which we have viewed the activities of the public sector, including the administration of social policy. This takes as its starting point the structure, patterns and arrangements among the people and groups involved in large-scale administration. However, within this overall label it is possible to identify a number of different approaches. The traditional view was primarily concerned with the structures and relationships between the principal units and subjects of an organisation, together with the location of authority and its delegation. This would have included the mapping of civil service or local government structures and so on. Systems theory (such as Easton's, outlined earlier in this chapter), presented a rather different perspective which emphasised the need to treat organisations as complete entities, sometimes drawing analogies with biological organisms. As seen by most systems theorists, organisations are open systems interacting with their environment. More recently these two views have been criticised from a number of perspectives. They can be viewed as hierarchical and authoritarian in nature, neglecting the creative potential and abilities of employees of bureaucratic organisations. The traditional view can also be criticised for ignoring the environment of governmental organisations and the impact of other tiers of government and other public and private organisations on the administration of public policy. Finally, all of these views generally assume that public policy and administration are performed by government employees. Yet much of the work of government is undertaken by other public, quasi-public and private organisations whose role and powers may not easily be analysed by traditional models of administration. For example, central government devolves many of its duties to local government, to agencies, to quasi-governmental organisations, and increasingly to the private sector, through a wide range of funding and support mechanisms. In areas such as community care the range of funding, regulation and provision spreads across a whole range of public, private and voluntary sector organisations, making it hard to draw firm conclusions about their roles, relationships and responsibilities. Yet, despite this complexity, organisation theory remains important in contributing to our understanding of how many of the organisations involved in social policy work.

Perhaps one of the most direct attempts to apply state theory in Britain which has had clear and direct relevance to social policy has been the use of 'dual-state' theory to analyse the roles of central and local government. Saunders (1981) and Cawson and Saunders (1983) pointed out that the state has two major economic functions: social investment (such as physical infrastructure) and social consumption (such as public education, health care and housing). Applying this to the UK, they argued that local government's major concerns are with social consumption, whilst regional and central government are concerned with social investment. Whilst there are a number of weaknesses to this view, such as its assumption that the local level is not concerned with consumption (or 'investment'), where it is at odds with regime theory (as discussed below and in Chapter 3), it provided a new perspective on the functions of different levels of government which still retains some relevance at the end of the twentieth century.

In the late 1980s 'regulation theory' also gained in influence (Jessop, 1990). It focuses on the organisation of western economies and the ways in which the contradictions of capitalism are regulated to ensure the continuation of capitalism. It argues that following the crisis of the 1970s a new regime of capital accumulation occurred. Rather than the Fordist regime with mass production of consumer goods by large, hierarchically organised business organisations aimed at mass consumption and accompanied by an interventionist state, post-Fordism is based upon flexible forms of demand-led production and segmented marketing, the growth of the service sector and small and medium-sized enterprises, together with fluid labour markets and a growing marginalised, part-time, temporary labour force (Jessop, 1988). This transition to post-Fordism can be seen as having particular implications for central and local government, implying a more 'hands-on' local economic policy, more service provision by private and voluntary organisations and less bureaucratic management approaches. It may also encourage new forms of public involvement (Stoker, 1991). However, regulation theory can be criticised for being highly generalised and as a result allowing for considerable detailed criticism, for example emphasising 'changes' that are not new (such as the existence of a dual labour market). Nevertheless, given the traditional service-providing role of local government and the breadth of social provision for which it remains responsible, its potential explanatory power and the possible changes which may result from such developments are of significant importance for social policy.

Also from the late 1980s there has been the emergence of 'regime theory', explored further in Chapter 3. The concern here has been primarily on modern urban governance. In itself this is of importance because of the role of different forms of urban government in economic and social policy and provision. However, some of its ideas are arguably of relevance in focusing our attention on aspects of the policy process in general. The emphasis from this perspective on 'the interdependence of governmental and non-governmental forces in meeting economic and social challenges, focuses attention upon the problem of co-operation and co-ordination between governmental and non-governmental actors' (Stoker, 1995, p. 54). In the UK, developments under successive Conservative governments, such as the growth of competition between cities for investment (both public and private), the role of business interests in local decision making, decentralisation, increasing financial constraints, and privatisation and contracting-out of services, mean that local governments are increasingly working in collaboration and partnerships of various types with other organisations. Regime theory addresses questions such as the implications of social complexity for politics, the privileged position of business in decision making and its implications for politics, and the role for democratic politics and potential input from disadvantaged groups.

Abstracting from the work of Stone (1989), Stoker (1995) identifies a number of key insights from regime theory. Complexity and fragmentation limit the capacity of the state as an agent of authority and control so that politics in complex urban systems is about government working with and alongside other actors and interests. There is no single focus of direction and control but networks co-ordinate social life, with co-operation obtained and sustained through the establishment of relations based on solidarity, loyalty, trust and mutual support rather than through hierarchy or bargaining. Regime theorists do not see governments as likely to respond to groups on the basis of their electoral power or the intensity of their preferences; rather governments are driven to co-operate with those who hold resources essential to achieving a range of policy goals. However, electoral politics and participation are recognised, as opposition to policy agendas can be mobilised and disrupt established policy regimes. Regime formation is about achieving a shared sense of purpose and direction and also about being able to mobilise resources necessary to achieve the main policy agenda.

Stoker (1995) also highlights some of the major criticisms of regime theory: there can be difficulties in applying abstract categorisations to empirical examples; regimes must be seen in the context of wider processes of change, and in particular regimes' interaction with non-local forces of change must be recognised; regime studies need to explore the dynamics of regime change as well as regime continuity.

Conclusion

This chapter has sought to examine some of the main ideas that can underpin the study of the social policy process. It is clear that on much of the terminology there are significant differences between writers and that different people also use different phrases to describe the same or similar phenomena. However, it is also apparent that in order to understand more completely the nature of social policy it is necessary to have a good grasp of the exercise of power in the making and implementation of policy. The value of this approach can be demonstrated through the case study of higher education provided above. We therefore suggest that we need at least to have an understanding of the different ways in which concepts such as 'policy', 'administration' and 'management' are used and applied. The entire policy process is not only concerned with, but also itself impacts upon, which policies and programmes do or do not emerge and the way in which they are implemented. We also need to recognise that not only is the subject of social policy itself continually evolving, but that the tools and methods with which we analyse policy and the theoretical perspectives that underpin our understanding are also contestable and changing. In some cases this can in turn impact upon policies, as with the adoption of some 'rational choice' ideas by the Conservative governments of 1979 to 1997. Finally, many of the developments from the 1980s can perhaps be summed up in the wider use of the term 'governance' rather than 'government', with the implication that we have shifted away from a position where governments had the ability to control and shape policy and society to one where governments have to operate in a complex, fragmented and decentralised environment, and have less of a capacity to bring about change through their own policies and actions.

The remainder of this book sets out to provide material to assist our knowledge and understanding of the social policy process, using both abstract theoretical concepts and frameworks and reference to the real world. Chapters 2 and 3 introduce a number of theories and models which help provide an understanding of the policy process and the exercise of power, whilst Chapters 4, 5 and 6 discuss the 'system' within which policies are made and implemented; Chapters 7 and 8 then focus upon two areas which have seen considerable emphasis under the Labour governments from 1997, the former considering the idea and reality of participation and the latter the area of evaluation of social policies.

FURTHER READING

For an extremely thorough view of a wide range of concepts associated with the policy process see: Parsons, W (1995) *Public Policy: An Introduction to the Theory and Practice of Policy Analysis* (Aldershot: Edward Elgar).

Other useful works include, on policy analysis: Hogwood, B and Gunn, L (1984) *Policy Analysis for the Real World* (Oxford: Oxford University Press); on public administration and public management: Greenwood, J, Pyper, R and Wilson, D (2002) *New Public Administration in Britain* (London: Routledge); Horton, S and Farnham, D (eds) (1999) *Public Management in Britain* (Basingstoke: Macmillan); and on careers for social policy graduates see: May, M and Bochel, C (2003) 'Careers and Social Policy Graduates' in P Alcock, A Erskine, and M May (eds) *The Student's Companion to Social Policy* (Oxford: Blackwell).

Perspectives on Policy Making

> **CHAPTER OVERVIEW**
>
> This chapter begins with a general discussion of policy and decision making. It then considers why it is that we use models to explain aspects of policy making, before moving on to consider the process of agenda-setting and a number of models themselves, including rational and incremental decision making and models of the influence of bureaucracies. The way in which these perspectives inform our understanding of the making and implementation of social policy are discussed. In addition, this chapter emphasises the importance of implementation in the social policy process and the impact which implementation can have on the outcomes of social policies. Theoretical perspectives such as the top-down model, the role of 'lower level actors' and the problems of implementation are covered, whilst the variety of factors that can affect the implementation of policies are highlighted.

Having illustrated in Chapter 1 some of the complexity and variety that can be identified around the analysis of the policy process, this chapter moves on to a consideration of a range of theoretical insights that can inform our understanding of the making and implementation of policy, and through that provide a greater appreciation of the forces that can exert an influence over the shaping of social policies. Academics from a variety of fields such as public policy, public administration, economics and sociology have made contributions to these debates by producing models, introducing concepts and formulating categorisations designed to explain particular perceptions of the process or parts of it.

For the purpose of analysis the making of policy in its broadest sense is often conceived of as a series of processes. However, whilst this approach has its uses, taken at face value it can project a somewhat misleading view of the development of policies. Policy making is clearly not a simple, straightforward process. Policies evolve over time and according to the needs of the population, the state of the economy, the world economy, the ideology of the particular government in power and many other factors. It is a complex process. According to Lindblom and Woodhouse: 'Deliberate, orderly steps. . . are not an accurate portrayal of how the policy process actually works. Policy-making is, instead, a complex inter-active process without beginning or end' (Lindblom, and Woodhouse, 1993, p.11).

Furthermore a whole range of actors, not limited to elected representatives such as local councillors and MPs, are involved in a variety of aspects of the policy process, from formulation into implementation, evaluation and feedback. Up to around the mid-1980s it was possible to argue that 'Politicians do not necessarily cease to try to intervene in the policy process once the law-making process has ended' (Hill and Bramley, 1986, p. 139). However, since then the picture has changed significantly and there is considerable evidence at both central and local government levels that this intervention has increased in recent years, whether it be councillors becoming involved in the running of social services or ministers in debates about education practices. Similarly the policy-making process is not restricted to central government but occurs at all levels of government, with local government frequently seeing itself and being seen as making policy within a broad statutory structure established by central government. At the start of the twenty-first century there are also new representative bodies, such as the Northern Ireland Assembly, the Scottish Parliament and the National Assembly for Wales, which are starting to have an impact not only upon the policy process but arguably also in diversifying further the processes by which social policy is made and also social policies themselves (see Chapter 5). Quasi-governmental organisations (discussed in Chapter 6) also have considerable importance and influence in making and implementing social policy.

Some writers have produced models or formulated categorisations designed to make this complex process simpler to understand. The notion of 'stages' is one which forms part of the perceptions of both academics and practitioners. For example, Burch and Wood (1990) propose three stages: 'initiation', 'formulation' and 'implementation', whilst Hill and Bramley (1986) posit two stages: 'development up to the point where legislation is enacted' (p. 139) and implementation from there on. They draw attention to the structural discontinuities that are likely to exist within the policy process, noting that 'Changes in actors are often involved, from politicians and their advisors to administrators' (p. 139) and that often different levels of government are involved in these stages, with legislation being provided by national government and implementation being undertaken by sub-national or local government. However, upon closer examination divisions such as these can appear to be somewhat arbitrary since there is likely to be overlap between both the stages and the actors involved in policy making and implementation. In addition, the notion of structural discontinuities can be misleading since such a separation between formulation and implementation suggests that once implementation gets under way there is no more policy making, whereas in practice the processes are inseparable.

What must be recognised is that there is likely to be overlap of various kinds in the course of making and implementing a policy. Nevertheless, it can be helpful to recognise different stages in the policy process so long as it is recognised that in reality the policy-making process is a continuous cycle in which there are many actors involved at different levels and stages.

Why do we use models of policy and decision making?

Models can be used as tools for analysis to help us shed light upon the distribution of power and the role of different groups in decision making. By applying particular models to specific legislation and policies we can gain an understanding of the role of different groups in the policy- and decision-making process, their power relative to one another, the motivations behind the development of policies and/or legislation and so on. Models and theoretical perspectives such as those set out in the remainder of this chapter provide tools which can help those interested in the policy process to analyse the way in which decisions in the policy process have been made. However, we should also recognise that many politicians and policy makers are concerned to improve the quality of the decision-making process and potentially, therefore, decisions themselves. Whilst they rarely set out to follow the processes set out in these models, they may therefore, from time to time, draw on the academic literature in order to try to improve the quality of the decision-making process.

Agenda-setting

The portrayal of the setting of agendas, or 'problem definition', as the first 'stage' in the policy process, may not always match reality, as some issues may be kept off the agenda (see, for example, the discussion of the three dimensions of power, below), some policies may arise as unintended consequences of other actions, and in other cases attempts to implement one policy will create problems which may need new policy responses. However, the question of how issues emerge onto policy makers' agendas is of clear importance in social policy, and arguably reflects the distribution of power in contemporary society.

Some accounts suggest that policy is made and implemented in response to a perceived social problem, and that to be considered as on the agenda an issue must usually be seen to require the attention of policy makers. This might be general topics such as rising crime rates or hospital waiting lists, or specific issues such as the food scares that occurred during the 1990s or the problems when examination boards adjusted A-level grades in 2002. However, this can be argued to be a rather simplistic and unrealistic view, with, for example, Cobb and Elder (1972) identifying two types of agenda: systemic, consisting of issues that are seen by members of the political community as worthy of attention, and as appropriate matters for existing government authority; and institutional, which are the problems or issues which policy makers see as appropriate for serious and active attention. Whilst reaching the institutional agenda does not guarantee that there will be action, the chances are significantly higher than if an issue is only on the systemic agenda, as it is the institutional agenda which are effectively the agenda for action.

Kingdon (1984) has suggested that agenda-setting can be seen as comprising three largely independent streams of activity (problems, proposals and politics), and when these converge there is a 'policy window' which permits some issues to reach the governmental agenda. The problem stream consists of those problems or issues with which policy makers become concerned; the proposals or policy stream is composed of policy communities with a wide range of ideas being developed, for example by academics, pressure groups, civil servants or local government officers, some of which are taken seriously whilst others are discarded; and the politics stream includes elements such as changes in public opinion, elections and other changes in government, and pressure group or media campaigns. Kingdon suggests that policy windows open because of a compelling problem or because of developments in the political stream, and when this occurs the policy stream has the opportunity to push an alternative policy. If all three streams come together then a topic has a good chance of reaching the top of the decision-making agenda. If there is no such coincidence then the policy window slips by and it is necessary to wait for another time when conditions are appropriate.

However, Anderson (1997) suggests that Kingdon's view, while useful, over-emphasises the role of timing and luck in agenda-setting, and that it is necessary to be aware of the range of other factors such as the role of political parties and pressure groups (see Chapter 7), political leadership (Chapter 4) and parts of government, as well as the role of the news media in shaping opinion and helping structure policy agendas. In a similar vein, Majone (1989) and Baumgartner and Jones (1993) have argued that policy options may be limited by existing institutional arrangements and the exclusion of certain ideas and interests, a perspective reinforced by the discussion of the three dimensions of power, below.

The role of the media in setting agendas has been widely considered, with one of the most influential pieces of work being that of Downs (1972) (see Figure 2.1). This sees there being a 'cycle of attention' for issues. Although developed by Downs in relation to environmental policy, it has been generally seen as having wider applicability, and in particular for understanding why issues may come to prominence and appear to fall off the agenda from time to time.

Three dimensions of power

The potential importance of agendas in policy making can be demonstrated by a consideration of the debate over the three dimensions of power. As discussed in Chapter 3, early pluralist accounts of democracy tended to assume that power was widely distributed within society with the policy-making process being driven by public demands and pressure. Perhaps the best-known account of this was by Dahl, who set out in his famous study of New Haven in the United States to ask *Who Governs?* (1961): an elite or ruling class, or something more complex? Dahl examined what he called 'key' decisions in three areas – nomination for political office, education policy and urban redevelopment. He claimed that no group won out consistently in these areas of decision making and that therefore there could not be a ruling elite. Dahl argued that in the United States power was widely distributed and the political system worked in a way that meant that the policy process was largely driven by public opinion and public demands.

Figure 2.1   Downs's issue attention cycle

Five stages:

1.   The pre-problem stage – the problem exists, and may be recognised by experts and groups in the field, but there is little public interest.
2.   Alarmed discovery and euphoric enthusiasm – often the result of a crisis or catastrophic event, such as the murder of Stephen Lawrence, or a child abuse scandal. The public is alerted and there is enthusiasm for dealing with the problem, including demands for government action.
3.   Realisation of the cost of significant progress – the public and policy makers become aware of the costs of tackling the problem.
4.   Gradual decline of public interest – having realised the cost of solutions, people become discouraged, bored or refuse to contemplate the problem any more. This process is assisted by the emergence of new issues which drive out the old.
5.   The post-problem stage – the issue has lost its position on the agenda and receives only spasmodic attention, although it may remain in a better position than at stage 1.

Source: A Downs, 'Up and Down with Ecology: The Issue Attention Cycle', *Public Interest*, vol. 28 (1972), pp. 38–50.

However, this 'one-dimensional' view can be criticised in a number of ways. For example, it implies that the exercise of power can only be analysed where there are cases of conflicting preferences. This approach therefore focuses on the analysis of 'concrete key decisions', with the assumption that the powerful are those who get their own way in these instances. Yet this is a simplistic view of power and, for example, does not take into account the careful preparation of demands to avoid opposition, nor who decides what is to count as a 'key' issue.

One of the most powerful critiques of Dahl and the pluralist view was put forward by Bachrach and Baratz (1963) who argued that such an approach failed to take into account the extent to which power could be exercised through the exclusion of issues and problems from the policy-making agenda. They therefore introduced the concepts of the 'mobilisation of bias' and 'non-decisions' into the debate, highlighting 'the practice of limiting the scope of actual decision making to "safe" issues by manipulating the dominant community values, myths, and political institutions and procedures' (Bachrach and Baratz, 1963, p. 632). They argued that:

When the dominant values, the accepted rules of the game, the existing power relations among groups, and the instruments of force, singly or in combination, effectively prevent certain grievances from developing into full-fledged issues which call for decisions, it can be said that a nondecision-making situation exists (Bachrach and Baratz, 1963, p. 641).

Such an approach therefore suggests that those with power can keep issues off the agendas that they control. Clearly there is an immediate methodological problem here – if non-decisions cannot be observed then how can we identify and analyse them? When Bachrach and Baratz applied their ideas in practice they examined race relations in Baltimore in the 1960s. They argued that the pluralist position failed to appreciate the extent to which those with power are able to exclude issues and problems from the policy agenda and that due to non-decisions by political leaders in the white community the black population was unable to generate a politics of conflict. The city's decision-making machinery was inaccessible to many black people so that there was effectively a closed political system.

This has immediate implications for the study of social policy. Parsons (1995) suggests that in the early stages of development of social movements it is relatively easy for decision makers to ignore such issues if they choose, giving the example of 'women's issues'; disability issues or environmental issues would perhaps be equally relevant examples. There is therefore an immediate challenge for social movements and lobby groups in forcing issues onto the policy agenda. Similarly Saggar (1991) shows how the issue of race was excluded from local politics in two London boroughs in the 1960s and 1970s, arguing that radical policy proposals were not heard largely because they were threats to the existing policy framework.

This 'two-dimensional' view clearly criticises the one-dimensional view's preoccupation with observable decisions. It point outs that if we wish to analyse the distribution of power within a society or community we need to focus not only on what gets discussed but also on 'non-decisions'. It also introduces the idea of the 'mobilisation of bias', which may not involve deliberate fixing by named individuals but is rather the systematically discriminatory impact of working within particular institutions or following particular rules of procedure (for example, the socially discriminatory consequences of selection procedures for higher education). It therefore shifts the focus to the question of who systematically gains and who loses by an institution's rules.

However, Lukes (1974) took the argument a stage further, describing three faces of power: firstly, that which can be identified in relation to decisions; secondly, that which is manifested in non-decisions; and thirdly, that which involves the shaping of people's attitudes and preferences so that no visible conflict may occur at all.

Lukes's three-dimensional view not only clearly accepts the idea of the mobilisation of bias (so denying that the study of the exercise of power should be restricted to the deliberate action of individuals), it also denies the centrality of conflict in the analysis of power. This involves the examination of claims such as those of false consciousness, and requires the separation of people's real interests from their expressed preferences. However, there are immediate methodological challenges to the testing of such ideas posed by the need not only to be able to identify 'real interests' but also to analyse the exercise of power where there is apparently no observable conflict and where beliefs are shaped by a system which ensures that its myths, beliefs and values dominate.

A study by Crenson (1971) is however highlighted by Lukes as being at least on the border between the second and third dimensions in its approach. In *The Un-Politics of Air Pollution* Crenson studied the failure of cities in the United States of America (USA) to tackle air pollution as quickly as might have been expected. He argued that since no one wishes to breathe polluted air, if some cities were not active in addressing the issue whilst others were, there would be a strong empirical case for non-decision making. Crenson looked at the steel-producing towns of East Chicago and Gary (in Indiana) and pointed out that whilst East Chicago tackled the problem quickly, introducing controls in 1949, Gary did not, introducing controls only in 1962. He suggests that this was because Gary was dominated by one major polluter, US Steel. The company did not make any threats, but its reputation influenced not only those decisions that were taken but also those that were not taken. When this analysis was extended to 52 other US cities, Crenson concluded that, where a city was dominated by one major polluter, clean air was unlikely to emerge as an issue on the policy agenda. From this perspective, power may be exercised as much in ensuring inaction as in taking action. Indeed, Crenson argues that merely the reputation for having power, as in the case of US Steel in Gary, may be sufficient to prevent some topics from becoming issues.

Crenson extends his analysis to suggest that there is a greater order and rationality to issues than may at first be apparent. For example, concerns about air pollution might apparently lead to the issue of government reforms to tackle the issue. However, if there is a commitment to maintaining employment or economic growth, the agenda is likely to be framed in a fashion that will play down the environmental costs. He also posits the view that power can be exercised at an 'ideological' level through the promotion of particular perceptions of social issues and conflicts and that the issues on a political agenda may be linked to 'an ideological vision of the political system' (p. 173) rather than to each other. Lukes (1974) builds yet further on this when he argues that power is exercised through the control of ideas, such as through the mass media and the processes of socialisation.

These three different underlying views of the exercise of power can be summarised as follows:

- Dahl – power is getting someone else to do something that they would not normally do – 'A has power over B to the extent that he [or she] can get B to do something that B would not otherwise do' (1957, pp. 202–3).

- Bachrach and Baratz – 'Power is also exercised when A devotes his [or her] energies to creating or reinforcing social and political values and institutional practices that limit the scope of the political process to public consideration of only those issues which are comparatively innocuous to A' (1970, p. 7).

- Lukes – power is exercised not only when preferences are prevented from having an impact on policy outcomes but also when preferences are moulded through socialisation, so that 'A exercises power over B when A affects B in a manner which is contrary to B's interests' (1974, p. 34).

Rationalism and incrementalism

Moving on from the setting of agendas, rationalism and incrementalism are perhaps the two best-known models of the policy-making process. Often seen as representing opposite ends of a spectrum, they make different assumptions about the nature of policy making and about the possibilities of change. However, such a view is rather simplistic for, whilst there are a number of differences, they do also have some similarities. Furthermore, the debate around rationalism and incrementalism is to some extent artificial because rationalism is generally portrayed as an ideal state of affairs, whilst incrementalism aims to show the world as it actually is. In that sense, therefore, the debate about their relative merits can be rather misleading.

The rational model

This model is usually traced back to Herbert Simon's book *Administrative Behaviour*, first published in 1945 and revised in 1957, in which he put forward a strong argument that rationality should be a goal in decision making. He suggests that in organisations 'rational' decision making can be seen as being a choice between alternatives which will help achieve previously selected goals, these goals reflecting the values of the decision maker. In order to achieve this there should be a comprehensive analysis of the alternatives and their likely consequences prior to the decision being made.

   Whilst there are number of weaknesses with this approach, some of which are discussed below, Simon argues that it is because of the limits to human rationality (he notes, for example, that knowledge, particularly of consequences, is always fragmentary, and that it is impossible to consider all possible alternatives) that it is necessary to attempt to improve decision making in organisations so that when there are a variety of possible ways of meeting a particular goal the decision maker chooses that which is most likely to achieve the desired outcome (see also Figure 2.2). Decision makers should therefore attempt to identify the desired objectives, or ends, and the different means of reaching these using a 'means–end rational model':

- identifying the goal;
- listing all the alternative strategies;
- assessing the consequences of each of these strategies including their costs and benefits;
- choosing the preferred strategy in order to achieve the desired outcome.

   In setting out this model Simon recognises that it is rarely possible to separate facts and values, and that values will often affect the aims of policies and the chosen means of achieving them. The rational model assumes that a given problem will be tackled by following cumulative and logical steps in the search for the best response. It is inevitably an idealised view of decision making, yet one which Simon suggests should lead to greater achievement of desired ends.

In many senses this model may provide an ideal-type for many organisations, but it fails to take into account that they are constrained by what has gone before and by existing demands, which introduce other pressures into the decision-making process. In the second edition of *Administrative Behaviour* (1957), and in a series of works since then, Simon sets out to discuss what he terms 'bounded rationality' in organisations, arguing that people's decisions are inevitably limited by a variety of factors which arise from the organisational and psychological context within which they are made, such as values, attitudes, culture and experience. These limits mean that decision makers are not choosing alternatives from the full range of possibilities, but that a form of rational decision making can still be applied within the restrictions that exist.

In later work (1960) Simon extended his argument to link his ideas about the rationalisation of decision making with the then emerging use of computers, by suggesting that, whilst organisations do not work entirely rationally, new techniques and technology could improve this. For example, he suggested that decision making could be made better by improving approaches to what he calls 'programmed' decisions: those routine, standardised decisions which he argued might benefit from techniques such as the application of computerisation (including simulations), set procedures and mathematical approaches. Overall, therefore, whilst recognising the many factors which work against it, Simon puts forward a strong case that rationality should be a goal in decision making.

Yet, despite attempts by Simon and others to respond to some of the weaknesses of the rational approach, a number of criticisms remain. Perhaps one of the most obvious problems with the rational approach to decision making is that whilst it may be possible to set out processes in a model as a logical series of steps which it is necessary to go through in order to achieve the desired outcome, in practice the reality is normally far more complex. For example, the formulation and development of any policy, whether it be for community care, criminal justice, education, housing or poverty, rarely proceeds in such an orderly fashion as described by Simon. Policy making is a complex process in which many different actors, from central government (ministers, MPs and civil servants), local government (councillors and officers), quasi-government, pressure groups, the media and political parties are involved. All of these groups and organisations have their own values and agendas. They have vested interests in the policy-making process. And the relative power of these groups or organisations in relation to one another will inevitably affect the process of policy formulation and development. Thus there are many push and pull factors which constantly work for and against one another.

The recognition that there are different values and objectives raises the question of whose values and objectives should be used in the decision-making process? Within any organisation, whether it be the Prison Service, a local authority department, a housing association or a school, there are a variety of individuals and groups who may have different values and objectives to those set by the organisation itself, and who certainly often have discretion in the interpretation and implementation of 'policy'. Within the NHS, for example, managers may be concerned with their perception of the most efficient use of resources, whilst health professionals may see their primary goal as being to provide good quality care. Whilst these aims do not necessarily conflict, there is certainly the potential for them to do so. Lipsky (1976, 1980) uses the term 'street-level bureaucrats' to describe those who actually implement the policy goals set by management. These people frequently have discretion in the way in which they interpret and implement policies. As a result, policies may be adapted or reworked by officers during the implementation process in order to make them workable in practice, for both those delivering and those receiving them. (Lipsky's work is discussed in more detail in the section on 'Bureaucracies', below.)

Overall, the rationalistic approach is often seen as utopian: it represents the planners' dream; but in the real world decisions are often not as clear-cut and evaluation is not systematic as this model implies. However, despite the very real shortcomings, it should not be assumed that this approach has not had a significant influence over decision making. The idea of rational decision making has actively influenced a whole range of attempts, particularly in the UK and the USA to improve the quality of the policy-making system. During the 1960s and 1970s initiatives such as that designed to improve planning on public expenditure, overseen by the Public Expenditure Survey Committee (PESC), and the spread of planning units within government departments, recognised many of Simon's criticisms of policy making and were attempting to move towards a 'better' system. For social policy, failures such as that of PESC to bring economic and social policy closer together, and the ambitious Joint Approach to Social Policy, designed to improve collaboration between government departments (see Challis et al., 1988), were two of the most obvious examples, although there were also a variety of initiatives designed to 'improve' policy making in many parts of the welfare state including the health service and the personal social services.

Indeed, it is possible to argue that governments continue to use a number of mechanisms which, to a greater or lesser extent, can be analysed using the rational model. For example, Royal Commissions, such as that established by Labour in 1997 to examine Long Term Care for Older People, display some elements of rational decision making, as they involve consideration of a range of options, generally by a group of experts, to enable the government to choose a preferred option, based upon the Commission's recommendations. However, they also illustrate some of the shortcomings of the rational approach, as governments may also utilise them for other reasons, including a desire to be seen to be doing something about a problem or issue, or to delay having to make a decision. Similarly, Labour's creation of the Social Exclusion Unit might also be said to be an example of a partially rational approach to policy making. The Unit has a specific remit, involving the co-ordination of work across government departments, and is based in the Cabinet Office. It was established to report directly to the Prime Minister and combines civil servants and others from outside Whitehall including the police, probation, business, the voluntary sector and local government. Its aims were to improve understanding of problems, to encourage more co-operation across departments (including persuading Whitehall to listen and learn from what works on the ground) and to make recommendations to tackle social exclusion more effectively. Similarly a Performance and Innovation Unit was also introduced as part of the attempt to enhance 'joined-up government'. Such initiatives can be seen as a move towards rational policy making in that they seek to improve policy making and implementation in their approach to social problems, their focus on mechanisms for co-operation and co-ordination, the manner in which they were intended to feed into other aspects of the government's activities, such as Comprehensive Spending Reviews, and their role in the construction of key indicators such as those of social exclusion.

The concept of rationality adopted by policy makers in government has tended to be based on an intuitive and 'common-sense' view of rationality, perhaps more along the lines of 'bounded rationality', than on the more refined concept of rationality as initially devised by Simon. However, the rational model remains a useful tool with which to analyse the actions and decisions of policy makers. In addition, the literature produced on the analysis of decision making may have value to decision makers in trying to improve the quality of policy making.

The incremental model

One of the main critiques of Simon's rational perspective came from Charles Lindblom, initially in his 1959 article 'The Science of "Muddling Through"', and since in a variety of sometimes rather different forms. One of Lindblom's main targets was the suggestion that rational approaches and techniques could replace the need for political agreement and consensus. In contrast, he argues that 'muddling through' is an important part of decision making. He also makes the points that the pure rational model is rarely, if ever, achieved in the real world and that policy makers are generally more concerned about coping with problems than solving them. Whilst sharing Simon's view that the choices available to policy makers are restricted by a variety of factors, Lindblom believes that rather than seeking to achieve rational decisions we should be more aware of the strengths of 'non-comprehensive analysis'. Lindblom's preference is therefore for an 'incremental' approach to policy making, both as a model for how policies should be made and as a better description of how they are actually made. The incremental model emphasises the extent to which policy makers tend to stick with the known, the accepted, the familiar and the manageable. It avoids the global, fundamental and wide-ranging analysis sought by proponents of the rational view (see Figure 2.2).

Burch and Wood (1990) identify five central characteristics of incrementalism:

1. Policy making is restricted – policy makers do not wander far from the status quo; new policies or responses to problems differ only marginally from existing policies – they keep to the familiar.
2. Means rather than objectives determine policy.
3. Incremental strategies are remedial – they deal with problems as they arise and there is little looking ahead. For policy makers the status quo is largely satisfactory until it cannot be maintained.
4. Incrementalism is reconstructive and serial – policy makers realise that problems change over time and solutions will raise new problems. Policy making therefore becomes a never-ending activity.

5.   Incrementalism is fragmentary – the involvement of different groups of people and different institutions in policy making varies with issues and across time.

Figure 2.2   Lindblom's comparison of rational and incremental approaches

Rational comprehensive model	*Successive limited comparison (branch) (incremental model)*
Clarification of values or objectives distinct from, and usually prerequisite to, empirical analysis of alternative policies. Policy formulation is therefore approached through means–end analysis; first the ends are isolated, then the means to achieve them are sought.	Selection of value goals and empirical analysis of the needed action are not distinct from one another but are closely entwined. Since means and ends are not distinct, means–end analysis is often inappropriate or limited.
The test of a 'good' policy is that it can be shown to be the most appropriate means to the desired end.	The test of a 'good' policy is typically that various analysts find themselves agreeing on a policy (without necessarily agreeing that it is the most appropriate means to an agreed objective).
Analysis is comprehensive, every important and relevant factor is taken into account.	Analysis is drastically limited: important possible outcomes are neglected; important alternative potential policies are neglected; important affected values are neglected.
Theory is often heavily relied upon.	A succession of comparisons greatly reduces or eliminates reliance on theory.

Source: C. Lindblom, 'The Science of "Muddling Through"', *Public Administration Review*, vol. 19 (1959), pp. 78–88.H

In *The Intelligence of Democracy* (1965) Lindblom developed his argument further, introducing the notion of 'partisan mutual adjustment' to reflect the processes of negotiation, bargaining and concession between decision makers that takes place in pluralist societies. From this perspective the adjustments and compromises of decision making also help to develop consensus and co-ordination. At the same time it can also be argued that such discussion and concession or compromise themselves eat into radical proposals, as different actors recognise that they need the support of others. Aspirations are therefore checked and small steps result. However, as Harrison, Hunter and Pollitt (1990) point out in their discussion of health policy, incrementalism does not necessarily equate with conservativism or slow change as, if there are frequent small steps over a fairly short period of time, the degree of policy change can be substantial. If this is the case then at some stage the nature of such policies might have to be reconsidered.

As a prescriptive view, Lindblom argues that the dominant style of decision making in government is incremental and that there are good reasons for policy makers adopting such a strategy. For example, policy making is made manageable by successive limited comparisons with the status quo. This limits the number of alternatives considered and also ignores consequences of policies. Disagreements over objectives can be avoided because objectives are seldom considered; the information and intellectual skills needed are more likely to be available; and for most actors, focusing on the familiar is more comfortable than assessing the unknown. Even where radical change is required, taking 'many smaller steps in a relatively short period...is often – but not always – both more politically feasible and more prudent analytically than leaping well beyond the limits of understanding' (Lindblom and Woodhouse, 1993, pp. 27–8)

One of the main weaknesses of Lindblom's earlier discussion of incrementalism lay in his optimistic pluralism. Like the influential pluralist writer Dahl (see the discussion of the three dimensions of power earlier in this chapter), he came to recognise that power is skewed in favour of certain groups, and in particular in favour of big business. One of the ways in which he responds to this is to argue that one of the roles of planners in the policy-making process is to give a voice to those who are less able to access and influence decision making.

Perhaps related to this are the criticisms that incrementalism can be a force for conservatism and a barrier to innovation. For example, by taking the status quo as a starting position, incrementalism may ignore problems such as how fair and equal the distribution of resources in society is. It can also be accused of conservatism in its emphasis on remedial and short-term change, which again may mean that an incrementalist approach risks ignoring fundamental issues and perhaps the need for radical change.

As an evaluative tool, one of the problems of incrementalism is the difficulty of making a clear distinction between incremental and non-incremental change. For example, was the decision of the Conservatives to introduce massive sales of council houses in 1980 incremental or not? There had been sales of council houses for many years, but the scale of these in the 1980s far exceeded what had gone before. Similarly when Labour returned to government in 1997 and introduced the New Deal there was considerable debate about the extent to which this was a new initiative or whether it was effectively building upon previous schemes designed to reduce unemployment, whilst at local government level the similarities and differences between the Conservatives' introduction of compulsory competitive tendering and Labour's use of Best Value (see Chapter 5) also raised questions about the distinction between incremental and radical change.

Alternative models

A number of commentators have been critical of both the rational and the incremental views of policy making. As noted earlier, rationalism and incrementalism have sometimes been treated as two models at either end of a spectrum, but in reality this is not the case. For example, Simon (1960) recognises that decision makers examine the options until something satisfactory (usually less than the optimum) is discovered. If nothing satisfactory is found, the level of aspiration will be reduced until eventually what is desired matches what is available in policy terms. Such an approach can arguably be interpreted as similar to Lindblom's incrementalism, where means rather than objectives are seen to be determining policy.

Perhaps the most common criticism has been that the rational model over-emphasises significant changes in policy whilst the incremental model suggests that any change is difficult to achieve. If we take Simon and Lindblom as at either end of a spectrum (although the artificiality of doing this has already been noted above), other views can then be located as more central relative to them. Perhaps the two best-known alternatives are Etzioni's (1967) 'mixed-scanning' and Dror's (1964) 'optimal model'.

Whilst criticising the rationalistic approach for being both unrealistic and undesirable, Etzioni also perceives flaws with incrementalism, particularly over how to deal with 'large' or 'fundamental' decisions, such as a declaration of war or those that may have significant long-term impacts on state budgets. He drew upon the weather observation and forecasting techniques of the time to produce a mixed-scanning approach. His analogy was that a rationalistic approach would require an exhaustive, detailed survey of weather conditions as often as possible, resulting in a great deal of detailed information which would be expensive to analyse and which would reduce the capacity of decision makers to respond. On the other hand, an incremental approach would tend to focus on areas where there had been particular weather patterns in the past and might neglect to observe developments in unexpected areas.

His mixed-scanning strategy includes elements of both approaches, with a broad overview of all parts of the sky, together with an examination of those areas identified from the broad picture as potentially requiring more in-depth attention. Etzioni argues that 'While mixed-scanning might miss areas in which only a detailed camera could reveal trouble, it is less likely than incrementalism to miss obvious trouble spots in unfamiliar areas' (p. 389). Applied to policy making, mixed-scanning implies that from time to time a broad scanning be undertaken to check for distant but 'obvious' dangers or problems, whilst allowing the generally incrementalist nature of most decision making to continue. In Etzioni's opinion this would allow more detailed consideration where fundamental decisions are required.

Dror (1964) also criticises both rationalism, for its failure to reflect the reality of decision making, and incrementalism, for its conservatism and support for the status quo. He proposed a 'normative optimum model' which aimed to increase the level of rationality in decision making but which recognised the extra-rational processes which are significant in policy making, including intuitive judgement and creative invention of new alternatives. He therefore produced an 18-phase model from the processing of values to communication and feedback which operates at the two levels of rationality and extra-rationality (1989), designed to encourage decision makers to use rational analysis but also to think creatively, to draw on holistic impressions and to use their intuition.

Both Dror and Etzioni set out to produce models that are both descriptive of the reality of policy making and prescriptive in that they argue that policy making would be improved through the use of these approaches. However, both can also be criticised, with Parsons (1995) noting that Dror has 'very little regard for the public in policy-making' (p. 296), relegating them to a marginal evaluative role, whilst Ham and Hill (1984) question both the significance of Etzioni's 'fundamental' decisions and how to distinguish between fundamental and incremental decisions.

The power of bureaucracies

Bureaucracies are an important part of the machinery of government and play a very significant role in the process of social policy making, from formulation to implementation and evaluation. They have been the object of considerable academic interest to students of the policy process from Weber onwards. The reliance on and part played by bureaucracies within different forms and levels of government is discussed in Chapters 4 and 5 and to some extent also in Chapter 6. Here the concern is with a variety of perspectives that can give rise to thought about and lead to an appreciation of the role and power of bureaucracies and the ways in which they can influence the policy process. This is a situation which has not always been recognised in the study of social policy, although in line with the generally greater awareness of the importance of the policy process, there is now more attention paid to this issue than has sometimes been the case in the past.

Terms such as 'bureaucracy' and 'bureaucratic' are widely used in a critical or negative sense, yet it is perhaps impossible to conceive of a modern society without such organisations. Much of the writing on bureaucracy has built upon the work of Weber, which has had very great influence on the study of these entities. The meaning of the term has evolved considerably but generally contains connotations of both government by a bureau of officials and the structure of modern large organisations. Finer (1997) provides a succinct summary of the characteristics of bureaucracy: 'it is hierarchical; permanently in function; specialised into its various fields; educationally and/or vocationally qualified; paid and full-time; rule governed' (p. 64). R G S Brown (1971) expands on this:

> The members of a bureaucracy are career officials, who are selected, controlled and as far as possible promoted according to impersonal rules. They occupy positions in which they carry out prescribed functions. The authority which they exercise (on behalf of the head of the organisation) belongs to their office, not to themselves. They are expected to work impersonally, regardless of their own feelings. Senior positions are filled

by promotion. The security of a salary and a life career protects them from any personal consequences of their decisions, so long as they have been taken in accordance with the rules (Brown, 1971, p. 125.)

Even a brief consideration of the agencies responsible for policy making and the implementation of social policy in the UK makes it obvious that bureaucracies play a significant role. The civil service is probably the best-known example of a 'bureaucracy', and the role of government departments such as the Department for Education and Skills, the Department of Health and the Department for Work and Pensions in social policy are immediately apparent. Many other 'bureaucratic' organisations staffed by public sector employees are also directly involved in the social policy process, such as local government providers of education and housing, and the National Health Service. In addition, the size and structure of some large voluntary organisations means that they too can have bureaucratic characteristics.

Work by Billis (1984) on welfare bureaucracies is of particular interest to students of social policy. He describes these organisations (whether public, voluntary or private) as occupying the middle ground 'between political statements of policy and the citizen receiving services' (p. 2), a depiction which itself implies that they are in a position of potentially great influence. He recognises that there can be a tension between 'welfare' and 'bureaucracy', including the role of the welfare 'professions', but notes that both have a central place in the study of social policy. This is because, in addition to their role in the formulation of policy, welfare bureaucracies are important in social policy because they are responsible for overseeing the delivery of services to the consumer and ensuring that services are provided and that statutory duties are fulfilled. Amongst their roles are the processing of requests or applications for provision, such as social security or social housing, and they often determine eligibility according to rules set by central government and on that basis either provide or refuse a service or payment. Welfare bureaucracies therefore deal with vast numbers of people on a daily basis and make decisions that have an immediate impact on their lives.

Finally, as outlined earlier and covered in greater depth later in this chapter, Lipsky (1976, 1980) and others have identified the significance of the role of 'street-level bureaucrats'. This has particular relevance to social policy where there is considerable interaction with the consumers of services, for example in the allocation of social housing, responding to claims for benefits, and in the classroom. This is considered in greater depth later in the chapter.

Perspectives on bureaucracies

A number of perspectives exist that can help us to understand the role and influence of bureaucracies in the policy process in its broadest sense. This section draws heavily on writing on the civil service, in part because it is perhaps the most obvious and the most powerful bureaucracy, and in part because there is by far the greatest amount of literature on it. However, many of the perspectives and critiques are applicable to other bureaucratic organisations involved with policy making and implementation in contemporary social policy, including local government, the National Health Service and other welfare bureaucracies.

The public administration model

Essentially this perspective is based upon the view that it is elected politicians who make policy whilst bureaucrats provide policy advice and implement decisions. Within central government therefore, neutral civil servants provide information and implement policies whilst it is ministers who make and defend policy decisions. Arguably this has been not only the traditional model put forward in textbooks but also the dominant view held by civil servants and ministers. A similar view would also hold, for example, in relation to local government where the elected politicians would be seen as making policy that is then implemented by officers.

During the 1970s both the accuracy and the utility of this model were increasingly questioned and a number of alternative, more 'realistic', views on how far the real decision-making power lies in the hands of civil servants were put forward. In particular, criticisms centred on the perceived neutrality of civil servants and the advice that they give to ministers, and the argument (discussed in Chapter 1) that there is actually significant overlap between policy and administration and that it is impossible to draw a firm distinction between them.

The liberal-bureaucratic model

This view builds upon the ideal that politicians are able to control bureaucrats, but aims to take into account the reality of departmental decision making and the factors that can increase the role that bureaucrats have in making policy. Whilst this perspective does recognise that a minister can still dominate a department, it acknowledges that there are a variety of factors that can shift power away from the elected politician and towards the permanent officials. These would include the permanence and experience of bureaucrats and their ability to control advice and information passed to politicians. Former ministers such as Benn and Crossman have claimed that civil servants obstructed their attempts to introduce more radical policy change. From this perspective there is a considerable degree of struggle between politicians and their officials. However, other former ministers, including Carrington and Healey, have argued that civil servants can be controlled. Indeed, upon their return to power in 1997, one of the most commented-upon developments under Labour was the greater use by ministers of political advisers, arguably at least in part to counter the influence of civil servants. In addition, there is general agreement that when a strong minister has a clear policy line, and particularly with the support of a significant electoral mandate, they are able to introduce radical policy changes. This view is useful in drawing attention to the factors that can affect the power of bureaucrats. Again, such arguments are equally applicable to other bureaucratic organisations such as the NHS or local government.

The power-bloc model

This view is based upon the fact that senior civil servants continue to be drawn largely from the elite and privileged sections of society, with many, for example, having public school and Oxbridge backgrounds, and that this introduces an inherent conservative bias. This group deploys its expertise to protect the ideals and interests of the sections of society from which they are drawn, and at the same time may use both their administrative skills and their permanent positions to ensure that only minimal change takes place. This model was initially associated with the political left, linking closely with Marxist arguments; however, some ministers in the Thatcher governments also claimed that the civil service tried to block some of those governments' more radical policies. On the other hand, it is possible to argue that simply because senior civil servants are drawn from a particular social group it does not follow that they will not implement radical policies, nor that they necessarily share the same views, aims and values.

The bureaucratic over-supply model

Sometimes termed 'the budget-maximising model', this perspective is linked to neo-classical economic views and was to some extent associated with the rise of New Right views in the 1970s and 1980s, suggesting that bureaucrats are primarily interested in promoting their own interests and that they do this at the expense of the public interest. Niskanen (1971) argues that those who work in bureaucracies seek to maximise the size of their agency and its budget because these are the only ways in which they can maximise their utility. Similarly, Tullock (1993) suggests that bureaucrats' welfare (in terms of security, pay, size of offices, and so on) increases with a rising agency budget and that they therefore attempt to maximise their personal welfare by expanding their agencies' budgets. This is only possible because the allocation of resources is made in a different way from the market. Whilst business people in the market are assumed to be profit maximisers and therefore will not produce additional output whose market price is less than the costs of production, according to Perlman (1976) government departments typically over-supply up to twice the level that would be produced by private firms under market competition conditions.

This perspective was reinforced by the argument from the New Right that political control over the bureaucracy is often ineffective, and the accusations of the 1970s and 1980s that the civil service supported interventionist government and high levels of public expenditure.

Bureau-shaping

Taking an alternative approach, Dunleavy (1986, 1991) sought to create an alternative model of bureaucratic behaviour based upon public choice theory. In looking at the privatisations of the 1980s and the experience of the civil service, he argues that bureaucrats' self-interest need not be expressed through size and budget maximisation, as in public service systems pay and conditions are often designed to maintain existing positions in the occupational class structure, whilst bureaucrats' perceived welfare is also linked to the type of work and status of their organisation. Dunleavy therefore argues that their behaviour is better characterised by their attempts to 'shape' their organisation so that 'Maximising a bureau's conformity to an ideal, high status organizational pattern... provides a powerful explanation of a wide range of observed administrative behaviour' (p. 205).

It is also possible to argue that New Right arguments about over-supply and budget-maximisation do not fit easily with the diminishing size and budgets of bureaucracies in the 1980s. Also, in explaining why there was relatively little resistance in Whitehall to privatisation, Dunleavy suggests that developments such as hiving-off and contracting-out can, in some circumstances, have the potential for senior officials to transform radically the character and status of their organisation. It is therefore possible to argue that the interests of senior civil servants were best served by shaping their departments and budgets to fit with the direction taken by politicians and business, rather than attempting to preserve budgets and staffing.

The bureaucratic co-ordination model

This approach centres upon the fact that elected policy makers overseeing large organisations such as central government departments or other substantial bodies are unlikely to be able to be in complete control of all that goes on within their area of responsibility. For example, given that there are large numbers of civil servants in each department and only one minister, he or she, no matter how well organised, is unlikely to be in complete control of everything that goes on within their department. This would apply to all actors within the core executive and arguably to those in similar positions in devolved and local government.

Thus bureaucrats tend to play the major role in the co-ordination that is necessary to the smooth running of government, whilst elected politicians are often relegated to more of a backseat role. At central government level, in particular, this would imply that no matter which political party is in power, there will never be total control over detailed policy making and that politicians will inevitably have limited power simply because they cannot oversee every aspect of policy formulation and implementation.

Street-level bureaucrats

A rather different view of the importance of bureaucrats, and one that can have a particular resonance for social policy, is that which is often associated with the work of Lipsky (1976, 1980), as mentioned earlier in this chapter, who developed a model to explain the behaviour of what he termed 'street-level bureaucrats' – those who work in bureaucracies at local level and (a) interact constantly with citizens in the course of their job; (b) have a significant degree of independence in their job, including discretion in making decisions; and (c) have the potential for a fairly significant impact on the citizens with whom they deal. Lipsky argues that at 'street level': 'public policy is not best understood as made in legislatures or top-floor suites of high ranking administrators, because in important ways it is actually made in the crowded offices and daily encounters of street level workers' (Lipsky, 1980, p. xii).

He argued, in addition, that the reality of policy making at this level is that it is more concerned about the development of practices that enable officials to cope with the pressures that they are under, than with the achievement of public service ideals. This situation arises because the nature of the work is such that the demands upon those who work in these services are often so great that they can become unmanageable. Street-level bureaucrats therefore develop methods that process their clients in a largely routine manner and adjust their work habits to lower expectations of themselves and those who use their services. Yet at the same time, street-level bureaucrats, such as lecturers, teachers and social workers, are sometimes seen to have a significant degree of freedom and autonomy, as well as power over service consumers. For example, they exercise discretion in a situation where demand for resources exceeds supply, by deciding which services a consumer may or may not receive; they also have considerable autonomy from the agency which employs them because large classes, huge caseloads and inadequate resources mean that instead of dealing with consumers on a one-to-one basis they must deal with them on a mass basis; Lipsky also observes that these can be further enhanced by the fact that their jobs frequently have ambiguous or even conflicting goals and that it is difficult to measure their performance.

The power of street-level bureaucrats can be seen in a number of different ways:

- Control of clients – through differentiation, for example, between the deserving and undeserving, the ability to withhold information from clients, and perpetuate or delay service delivery. Such activities may help to limit client demand, and whilst the services can always be presented as in best interests of clients, yet they may often run in the interests of bureaucracy.
- Control of their own activities – the ability to modify their own activities and perceptions of their jobs and clients and also to modify their objectives to match their ability to perform.
- Power over their own agency – street-level bureaucrats carry out much of the difficult rationing at client level and it is often convenient for organisations to permit this discretion to continue, as the exercise of the street-level bureaucrat's discretion can be functional to the organisation.

In the light of these powers, in situations of pressure, street-level bureaucrats develop techniques that enable them to fulfil their work within the resources available. They may, for example, deal with clients in a largely routine manner and adjust their work habits to lower expectations of themselves and those who use their services. In the case of teachers, if resources do not allow them to work with children on an individual basis as they might prefer, they develop techniques such as encouraging children to read in groups and to help one another, or teaching them on a mass basis. Similarly, social workers who are unable to visit all their clients on a regular basis may introduce systems of prior-itisation, only seeing those deemed in greatest need frequently.

The exercise of such discretion is a key feature of Lipsky's model. The ability to exercise discretion is a source of power, whether it be for housing officers to make decisions about who gets housing and if so whether it be a flat in a tower block, a house or a room in shared accommodation, police who decide which offences to turn a blind eye to and which to record, or health care workers who decide who should and who should not receive treatment. The exercise of discretion is often related to the rationing of resources, but for many welfare agencies there may be no limit to the demand for free services, and changes in the level of resourcing will not necessarily result in significant changes for individual workers.

There are potentially important implications for social policy arising from these arguments. In particular, they imply a pessimistic outlook for top-down policy changes. For example, McDonald (2002) applies the notion of street-level bureaucrats to GPs in the NHS, noting that such an approach may be more appropriate than the frequent references to the 'power of the medical profession', as the degree of cohesion and uniformity of belief and action may be inadequate at the micro level. She points out that the professional status of GPs is such as to justify relatively weak forms of top-down control and that as a result they are able to adopt 'implicit rationing to cope with service demands' (p. 134) and that this can conflict with attempts to introduce more 'rational' and systematic managerial techniques. Similarly, Lipsky's arguments could sug-gest that given the raft of changes introduced by the Labour governments aimed at improving education in schools, teachers would be likely to accommo-date themselves to the new demands, but in a way that would not mean sub-stantial change from the preceding situation, therefore limiting the impact of these new policies.

Implementation

At its most simplistic, 'implementation' is the process of putting policies into practice. For example, central government might formulate education policy which local authorities are then expected to implement in the schools for which they are responsible. Such a view fits well with the traditional top-down public administration model of neutral bureaucracies implementing policies deter-mined by elected politicians, so that the original thinking around theories of implementation 'evolved from a starting point in which the translation of policy into action was seen as being, under normal circumstances, an unproblematical process so long as bureaucracies were clearly subservient to their political mas-ters' (Hill, 1997b, p. 213). However, this perspective arguably bears little resemblance to the realities of implementation in contemporary society, and in practice both the numbers of actors and their role in the policy making and implementation process are far more complex.

Instead, there is a strong argument that implementation should be seen as part of the continuum of the policy process, rather than as a distinct component of it. For example, implementation is often said to start only when a policy or programme has been formally ratified, but such a chronological separation from policy formulation can be unreal and potentially misleading. In addition, some policies do not need formal ratification, but simply emerge from statements of intent or practices in the field (for example the movement of resources towards community care from the 1960s in the UK cannot easily be traced to specific government legislation). Such a separation also suggests that once 'implementation' commences there is no more policy making, whereas in reality the processes are inseparable since policy making is a never-ending process with bargaining and flexibility involving other agencies.

Top-down approaches

One of the first works to make a significant impact upon the until-then widely accepted distinction between policy making and policy implementation was Pressman and Wildavsky's *Implementation* (1973), a study which examined the implementation of economic development in a Californian city from which the writers became aware that the problems of policy implementation were rarely considered. This work was effectively grounded in a 'top-down' approach to policy making, arguing that successful implementation requires a top-down system of control and that policy makers should only promise what they are actually able to deliver. Subsequently British writers such as Hood (1976), Gunn (1978) and Hogwood and Gunn (1984) expanded upon this with examinations of what would be necessary to achieve 'perfect' implementation. In many policy areas, and in particular those requiring the participation of a wide variety of agencies, such as community care (with a plethora of organisations involved, including those responsible for health, housing and the personal social services), the problems of inter-agency collaboration have often been cited as contributing to difficulties with implementation, thus apparently encouraging the need for a top-down approach. Hogwood and Gunn produced ten preconditions that they argued would have to be satisfied for perfect implementation:

1. That circumstances external to the implementing agency do not impose crippling constraints.
2. That adequate time and sufficient resources are made available to the programme.
3. That not only are there no constraints in terms of overall resources but also that, at each stage in the implementation process the required combination of resources is actually available.
4. That the policy to be implemented is based upon a valid theory of cause and effect.
5. That the relationship between cause and effect is direct and that there are few, if any, intervening links.
6. That there is a single implementing agency which need not depend upon other agencies for success or, if other agencies must be involved, that the dependency relationships are minimal in number and importance.
7. That there is complete understanding of, and agreement upon, the objectives to be achieved; and that these conditions persist throughout the implementation process.

8. That in moving towards agreed objectives it is possible to specify, in complete detail and perfect sequence, the tasks to be performed by each participant.
9. That there is perfect communication among, and co-ordination of, the various elements involved in the programme.
10. That those in authority can demand and obtain perfect obedience.

(Adapted from Hogwood and Gunn, 1984, pp. 199–206).

This list clearly illustrates why this is called the top-down approach. Its central purpose is essentially to provide advice to those at the top on how to minimise implementation problems, and 'policy' is taken to be the property of policy makers at the 'top'. Hogwood and Gunn recognise that these pre-conditions are unlikely ever to be achieved in practice, but they retain 'a measure of sympathy with the top-down view, if only on the grounds that "those seeking to put policy into effect" are usually elected while "those upon whom action depends" are not' (p. 207). They cite the case of civil servants and health service employees as examples of the latter. They also note that there are many examples of national top-down policies that have been so mis-conceived that they should never have occurred, or have been insufficiently thought through, as with Trowler's (1998) example of the development of the National Curriculum, where the desire to place greater emphasis on the '3Rs' was ultimately undermined by the need to fit these elements into a primary school curriculum already over-full with other subjects. However, they also observe that in some instances a top-down approach can be attractive, giving the example of a Home Secretary attempting to reduce racism within the police force, rather than accepting the persistence of racist attitudes and actions at 'street level' within the police. However, Pettigrew et al. (1992), examining reforms in the NHS, point out that historically top-down attempts to intro-duce ambitious change, such as large-scale administrative reorganisation, have faced the 'the likelihood of rapid regression as soon as top-down pressure diminishes' (p. 32).

Top-down models of implementation can also be seen to be associated with managerialist approaches to the achievement of policy objectives that became dominant in much of the public sector from the 1990s, so that Parsons (1995) is able to include 'operational management', 'corporate management' and 'person-nel management' in his exploration of implementation.

Bottom-up approaches

Perhaps the most important criticism of the top-down approach is its failure to take into account the variety and importance of other actors involved in policy implementation. This is one area which arguably owes its prominence to social policy academics who 'particularly discovered a "bottom/up" perspective – effective implementation was more likely to be a function of street-level adjust-ment than of perfect policy design' (Dunsire, 1999, p. 372). Essentially this criticism makes some of the same points as Lipsky's model of street-level bureaucrats discussed earlier in this chapter. Critics argue that control over people is not the best way of achieving successful implementation and that it is necessary to take account of the exercise of discretion in the implementation of policy, with professionals, such as doctors, police officers, social workers and teachers all playing a part in controlling and delivering the services for which they are responsible, so that the actual outcomes of policy may be very different from those intended by policy makers. In addition, supporters of a bottom-up approach argue that the reality is:

> Not of imperfect control, but of action as a continuous process of inter-action with a *changing and changeable policy*, a *complex interaction structure*, an *outside world which must interfere* with implementation because government action impinges upon it, and implementing actors who are *inherently difficult to control* (Hill, 1997a, [italics in original], p. 139).

Thus whilst the top-down approach stresses the creation of implementation deficiency, the bottom-up view stresses the continual re-creation of policy. This latter viewpoint has led some to suggest that there is a need for 'backward map-ping' (Elmore, 1980), from the problems and choices facing individuals and organisations to the policies required to change those things. Elmore criticises the dominant top-down perspective, 'forward-mapping', for its 'implicit and unquestioned assumption that policymakers control the organizational, polit-ical and technological processes that affect implementation' (p. 603). He sug-gests that backward-mapping, starting at the lowest level of the implementation process and working up, level by level, looking at the ability to affect the behav-iour that is the target of the policy and the resources that would be needed to have that effect, is more realistic, and argues that this would produce policy objectives that would be achievable.

A policy continuum

Others have tried to draw upon both top-down and bottom-up perspectives to: 'consider implementation as a policy/action continuum in which an interactive and negotiative process is taking place over time between those seeking to put policy into effect and those upon whom action depends' (Barrett and Fudge, 1981, p. 25).

It is apparent that whilst the top-down approach reflects the view that it is a policy elite (however that may be defined) that 'makes' policy, the bottom-up perspective is perhaps more realistic in recognising that at each level of government there are a variety of often interacting policies that those at local level are affected by and seek to use in the pursuit of their own goals; it also reinforces the view of 'policy making' as a continually developing continuum. As Hill and Hupe (2002) note, from the mid-1980s there have been increas-ing attempts to produce 'synthesised' or other alternative approaches to implementation, and indeed it is arguable that the use and application of any model in researching policy implementation should depend upon the subject and its context.

Conclusion

This chapter has outlined a number of approaches to agenda-setting and policy making. Even before issues reach the agendas of policy makers it is necessary to be aware of the ways in which ideas emerge and agendas can be managed, and when decisions are being made. It is apparent that there are strengths and weaknesses in both rational and incremental approaches as normative models, and that whilst incrementalism may often provide a more accurate picture of what happens in real-world policy making, the idea of rationalism still exerts a powerful appeal. There is often therefore a conflict between 'the desirability of a prescriptive approach and the reality of the need to recognise that implementation involves a continuation of the complex processes of bargaining, negotiation and interaction which characterise the policy-making process' (Ham and Hill, 1993, p. 112).

The variety of perspectives on the working of bureaucracies can provide potentially important insights into some of the organisations that are responsible for the making of social policy and the delivery of substantial parts of welfare in the United Kingdom, whilst debates over street-level bureaucracy are also important in relation to arguments over top-down and bottom-up approaches to policy making and implementation. The past twenty years have seen some clear examples of top-down policies, such as sales of local authority housing and the introduction of the National Curriculum in education (arguably successful) and the poll tax and student fees (arguably unsuccessful). Yet in many areas it is much harder to be certain about what the central goals of policy have been, for example in community care, employment policy or penal policy, requiring us to look carefully at the models that can inform our understanding of the policy process.

FURTHER READING

Dunleavy, P (1991) *Democracy, Bureaucracy and Public Choice: Economic Explanations in Political Science* (Hemel Hempstead: Harvester Wheatsheaf).

Lipsky, M (1980) *Street-Level Bureaucracy: Dilemmas of the Individual in Public Services* (New York: Russell Sage Foundation).

Lukes, S (1974) *Power: A Radical View* (London: Macmillan).

Parsons, W (1995) *Public Policy: An Introduction to the Theory and Practice of Policy Analysis* (Aldershot: Edward Elgar).

Power and Policy

3

CHAPTER OVERVIEW

This chapter examines a number of what might loosely be termed 'theories of power' that are relevant to analysing and explaining social policy making in contemporary Britain. This includes a variety of interpretations including pluralism, corporatism, Marxist and public choice interpretations. Concepts such as elites and elite theory are also discussed. The sources of power in social policy making will be perceived differently depending upon the theory adduced. Implications of these perspectives for the making and implementation of social policy are therefore considered.

Whilst the preceding chapter outlined a variety of perspectives that can provide us with one form of framework with which to analyse and interpret the social policy process, there are other different approaches that we can also use to enhance our understanding. This chapter therefore explores different explanations of the exercise of power, and in particular the role of the state and state institutions, in order to enable us to examine the policy process in a more rounded way. The state can, for present purposes, be defined in terms of the institutions of which it is composed and in terms of the functions that it performs. For example, Chapters 4, 5 and 6 are concerned largely with the social policy process in different sections of the state. In the United Kingdom state institutions include representative bodies such as the Westminster Parliament, the Scottish Parliament, the Welsh Assembly and local government, executive bodies such as government departments and some quangos and judicial bodies such as the law courts. However, recent years have also seen European institutions having a greater influence over UK policy making, including the European Union and the European Court of Human Rights.

State institutions perform a wide variety of functions. Historically the most important were the maintenance of law and order and peace (or war), the protection of property rights and the system of justice. From the nineteenth century the state has increasingly been drawn into other areas of activity including the management of the economy and the provision of a wide range of services. In the UK one of the most important areas of state involvement in service provision has been with the welfare state, traditionally seen as primarily concerned with education, health, housing, the personal social services and social security. However, other aspects of the state's role are also important for social policy. For example, as indicated in Chapter 1, the state's management of the economy has had direct and indirect implications for social policy, for example with its impact on taxation (and as a result not only on individual incomes but also on the amount of money available for services) and on employment and unemployment (again with significant ramifications for both individuals and services).

Perspectives on the exercise of power by and within the state can be presented in a variety of ways. Here the emphasis is on providing overviews of some of the main viewpoints which can contribute to our understanding of the exercise of power in the social policy process. Like many of the concepts that are presented in this book, the primary emphasis is on their utility for analysis and increasing our understanding of social policy; in other words, they are to some extent empirical, attempting to explain reality in the form of the nature of social policy decisions. However, these ideas are also seen by some as ideal models, normative views of how the world should be, towards which societies can work for a better future. In both cases they are also generally highly political and contestable concepts. It is important to bear these issues in mind when considering some of these ideas and their discussion in the wider literature.

Pluralism

Pluralism is the theory that has generally been dominant in studies of British politics and policy making. The central feature of pluralist theory is its contention that, in western industrialised societies such as Britain, power is widely distributed among different groups. This plurality of power centres makes available a multiplicity of channels of influence, so that in the long term any legitimate interest can be represented at the political level, and no one group is dominant in the decision-making process. There is, however, some debate within pluralism over the role of the state and government institutions. Some pluralist writers emphasise the even-handedness and the basic 'public interest' orientation of administrative agencies, whilst others argue that they are only one set of pressure groups among many others; for some this has involved an acceptance of criticisms that early pluralist writings often failed to take account of the constraints on decision making imposed by the capitalist economy.

As noted in Chapter 2, pluralist theory owes much to the work of Robert Dahl in the United States during the 1950s and his view that, in relation to the issues that he defined as 'key', no one person or group was dominant and that there was no consistent pattern of success or failure (Dahl, 1961). This is widely seen as underpinning both subsequent pluralist analyses of decision making and to some extent as providing a normative view which supports the operation of liberal democracy. However, Dahl's views have continued to develop and be clarified over the years to a position which might more accurately be equated with 'neo-pluralism' (for example, Dahl, 1985 and 1986).

In Britain interest in pluralism and the activity of pressure groups grew rapidly during the 1960s, as government, academics and the public became increasingly aware of the existence of a wide variety of groups. For example, as governments attempted to manage the economy, they found it necessary to bargain with organised groups, in particular employers' associations and trade unions. Both Labour and Conservative governments found it desirable to seek the advice and co-operation of these associations. Similarly, the growth of the state and its activities, particularly the welfare state, stimulated action not only by workers, including a wide variety of professional groups (such as the British Medical Association and the British Association of Social Workers), but also by consumers such as tenants and patients. The 1960s and 1970s also saw a growth in pressure groups involved in welfare politics including what Whiteley and Winyard (1984) described as the 'new poverty lobby', with the emergence of organisations such as the Child Poverty Action Group, the Disablement Income Group and Shelter. In an attempt to win votes, and arguably also to achieve 'better' policies, governments also consulted and bargained with these new consumer groups. This period possibly saw the heyday of pressure-group influence in Britain, both in social policy and other areas of state activity, so that by the late 1970s Richardson and Jordan (1979) were able to contend that policies in Britain were being developed in negotiations between government agencies and pressure groups organised into policy communities. According to them, pressure groups were able to influence public policy from the stage where issues emerged onto the agenda to the stage of implementation. In the welfare arena there were many examples of successes for these groups, such as those documented by Donnison (1982) on the Supplementary Benefits Commission, Field (1982) on the Child Poverty Action Group, and Raynsford (1986) on the Housing (Homeless Persons) Act 1977, which demonstrated that groups, acting both inside and outside the formal state organisation, could have an influence on policy formulation.

The election of the first Thatcher government in 1979 marked a significant change in pressure-group politics in the UK. As a conviction politician Margaret Thatcher was not easily amenable to open discussion with or persuasion from groups, even those such as the Confederation of British Industries (CBI) with which she might have been expected to share some common beliefs, and many were excluded from some stages of policy formulation (Baggott, 1995). Indeed, the Thatcher governments' attitude to many groups was actually confrontational, including professional groups such as teachers and doctors, local government organisations and the churches. Instead she sought and received ideas and advice from a newly influential set of bodies, the right-wing think-tanks, such as the Adam Smith Institute, the Centre for Policy Studies, the Institute of Economic Affairs and the Social Affairs Unit. For example, Trowler (1998) argues that between 1979 and 1997 there was a decline in the pluralistic nature of educational policy making, with teachers' groups and local education authorities being progressively excluded, so that, during the design of the National Curriculum in the 1980s, education professionals were not consulted about the reforms, but were largely excluded from the policy-making arena, whilst New Right think-tanks came to play a more central role. Despite this, there remained some instances of social policy where pressure groups did successfully make an impact upon government. For example, Parton (1991) noted the sophisticated and co-ordinated approach of the child-care lobby during the passage of the Children Act in 1988/9, whilst Bochel (1992) suggests that the disability lobby were able to exert considerable pressure on the Disabled Persons' (Services, Consultation and Representation) Act 1986. However, despite such examples, the impact of pressure groups on government policy was certainly less than in the 1970s. Bochel did, however, find that whilst MPs of all parties felt that lobbying was overdone, pressure groups were still seen as useful by backbench MPs in that they provided information and advice with which they could challenge government more effectively. Frontbench spokespeople also expressed appreciation for the specialist advice and information that could be provided by groups, whilst being less enthusiastic about their campaigning and pressuring role. Under John Major the government was less overtly hostile to the 'traditional' pressure groups, but nevertheless many continued to feel excluded from social policy formulation.

The return of a Labour government in 1997 saw a shift towards an apparently more consultative manner of government, with numerous consultation papers being issued and a greater use of inquiries and commissions which at least held out the prospect of some input from pressure groups. However, as much of the legislation and many of the policies introduced in the first three years of the government originated in Labour's policy agenda set before the 1997 general election, the extent to which pressure groups were able to successfully influence the formulation and implementation of policy remained unclear. Nevertheless, there was a general welcoming of the greater willingness to allow more open discussion on some social policy issues.

Despite a general level of acceptance among society, pluralism, as a theory of power, can be criticised in a number of ways. Firstly, the basic premise can be denied. For example, some analysts of poverty policy in Britain have argued that the poor are poor simply because they are powerless (for example, Miliband, 1974; Townsend, 1979; MacGregor, 1981). Following this line it is also possible to argue that access to political communication is severely skewed and that the pluralist notion of all groups being able to access power is erroneous.

Another critique of the position taken by Dahl, which is also relevant to pluralism generally, has emerged from more sophisticated theories of power. Lukes (1974) points out that a number of other writers see political systems, apparently open to all comers, as containing mechanisms that actually exclude the influence of legitimate interests. The exclusion of issues from agendas, the manipulation of voting procedures, the choice of community representatives for consultation, and the operation of secrecy in political affairs may all serve to slant power upwards (see also the discussion of the three dimensions of power in Chapter 2). It can also be argued that state policies are produced within particular political, economic and ideological constraints, and within British society policies can clearly operate more to the benefit of some sections than others.

Finally, whilst pluralists may view the existence of a wide variety of organisations and groups competing to influence a neutral state as constituting a pluralism of power, an alternative (Marxist) view might see the state and state institutions as indivisibly linked by the ideological ascendancy of certain class-based values and assumptions and inevitably acting in the interests of capitalism (W Jordan, 1985).

From a practical point of view it can be argued that much of the debate within the pluralist perspective in Britain has traditionally focused upon how political power is asserted at the central government level. Debates over the importance of the House of Commons were often grounded in a view which saw the Cabinet as important in policy making, but as responsible to the House of Commons. However, from the 1960s many commentators have perceived a weakening not only of Parliament but even of Cabinet government and a move towards a more 'presidential' or 'prime ministerial' style of politics, reducing the channels of access to power even further. At the local government level the position is perhaps less clear. Judge (1995) amends Hampton's (1991) statement that 'Pluralist theory underlies most of the case studies of local politics in Britain' (p. 238), suggesting that instead it is 'a critique of pluralist theory that has underpinned most British case studies', pointing out that in the 1970s and 1980s many local authorities sought to encourage greater involvement of local organised interests in decision making whilst at the same time there was a growth in the numbers and types of such organisations. However, at the same time there was evidence that business interests retained their privileged position in decision making (Stoker, 1991).

Pressure groups

As discussed further in Chapter 7, pressure groups are arguably of key import-ance to the pluralist approach, particularly in states such as the UK where a diverse range of groups seek to influence economic and social policy. Because of this clear link with pluralistic approaches to the policy process, it is perhaps appropriate to consider briefly here the impact of pressure groups on social pol-icy. There are a great many pressure groups which attempt to influence a wide variety of different aspects of social policy in the UK (see also Exhibit 7.2), varying from small *ad hoc* groups such as those that might oppose local school or hospital closures, through charitable organisations such as Child Poverty Action Group, Scope and Shelter, to large bodies such as trade unions, the Trades Union Congress (TUC) and the CBI. As discussed elsewhere in this chapter there are different views of the role of pressure groups in their attempts to influence government.

A pluralistic view would argue that pressure groups:

- are a valuable resource which allows citizens to mobilise with others who hold similar views so that their views can be communicated to others and to government;
- help with the dispersal of power downwards and help counter-balance the powers of central institutions;
- allow a greater degree of participation in the political system; and
- provide an outlet for citizens with grievances.

On the other hand, critics argue that in many respects pressure groups can be undemocratic since:

- resources and channels of influence available to groups are severely skewed and as a result the poor tend to remain excluded from power;
- much of the influence of 'insider' groups is exerted informally and in a manner that may not easily be observed;
- in some areas of policy a 'corporatist' bias operates, reinforcing the influence of major interests and reducing the input of elected representative bodies;
- pressure groups may be unrepresentative of the interests that they claim to represent, and even of their members; by their nature pressure groups have sectional or partial interests, rather than acting in the interests of the country as a whole.

Marxist and public choice theories would provide different insights. For Marxists, pluralist democracy is itself a facade, disguising the state's support for capitalism, and the most powerful groups will inevitably represent the interests of business. In addition, most members of elite groups will accept the existing dominant values so that pressure group activity is concerned with managing inequality rather than achieving genuine democracy.

From the public choice perspective pressure groups are seen as damaging to democracy, as they are concerned with their own rather than society's interests. In addition, their attempts to influence decision making mean that the executive and the legislature are forced to respond to the demands of these groups and therefore cannot represent the interests of all. In protecting their sectional interests, pressure groups therefore damage economic growth and encourage higher public expenditure, whilst their demands can lead to 'democratic overload'.

Neo-pluralism

In response to a number of criticisms, variations of pluralism have emerged, perhaps the most important of which is usually termed 'neo-pluralism'. Supporters of this view recognise that power and resources are not evenly distributed and therefore that the decision-making process is not equally open to all. Neo-pluralists therefore see the policy-bargaining process as lop-sided. In particular, big business is seen as occupying a particularly privileged position because it controls wealth, employment and expertise, and it can often veto public policies which it perceives as threatening to its interests. The state is also seen as important, with a recognition that as the state has grown it has acquired interests of its own and a large and powerful bureaucratic apparatus, for example around the welfare state. At the same time neo-pluralists also recognise that there has been a decline in the relative influence of representative political institutions, such as Parliament, the political parties and local government. Neo-pluralism therefore arguably gives a more realistic reflection of the contemporary situation than does pure pluralism.

Corporatism

During the 1970s in the UK considerable attention was paid to an alternative model to pluralism. Corporatism as a body of theory focuses upon major interest groups, particularly those that command resources that are essential for economic activity. The key to their influence over government is seen as lying in their organisational power and their ability to tap strong solidaristic loyalties in the population rather than in any electoral strength. For example, trade unions and business associations, along with some professional associations, are often organised into single, hierarchical, associations. In some cases these organisations can develop a special bargaining position with government and their close and permanent 'insider' relations with state agencies can create a 'corporate bias' in policy making which relegates other interests to a secondary position. In return for this, the leaderships of corporate groups not only represent their members to government but also control their members for the government. The group leaderships themselves are often integrated into government functions through appointments to the boards of, or other involvement with, quasi-government agencies.

Corporatist interest bargaining was often seen as decisive on economic issues, whilst a more open pluralist group process was seen as relevant to 'secondary' issues such as some areas of social policy. With a corporatist model there is no longer freewheeling interest-group activity such as in pluralism, nor open access for any potential group to influence policy.

The high point of a corporatist approach to policy making in Britain is usually seen as the 'social contract' of 1975–78 under which the then Labour government gave trade union and business leaders a voice in many domestic policy issues, in exchange for delivering their members' compliance with government wage norms. This agreement lent support to the view that corporatism was becoming an important part of British political life. Also, during the 1970s some commentators saw or sought for significant evidence of corporatism not only in central government (Middlemass, 1979; Schmitter and Lehmbruch, 1979) but also in local government (Newton, 1976; Saunders, 1979).

However, during the 1980s under the more right-wing and ideologically led Conservative governments, corporatist bodies such as the Manpower Services Commission and the National Economic Development Council fell from favour and were gradually abandoned so that by the 1990s it was hard to argue that there was significant evidence for corporatist decision making in British central government.

Like pluralism, corporatism can also be criticised for its view of the role of the state. Corporatist writers generally view the state as having moved from a position of supporting the process of capital accumulation to directing that process. The state, although constrained by major economic interests, is often seen as autonomous as a result of its control of legal, organisational and other resources and is therefore able to act in the interests of capital, labour or other resources. However, Marxists would again argue that the state is not a neutral entity but that it acts in the interests of capital.

Perhaps one of the strongest arguments against the applicability of corporatism in Britain is the lack of evidence of successful examples in practice. In contrast to the experience of some countries, such as Austria, the 'Social Contract' of the 1970s was not only short-lived but was widely perceived as a failure. Following the election of the Conservatives in 1979 the Thatcher governments distanced themselves from direct interest bargaining and let existing corporatist institutions fall into disuse. In addition, not only was trade union opposition to government policies ignored, large sections of the business community also felt that government did not listen to their pleas for changes to elements of economic policy.

Corporatism and social policy

Despite these criticisms, and the emphasis of much corporatist writing on economic policy, there remain important implications for the study of the social policy process from corporatism. For example, Cawson (1982), who examined corporatism with reference to social policy, believed that the corporatist approach could help in focusing attention on the reciprocal relationship between the state and organised interests in society in respect of the formation and execution of public policy. He argued that despite the variable influence of professionals between service areas (he suggested that they were strong in the health service, weak in housing and the personal social services, and so on), and between different parts of the same service (for example, the differential influence on public housing provision exerted by local authority housing departments, the Housing Corporation and the National Housing Federation), overall, social policy can frequently be seen as operating in the interests of service providers, rather than service users. In this sense social policy is often shaped by the advocates of a welfare state whose priority is to sustain itself rather than to address the discrepancies between public experiences of problems and professional constructions of them. However, whilst for Cawson, during the late 1970s, the NHS provided a clear example of corporatism, because of the close co-operation between the medical profession and the government, he also recognised that consumer groups, such as MIND (the National Association for Mental Health), were seeking to influence government in a manner associated with pluralism, but suggested that they lacked the leverage available to the medical profession as a producer group. It is also possible to argue that the Thatcher reforms of the 1980s reduced the corporatist tendencies of the NHS as they unsettled the relationship between the Department of Health and organisations such as the British Medical Association (BMA), and also introduced reforms such as the internal market in the face of sometimes bitter opposition from producer groups. With regard to education, Rust and Blakemore (1990) noted that there can be both 'strong' and 'weak' versions of corporatism, depending upon factors such as the degree of centralised control and the status of teachers' professional groups.

It is also important to recognise that in some areas of government a corporatist approach to policy making has arguably existed for a considerable period of time. Perhaps most notably, until the food scares of the 1990s, the relationship between the Ministry of Agriculture, Fisheries and Food (MAFF) and the National Farmers Union (NFU) long exhibited at least some of the characteristics of corporatism. The NFU had a significant input into policy making on agriculture and farming whilst it also gave the Ministry specialised information, advice and support, as well as representing its position to farmers. Many consumer groups and others in turn felt excluded from the policy-making process, for example over environmental and food safety issues, as a result of this close relationship. However, eventually, following a series of concerns including salmonella and BSE, the government passed many of the functions of MAFF on to the Department for Environment, Food and Rural Affairs, and created an independent Food Standards Agency to reflect the interests of consumers.

For social policy, therefore, the main 'corporatist influences' are arguably different from those active in bargaining over the economy. The most significant may be the professions and quasi-professions, and perhaps, in some cases, public sector trade unions, although in some areas, such as pharmaceuticals, business concerns should not be discounted. For the study of social policy in the early twenty-first century, corporatism perhaps retains two main implications. Firstly, in contrast to pluralism it focuses on the close relationships which can develop between government (of whatever tier) and powerful interests, and the type of arrangements that may occur in these cases. Secondly, it reminds us that in these cases power can be centred outside Parliament and other representative institutions and that decisions can be made in negotiation between the executive and powerful interest groups, potentially with little attention to the interests of consumers and with minimal democratic scrutiny.

The dual state thesis

Building upon both pluralist and corporatist ideas, Cawson and Saunders (1983) and Saunders (1984) developed what they termed a 'dualistic' theoretical approach to the analysis of British politics. They argued that it is necessary to use two different political theories, which have often been seen as incompatible, in order to make sense of two different types of political process which have developed side by side in the modern British state. The dual state thesis is summarised in Figure 3.1.

Figure 3.1   The dual state approach

Dimension	Class	Sector	Tension
Organisational	Central	Local	Centralised direction versus local discretion
Functional	Production	Consumption	Economic versus social priorities
Political	Corporate	Competitive	Rational planning versus democratic accountability
Ideological	Profit	Need	Private property rights versus citizenship rights

Source: P Saunders, 'Rethinking Local Politics' in M Boddy and C Fudge (eds) *Local Socialism* (London: Macmillan, 1984), p. 30.

For present purposes we are concerned primarily with the 'functional' dimension. Saunders (and Cawson and Saunders) argued that at the central government level power has tended to shift away from the elected representative agencies of government (notably the House of Commons) into a relatively exclusive 'corporate' sector consisting of bodies (including many quangos (see Chapter 6)) whose membership is not directly elected but is appointed from representatives of particular producer interests such as business, professional associations and the trade unions. This can be seen as part of the development of a 'corporate bias' which reflects central government's desire to insulate itself from the pressures of competing interests and to direct its policies in the light of the expressed needs and demands of particular (often private sector) interests. These interests therefore have direct access to government both formally, through the range of quasi- and non-governmental organisations, and informally, for example through links between the Treasury, the Bank of England and City-based financial institutions. Cawson and Saunders (1983) argued that the political process was therefore being bifurcated between democratic and corporate sectors. They recognised that there had been some increase in 'corporate bias' at the local level but argued that the scale and organisation of local government meant that it remained more accessible to a wider range of interests, involving competition between different 'consumption sectors'.

They therefore suggested that there was a division between a democratic or 'pluralist' sector of politics and a more closed and exclusive 'corporatist' sector and that this was reflected to a large extent in the division between local and central government. They also attributed part of the rising level of tension and conflict between central and local authorities in the mid-1980s to a reflection of the relative openness of local government to a range of popular interests that were not finding a voice within the corporatist sector at national level. Such arguments appeared to lose much of their force during the 1990s, in part as a result of local government's powers and expenditure being increasingly restricted by central government. Nevertheless, many of the criticisms of quasi-governmental organisations outlined in Chapter 6 echo Cawson and Saunders's concerns of a corporate bias towards business being reflected in appointments to these bodies. However, neo-pluralism might equally serve as an explanation for this situation.

Policy communities and policy networks

One of the responses to debates over the applicability of pluralist ideas to the United Kingdom came in the form of the notion of policy communities and policy networks, an area of analysis which developed rapidly from the 1980s. The terms 'policy network' and 'policy community' have each since been utilised in a variety of sometimes rather different senses. The importance of these ideas lies in the view that in most areas of policy or decision making there are a variety of government departments or agencies, advisory bodies and pressure groups with interests in the areas, as well as other bodies or individuals who may be affected by the policies or issues. In so far as there is any real distinction between the terms it may be that policy 'communities' involve organisations that are linked to each other by resource dependencies and that they are therefore normally smaller, and perhaps more stable, integrated and consensual groupings than are policy 'networks'. However, for many purposes the two can be used interchangeably. A policy network is therefore composed of those likely to be involved with or affected by decisions made in a particular policy area, as illustrated in Exhibit 3.1 (see also Chapter 5). Rhodes (1997) examines the variety of approaches to networks and suggests that there might be a continuum from 'policy communities', through professional, inter-governmental and producer networks to 'issue networks'. The key characteristics of policy communities are that all participants have some resources important to the policy area, with limited numbers of participants, frequent high-quality interaction between members, consistency of values, membership and policy outcomes and a significant degree of consensus on ideology, values and broad policy preferences. Issue networks, on the other hand, have larger and fluctuating numbers of members encompassing a broader range of interests, have more unequal power relationships, have less constant and intensive contacts, and, whilst there may be general agreement on policy, also contain a degree of conflict. He usefully summarises some of the key ideas of the policy networks approach explaining that it:

> emphasizes the need to disaggregate policy analysis and stresses that relationships between groups and government vary between policy areas. At the same time it recognizes that most policy areas involve few interests in policy making. Continuity of both outcomes and groups characterizes policy making in many policy areas. (Rhodes, 1997, p. 32).

EXHIBIT 3.1   POSSIBLE MEMBERS OF A POLICY COMMUNITY OR POLICY NETWORK AROUND HOUSING

In the case of housing the 'government' side might be represented by:
- ministers and civil servants from the Office of the Deputy Prime Minister (with perhaps representation from Northern Irish, Scottish and Welsh governments); the Housing Corporation (and Scottish Homes);
- the House of Commons' Office of the Deputy Prime Minister Select Committee.

Those from the 'non-governmental' side might include:
- local authorities, with their roles as both providers and strategic planners;
- independent social landlords, such as housing associations, either directly and/or through the National Housing Federation;
- pressure groups, both those associated with housing, such as Shelter, and those concerned with other issues, such as the environment;
- other interested bodies that might include mortgage lenders, financiers and construction companies.

However, it is worth noting that within this potential diversity there may exist tighter networks that continue to exert a strong influence over housing policy.

Of course, it is important to recognise that policy outcomes inevitably feed back into the policy community and thus will affect future policies and outcomes. In some cases government bodies will encourage the development of policy communities, as this may facilitate regular communication and the implementation of policy. However, the existence of a policy network should not be taken to mean that there is consensus or an absence of conflict. The emphasis is not so much on conflict or agreement, but rather on the shared framework in which decisions are made and policies implemented.

Indeed, there can be dangers in the existence of policy communities. As Grant (1995) points out, 'the idea of policy communities clearly provides a good fit with the available empirical evidence on how decisions are made in British government... [but] does raise some worrying problems for normative democratic theory' (p. 37). Some of these concerns are similar to those raised by corporatism and neo-pluralism, with issues around access and openness to policy networks, including the possibility that they may come to consist of 'insider' groups, and that some interests might be excluded from the policy-making process. Richards and Smith (2002) note that for much of the post-war years there was a closed policy community, with health policy centred around the Ministry of Health (later the Department of Health), the British Medical Association and the royal colleges representing hospital consultants, and as a result it was hard for other groups, such as patients or nurses, to have any say in the development of health policy. Associated with this is the danger that such exclusive processes may actually damage the quality of decision making, becoming more concerned with avoiding conflict and maintaining existing relationships than with tackling policy problems. An example cited as part of the discussion of corporatism earlier in this chapter again illustrates this well, as in the policy areas of agriculture and food the close relationships between the 'core' policy communities of farmers and food producers have sometimes been identified as excluding consumer and public health interests and as a result increasing the risk of problems such as BSE and other food and related public health issues. Indeed, writing on health policy in the early 1990s, Wistow (1992) noted that its disaggregation into two policy communities, 'relatively discrete (and competing) health service interests and agribusiness interests' (p. 71), had already had an impact in terms of food health scares over salmonella infection in eggs. Labour's creation of the Food Standards Agency in 2001 to be responsible for food safety and standards, and the Department for Environment, Food and Rural Affairs, was in part a response to this.

Where the role of technical experts is concerned, Sabatier (1998) and Sabatier and Jenkins-Smith (1993) have developed the concept of the 'advocacy coalition framework'. Rather than conceiving of agency officials and researchers as passive or indifferent in the policy process, this approach views them as having policy beliefs, being potentially involved in advocacy coalitions (subsystems of actors from a variety of organisations who are actively concerned over particular issues or problems, such as education or health, and who regularly seek to influence public policy in that area), and as engaging in co-ordinated activities with others in pursuit of their policy goals.

Regime theory

Regime theory again reflects the complexity of government and the exercise of power. As outlined in Chapter 1, it has developed largely from the study of urban politics to provide us with another perspective on power. Unlike many other accounts, it emphasises the interdependence of governmental and non-governmental forces in meeting economic and social needs; and it focuses attention on problems of co-operation and co-ordination between the different actors in policy making. It attempts to explain how, despite the number of competing interests and the complexity of government in the late twentieth century, a capacity to govern can emerge in the political system. Recognising the existence of a very complex web of relationships including a large number of institutions and actors, and in which there is considerable fragmentation and lack of consensus, regime theory sees interdependence between these institutions and actors as characterising modern urban systems. Stone (1989) suggests that the world is 'loosely coupled' and in some ways 'chaotic'. This type of society is not easily governed by direct and intense control but is more likely to see control limited to particular aspects of society. Regime theory therefore examines how these limited segments of power are combined to produce policy initiatives or developments.

For regime theory the 'regime' is the set of arrangements by which the division of labour between government institutions subject to some degree of popular control and the mainly privately controlled economy is bridged. At its most basic a regime can be presented as a political coalition, centred upon elected politicians and local bureaucrats and including the other forces with which they work. In some ways regime theory can be seen as drawing on Marxist or corporatist views, in that it recognises that business controls investment decisions and resources and thus has a privileged position in government decision making. On the other hand, regime theory also argues that politics does matter and, unlike some Marxist views of the state, this perspective does see decision makers as being able to exercise a degree of autonomy. Whilst there are limits to this autonomy, the possibilities do exist for political activities to have an impact upon government and policies. However, some regime theorists do suggest that the political system does not attempt to encourage widespread participation and involvement and that this can both reduce popular control over decision making and make government less responsive to the needs of disadvantaged groups (Elkin, 1987). Regime theory also clearly shares some common ground with pluralism, and particularly neo-pluralism, which sees business as having a privileged position, but also sees a range of organised interests competing to influence power. Indeed Judge (1995) uses regime theory as part of his argument that 'we are all pluralists now' (p. 30); however, in the same book Stoker (1995) suggests that this 'tells us more about the changing nature and diversity of pluralism' (p. 57) than it does about regime theorists.

From the perspective of regime theory the power of the state is seen as restricted by the complexity and fragmentation of the contemporary world. Unlike the pluralist view, the state is not there primarily to judge competing claims; rather the role of the state is as a mobiliser and co-ordinator of resources.

It is upon this type of government activity that regime theory focuses, and in particular in urban government and politics this is seen as of growing importance. For regime theorists, urban politics is about getting enough co-operation to bring the various community elements together to get things done. Politics is seen as about government working with other institutions and interests, and this involves forming regimes to facilitate action and empower themselves. Whilst Dahl (1961) asked *Who Governs?*, regime theory looks at the social production of power – achieving the capacity to act – and focuses on the power to do something rather than power over someone.

In his study of post-war Atlanta, Stone (1989) identified a continuous regime from 1946 to the late 1980s which had been committed to economic growth. This involved the need for considerable government spending and risk. Stone argued that two groups dominated the regime: the first was some of the city's big business – the banks, utilities, newspapers, department stores and Coca Cola – which had a long history of working together and which encouraged new business to join with them in their aims; the second part of the regime was based upon the post-war black electoral majority in the city, and in particular the black mayors. Stone argued that the black middle class manipulated this political resource well to their advantage. He suggested that both of these groups saw benefits to themselves from a rapid economic development (good housing, employment and small business opportunities for the black middle class, and expansion and profit for business). They also developed mutual trust and co-operation through civic institutions and informal exchanges. Both partners made themselves indispensable in strategic decision making in the city. Furthermore, both needed each other: business needed government support and thus an alliance with black leaders and the black middle class; whilst the black middle class needed business to provide much of the impetus for expansion. The result was a regime capable of pursuing a goal of economic development that was beneficial to both partners. However, more recently he has reflected upon change in the city to note the declining population, high levels of poverty and problems with education, and has suggested that 'the Atlanta regime seems currently to lack direction and vitality' (Stone, 2001, p. 20). Using this to re-examine regime analysis, he argues that the highly informal nature of the regime in Atlanta was not conducive to long-term and systematic consideration of policy problems and that as old issues, such as school desegregation, decline in importance, so it is possible for regimes to decline, and that in Atlanta 'that decline rests on a flawed capacity to construct a program of action to address the city's deepening social problems' (p. 33).

For social policy, the lessons from regime theory perhaps lie mainly in its focus upon the complexity of society and economy and the consequent need to bring together potentially diverse interests to mobilise the resources necessary to act. Given changes over the past two decades, it is not hard to think of the relevance of this approach. In Britain, as in many other countries, there is an increasing emphasis on public–private partnerships (see for example, Commission on Public Private Partnerships, 2001); there is growing competition between cities and regions for investment; there has been greater involvement of business interests in local policy making; and decentralisation and changes in responsibility within the state, financial constraints and privatisation of services have further added to the complexity of governing not only at the local, but also at the national level.

One attempt to apply regime theory to the UK has been J S Davies's (2001) analysis of urban regeneration and the relationships between local authorities and the business sector in regeneration activities. He argues that partnerships in urban regeneration 'do not share the collaborative characteristics of regime governance...[and] that the emergence of regime governance is very unlikely in the near future' (p. 195) but that the approach remains of value as 'The conceptual lens of regime theory invites comparisons and contrasts' (p. 211) and encourages consideration of the extent to which local politics still matters. An analysis of AIDS (Acquired Immune Deficiency Syndrome) politics in the city of Christchurch in New Zealand (M Brown, 1999) found the application of regime theory valuable, particularly given the complex arrangements that tend to be involved in the delivery of AIDS services, but noted that it was important to consider dimensions other than the relationship between state and market, such as the community, and the domestic and family sphere.

Stoker (1995) identifies three main criticisms or weaknesses in regime theory. First is that, perhaps because of the relative newness of the idea, it is still difficult to define and apply the regime view of power, and in particular the regime view is hard to test in practice, so that it is unclear to what extent the application of a regime perspective necessarily adds to our understanding of the exercise of power. Second, the focus on regimes at the local level means that it is necessary to put regimes in context – regimes exist within a broader regional or national environment and their capacity can be enhanced through access to non-local powers and resources or constrained by external forces. It is therefore necessary to consider the interaction between regimes and higher levels of government. Third, there is a need to explain regime continuity and change. For example, whilst Stone's study of Atlanta focuses on continuity, regimes do change and the influence of new ideas and policy solutions must be taken into account. When a regime's favoured policy approach becomes unpopular and new policies gain support, what is the impact of these on old regimes and the emergence of new regimes? And how are old regimes changed or replaced?

Whilst putting forward a number of arguments in favour of regimes as a prescriptive model, Elkin (1987) also highlights a number of difficulties, in particular the tension between what he terms a 'popular' regime (based upon popular political control) and a 'commercial rights-bearing' regime. Where the latter dominates, he sees the danger of systematic bias in favour of those who control the assets that urban governments require, such as land and capital.

Regime theory has arguably added a new perspective to studies of urban government. Particularly useful are its emphasis on the complexity of politics and its suggestion that in complex societies we should see power as the capacity to provide leadership and allow significant tasks to be achieved.

Institutional theory

Like pluralism, institutional theory is something of a 'traditional' perspective, and in contrast to policy-network and regime approaches, emphasises the centrality of institutions to understanding the exercise of power. Conventionally in political science this took an approach grounded in descriptions of institutions such as Parliament, the courts, political parties and the executive, and to some extent the formal relationships between them. It has frequently been used in attempts at comparison across countries as a means of seeking to describe and measure the differences in the role of particular institutions such as the courts or the legislature. Unsurprisingly, among the main criticisms of institutionalism was its emphasis on a highly historical and legalistic approach to the study of politics and a consequent failure to recognise and account for policy or power that occur or are exercised outside these formalistic mechanisms, or even the relationships between institutions and policies. Another frequent criticism was the reliance upon a rather descriptive, formalistic methodological approach by many institutionalists. For some critics these together could be characterised by an emphasis on the state without taking account of the society in which it operates, thus neglecting the role of actors such as voters and pressure groups. As a response to these criticisms there was a shift to a recognition of the role of less formal organisational networks (for example, as reflected later in this chapter in debates about policy networks) and an attempt to marry the traditional institutional approach with more 'behaviouralist' approaches, including public choice theory, discussed elsewhere in this chapter (Peters, 1999).

Rhodes (1997) has suggested that there are now three types of institutional analysis: constitutional studies, public administration, and the 'new institutionalism'. Inevitably the focus of the first has been on the analysis of, and frequently the reform of, the constitution, with one of the common concerns in the UK in the past having been the lack of a bill of rights. The study of public administration also places the study of institutions at the centre of its concerns, with an emphasis on their history, structure, functions and power. In some respects much of the coverage of Chapters 4 and 5 of this book draws on such an approach. Whilst some critics have suggested that there is little new about the 'new institutionalism', supporters of the notion have argued that it differs from the original, as it recognises the importance of taking account not only of formal institutions and practices but also of less formal organised networks and relationships (see also Peters, 1999). Colomer (2001), for example, has argued that political institutions (defined as the formal rules of the game, and in particular who can vote, how votes are counted and what is voted for) shape the strategies of actors, and that these in turn produce collective outcomes which can themselves only be explained in terms of the information, opportunities, incentives and constraints provided by institutions and the consequent strategies adopted by both citizens and leaders.

However, institutionalism is not restricted to political science and there are economic and sociological approaches too. In the field of economics the relationship between institutions and individuals' preferences has been a key area of debate, and in particular the extent to which institutions are created by individuals who are seeking to maximise their own utility, and/or the extent and means by which institutions shape individuals' preferences. From a sociological perspective it might be argued that there has been more of an emphasis on the process by which institutions emerge and develop and therefore on change.

For the analysis of social policy the institutional approach directs us at an examination of the formal organisations, rules and procedures of government and other bodies. However, it should be extended beyond political structures to a consideration of other forms of 'institution' such as the media, quasi-governmental bodies and even supranational organisations such as the European Commission and the World Health Organisation. It may also include policy communities and policy networks as discussed elsewhere in this chapter. It focuses on regularised patterns of behaviour and these, 'which we often call rules or structures... can affect decision-making and the content of public policy' (Anderson, 1997, p. 32). As was pointed out in Chapter 2, rules and structures are often not neutral in the impact that they have, and frequently favour certain policy alternatives or particular sections of society to the disadvantage of others. They may also give incentives to particular forms of behaviour. Thus, whilst the institutional approach has its weaknesses, it remains relevant, for not only do institutional structures, arrangements and relationships set the context for policy making, they themselves must be considered as part of the dynamic in the study of policy.

Elite theory

In contrast to the pluralist approach, elite perspectives on policy making contend that power is concentrated in the hands of a few groups or individuals. The processes of decision making will therefore work to the advantage of these elites. The 'classical' elite theorists, Mosca and Pareto, argued that the existence of elites is a necessary and inevitable feature of all societies, although Mosca later amended his view to a position that in a 'democracy' elites might compete through elections for the legitimacy to rule. Michels (1915) propounded the 'iron law of oligarchy' which suggests that, over time, elites in organisations will develop their own interests and goals which will be distinct from those of the membership. These three, however, were writing at a time when many were still opposed to emerging democracy, and to socialism in particular, and there were fears of the disorganised mass and demands for democracy and equality. Other writers have attempted to bring together the notions of democracy and elitism. Schumpeter (1974) argued that in a democracy elitism is legitimised by the political market, which is made up of the competing parties and rival elites. Lowell Field and Higley (1980) have similarly suggested that elites require support from non-elites, for which they must compete. Following from this it has been argued that the existence of elites is not incompatible with pluralist democracy (with its many competing interests), as competition between elites protects democratic government. In addition, the fact that different elites may operate in different areas of society (including social, political and economic arenas) has been seen by some as protection against domination by one group.

Some theorists have argued that social change in the modern state means that the position of elites is related to the development of large-scale organisations in many areas of life, and therefore there are different kinds of elite. For example, Bottomore (1966) suggests that elite power can arise from a variety of sources including formal office (such as Parliament), wealth, knowledge and technical expertise.

Nevertheless, modern elite theorists have drawn attention to institutional position as a source of power, and noted the overlap and connection between those occupying key positions in government, business and the military (Wright Mills, 1956). Other writers such as Miliband (1969) also point out that whilst there may be several elites, they have similar backgrounds and exercise power in the interests of a dominant class. However, whilst an important perspective, this makes the assumption that shared background implies a shared consensus of values among those in important positions. Yet just because a person originates from a particular class background, it does not inevitably follow that he or she will adopt policies that are designed to promote the class interests of that background.

For elite theorists, the fact that policies are made by these elite groups skews policy making. For example, it is argued that they focus on policies either which benefit them and their position – for example they tend to use different services, and in particular those from the private sector, whether it be education, health, housing or pensions, so that services used by the masses are neglected – or which they think are best for non-elites, but which most of them will have little or no experience of.

It is perhaps worth asking to what extent do the agendas of those in authority concur with the priorities of the population in general? By their very status as leaders, elites can influence the attitudes of citizens. They are not passive recipients of pressure from individuals and groups; indeed they are often responsible for placing issues on the agenda. A good deal of public participation is reactive: people respond to decisions or proposals by those in authority. In this way, matters assume an importance in the minds of individual citizens which they would not have possessed but for elite intervention. The acts or decisions of leaders frequently make news in their own right, and such publicity, sometimes fostered by elites themselves, can generate support. In a democratic society the mobilising role of groups is therefore an essential feature of the process of setting agendas.

One of the major problems for elite theorists is the need to demonstrate that elites do inevitably rule in democratic societies. For example, Birch (1993), one of the leading critics of such a view, has argued that in order to show that elite rule occurs in reality it would be necessary to show that at least one of the following is the case:

- Access to political office is restricted to a small and cohesive group whose members share common interests and values that are not shared by the majority of the people.

- Office holders are unresponsive to the views and interests of the public, rather using their own views and interests, and avoid public accountability either because mechanisms of accountability are inadequate or because they use other means to circumvent accountability.

- Office holders regularly take decisions on behalf of a small class or group with a non-political power base whose interests are different from those of the majority.

Birch suggests that none of the classical elite theorists was able to produce sufficient evidence of any of these to show there was any inevitability about elite rule.

From a different perspective, Scott (2001) identifies a number of specialised
elites within a modern state (legislative, government or executive, administrative,
judicial, local state, military and police and para-police elites) and notes that to
draw firm conclusions it would be necessary to look empirically at the extent to
which these overlap to form a single elite with a coherent policy and programme
(perhaps drawing on Meisel's (1958) 'three Cs' – cohesion, consciousness and
conspiracy).

Another weakness of the classical elite theorists lay in their negative assumptions about the possibilities for democracy. They believed that the public would
be unable and unwilling to exercise power and that an undemocratic elite would
therefore inevitably emerge. They did not consider that the people would develop
greater political understanding as society developed, and that it may be appropriate and acceptable for responsibility for decisions to be taken by a few, so
long as the mass retained ultimate control.

Elite theory and social policy

From the perspective of the exercise of power in social policy, elite theory directs
us to look in a number of directions. It may be the case that in most organisations there is a tendency over time for power to slide towards a few people,
whether through their energy, expertise, availability, or merely their willingness
to take on either tasks or decision making, and for such elites to avoid control
by the remainder of the organisation. The issues may therefore be to consider
who the elite (or elites) are in society, where they draw their power from and
how powerful different elite groups may be in relation to each other. Do they
have common interests and do they regularly make decisions which support
their interests? Ultimately, do these elites have control or are they dependent
upon public support which may be withdrawn?

Marxist perspectives

The Marxist concept of the state is distinctive, in that the state is seen as the
product of the historical struggle between classes and as an institutional super-
structure resting on the economic base. In 1884 Engels described the state as
the instrument by which: 'the most powerful, economically dominant class, which
by its means becomes also the politically dominant class ... acquires new means
of holding down and exploiting the oppressed class' (Engels, 1981, p. 231). For
Marxists, therefore, the state is not a politically neutral apparatus but instead it
represents and operates in the interests of the dominant class. Its legitimacy and
authority are irrelevant and exist only in the minds of the ruling class and the
false consciousness of those unaware of its true nature. Once the class struggle
has been resolved, following the proletarian revolution and the emergence of
a classless society, the state will wither away.

Neo-Marxists such as Gramsci and Althusser explained the persistence of the
state in capitalist society through its ability to elicit consent from members of

society, as well as the threat of force. Gramsci argued that the bourgeoisie helped to maintain dominance by making concessions to the working class, by accepting compromises which did not fundamentally undermine its position and therefore that of the state. Althusser stressed the importance of ideology and the ability of the bourgeois state to secure the acceptance of its values through ideological state apparatuses, such as the education system, the church and trade unions, rather than through repressive state apparatuses such as the police and the armed forces.

Miliband (1969) draws a distinction between the government and the state, arguing that the government is the most visible, although not the most important part of the state. He points out that the state also includes the bureaucracy, the police, the judiciary, local and regional authorities, many economic institutions (such as the Bank of England) and national, regional and local representative (elected) institutions. Winning control of the government through elections is therefore no guarantee of winning control of the state.

However, Miliband also suggests that the state does have a significant degree of autonomy which helps it operate in the interests of the dominant class but makes it appear neutral, and, like Gramsci, points out that it can make concessions to subordinate classes which help preserve the position of the ruling class. He argues that ultimately the state acts on behalf of the ruling class for three main reasons: the occupancy of key state positions (with people being drawn from the dominant class and having similar socio-economic characteristics and therefore similar economic and social values); the political power of business interests (for example, through funding of political parties, through the media, and through their ability to influence the economy and economic policies); and the constraints of a capitalist system (so that, for example, business interests are often equated with the national interest, whilst the capitalist system is portrayed as the only viable one). Miliband argues that in countries like Britain, therefore, the power of capitalism and the capitalist state rests not on its repressive capacities, but on a variety of more subtle and deep-seated influences.

Poulantzas (1973) takes a different approach, regarding the socio-economic characteristics of the ruling class as irrelevant, although he also argues that the state is able to develop some autonomy. He suggests that the state's role is not to eliminate class struggle but to regulate it, to keep it within manageable proportions, and to prevent any direct challenge to capitalism. This requires the state to have some autonomy from the ruling class.

It is also possible to look at the functions of the state in capitalist society. Its main function can be portrayed as assisting the process of capital accumulation: creating conditions in which capitalists are able to promote production for profit; in addition it is responsible for maintaining order and control within society. Assisting accumulation would include the provision of physical resources such as roads and industrial sites, as well as providing services such as education, health and housing to groups in the working population – these reduce the cost of labour power to capital. Maintaining order and control is carried out through repressive mechanisms such as the police, through systems such as education, and even through forms of social control such as provision of benefits.

Marxist theories therefore hold two rather different views of the role of the relationship between the state and the different classes. One is that the state is merely a tool of the economically dominant class, the bourgeoisie, who not only own the bulk of wealth but who also form an elite in terms of class origin, education, life-style and values. Whilst there may be occasional divisions of interest between different sections of the ruling class, the common interest in preserving and strengthening capitalism dominates. From this perspective, Britain is a 'capitalist' democracy rather than a 'liberal democracy', as economics takes precedence over politics. The working of the political system is determined by the economic system rather than vice versa. Inequalities of wealth and income arise from capitalism, and the British state does not challenge this. Hence 'rights', such as civil and political rights, are not really rights whilst there are enormous inequalities in wealth and life chances. Even apparently radical reforms, such as devolution, do not affect the power of the ruling class, nor do they significantly improve the position of the poor. Elections and Parliament serve primarily to legitimise capitalist democracy and to contain pressures from below. For example, Marxists would argue that, when in government, the Labour Party has done little to weaken capitalism but has sought merely to win some concessions for the working class. Regardless of which party is in government, the ruling class is permanently in power. The state is therefore inherently biased in favour of capitalism and against the working class.

The second Marxist (or neo-Marxist) perspective is that which propounds 'the relative autonomy of the state'. There are different approaches to this: firstly there are those, such as Gramsci, who focus on class domination through ideological, cultural and political means, as well as coercion; secondly there are some modern Marxists who see government politicians effectively as managers of the state, whose main aim is to further their self-interest rather than the interests of capital. However, since winning elections depends on electoral success, governments must use policies which are in the interests of capitalism. Therefore whilst theoretically autonomous they still need to ensure a healthy capitalist economy.

There are a number of potential criticisms of Marxist approaches. For example, in Britain there is substantial evidence that political elites come disproportionately from a propertied and privileged group who share significant cultural, economic, educational and social experiences, and it is therefore possible to argue that this may create bias, perhaps including favouring the capitalist system. However, it is also possible to argue that most, if not all, citizens benefit from capitalism, and therefore that the ruling class may not rule solely in its own interests.

It is also apparent that democratic governments spend large sums of money on welfare and environmental programmes which are funded in part by taxes from industry and finance. Marxists generally respond that such programmes help to legitimise the capitalist system and are therefore in the long-term interests of capitalism. Some, such as education, may also help to ensure that capitalism has a suitable supply of appropriately skilled labour, whilst income maintenance payments may help to maintain social order. However, it is possible to argue that capital has made some concessions to labour interests and that the working class can therefore negotiate benefits from capitalism in the form of state welfare. Yet Marxists also see these gains as illusory and acting only to preserve the power of the capitalist ruling class.

Marxist notions of 'false consciousness', that the thoughts and wishes of the working class are simply reflections of the ideology of the ruling class, can in turn be criticised for their outlook on society. For example, the view that people, and in particular the working class, do not recognise what their real interests are, can appear both elitist and dismissive of the working class.

Public choice theories

Public choice theories are rather different 'theories of power' from the pluralist, corporatist and Marxist analyses discussed in this chapter. Rather they can often be seen as drawing upon some aspects of the institutionalist approach, combining accounts of the behaviour of institutions with more behaviouralist explanations. These ideas, upon which the New Right drew heavily, do have significant implications for the study of the social policy process and were also of importance in setting the political and social policy agenda from the late 1970s into the 1990s.

Public choice theory as a body draws upon economic theory and techniques to analyse political processes. Whilst some, notably the work of Downs (for example, 1957), is written from within a pluralist context, much public choice writing has been associated with New Right views (for example, Niskanen, 1973; Olsen, 1968; Tullock, 1976; Buchanan, 1986). From this perspective self-interest lies at the heart of politics and policy making, so that actors are seen as acting in their self-interest. The application of some of these ideas to bureaucracies was outlined in Chapter 2.

Tullock (1976) argues that in order to win elections politicians are forced to 'bribe' the voters by offering benefits to different groups in order to attract their votes. It is in the interests of a voter to vote for the party offering the best package of policies for themselves, as the cost of these proposals will be spread across all taxpayers, not just those who share the characteristics of their group. The voter therefore does not pay the full price of the benefit they receive, but across the political system as a whole this results in excessive promises. Further, he examines the power of bureaucracies in the decision-making process and argues that one of the principal characteristics of the modern state has been that bureaucracies have been serving their own, rather than the public interest.

The existence and operation of pressure groups also create problems. Pressure groups are seen as diverting resources to their own self-interested ends (Tullock, 1976, 1988). This happens because the cost to individuals of a benefit is low when it is spread across the whole community. The net cost of organising to resist such a programme is relatively much higher than the net cost of organising to achieve it. The political system therefore becomes disproportionately skewed towards increasing public expenditure.

Like Tullock, Niskanen begins with the assumption of bureaucrats maximising their self-interest. He views government agencies as types of business and applies theories which attempt to model the behaviour of firms to state bureaucracies. Government agencies are therefore conceptualised as businesses which seek to maximise their budgets and their size, in the same fashion as private firms (see also the discussion of the bureaucratic over-supply model in Chapter 2). Whilst business people are assumed to seek to maximise their profits and will therefore not produce additional output whose benefit to the consumers (and hence the market price) is less than the costs of production, Niskanen argues that it is only through increasing their budgets that bureaucrats can maximise their self-interest and personal welfare. They do this through supplying outputs to the legislature in return for a budget. However, unlike a firm operating in the market, government agencies do not have to reveal the costs of a unit of output at different levels of production, and the legislature may therefore find it hard to ascertain the benefit of an agency's activities. Again, unlike in a market situation, bureaucrats have a monopoly of information about the costs and benefits of what they are doing, and this enables them to maximise their interests, and makes it hard for governments to maintain control. Rational officials therefore attempt to maximise their personal welfare by expanding their agencies' budgets. This leads to over-supply. Building upon this argument, the New Right frequently claimed that political control over government bureaucracies is ineffective and that, in attempting to achieve their self-interest, bureaucrats therefore divert resources which could be better used in other ways.

This approach can be used to support the view that society should merely lay down a basic set of general rights and that individuals should be allowed to operate freely with no other constraints (a negative view of freedom). It also supports the view that in a two-party system, where voters are forced to choose between what may be polarised alternatives, there may be excessive promises by politicians and inadequate control by citizens. Public choice theory is also attractive because it appears to provide a powerful model for explaining the widely held view that bureaucrats are primarily motivated by their own self-interest and are unresponsive to other demands. When applied to central or local government departments it may help to explain what is sometimes seen as a constant struggle for bigger shares of public expenditure.

A fundamental criticism of this perspective is that it is based upon a number of assumptions which are difficult to test. In particular it not only assumes that bureaucrats are motivated primarily by self-interest but also that those self-interests would also be best served by bigger departments and bigger budgets, which, as Parsons (1995) points out, is highly simplistic. In addition, the evidence from many countries, including the UK, in the 1980s and 1990s showed that in many cases the number of civil servants fell; this period also saw the introduction of markets and/or market techniques into public sector bureaucracies. Finally, what little empirical evidence does exist to support the ideas of Niskanen, Tullock and others, originates largely in the USA, and may not easily or appropriately be transferred to the different cultural, political and social situations that exist in the UK.

An alternative approach

Although a critic of New Right ideas, Dunleavy (1991) has produced an alternative model for bureaucratic behaviour which draws upon public choice theory (see the discussion of bureau-shaping in Chapter 2). In analysing the large-scale privatisations of the 1980s, Dunleavy points out that the relationships between types of bureaucrats and the differences in power are much more complex than

Niskanen and others have recognised. In particular, he argues that self-interest does not have to be expressed in terms of departmental size or and budgets so that they will advance their interests in a similar direction to politicians and private business. Senior civil servants therefore did not resist privatisation as it was in their class interests, although the cost was job losses and poorer working conditions for those lower down the civil service ladder. Dunleavy also produces a number of arguments which suggest that budget-maximisation is not the sole, or even necessarily the most important motivation for bureaucrats. In particular, he concludes that collective-action strategies for maximising welfare are only used by bureaucrats when other strategies have failed. Parsons is therefore able to state that:

> The arguments of Downs and Niskanen laid claim to being based on a realistic and empirically grounded analysis of the context of bureaucratic decision-making. It was an argument that has proved more powerful as a normative model than as an explanatory or descriptive one. The bureau-shaping model developed by Dunleavy, on the other hand, does have a far better fit with the experience of bureaucracy in contemporary society (Parsons, 1995, p. 320).

Globalisation

Taking another different approach to the notion of power, from the 1990s there has been considerable attention paid to what some have seen as the phenomenon of 'globalisation'. This is an argument that a complex set of processes – cultural, economic, financial, political and technological – increasingly mean that the boundaries of the 'domestic' political and policy-making system are being influenced by external pressures and developments.

One of the key changes is generally seen as being the transformation of the global economy, with new modes of production and trade, the spread of deregulation and the growing power of transnational corporations and institutions, reducing the ability of domestic policy makers to control their agendas and policies. From this perspective 'global issues and problems interact with national issues and problems and national issues and problems interact with the local level' (Parsons, 1995, p. 236). Meanwhile the boundaries between these different layers are becoming more interactive and permeable, and new tiers of policy making are also developing, for example with the 'Europeification' of policy making within the states of the European Union (EU). In addition, the growth of transnational corporations, which organise production on a global basis and which have the ability to move capital rapidly around the world, is fundamentally weakening the ability of national governments to determine their policies independently. The emphasis is increasingly on the world economy as much as on national or regional economies. And the globalisation of communications and the media means that news, ideas and values are increasingly also being spread and taking on a global nature.

Whilst this is not entirely a new state of affairs, since agenda-setting and policy making have long been affected and shaped by international or global influences, seen from this perspective the pace and nature of recent and continuing changes are such that our lives are increasingly affected by activities and events which take place in very different contexts from those in which we operate as individuals.

Some proponents of the globalisation thesis suggest that the importance of the nation-state as the context in which agendas and policy are formulated is in terminal decline. Not only are the processes of globalisation proceeding rapidly, but also the issues facing liberal democratic societies are essentially the same, such as ageing populations, crime, drugs, urban decay, the environment. In addition, the impact of global communications means that the way in which these problems are defined is increasingly the same, whilst socio-economic convergence is also causing the industrial democracies to exhibit similar problems.

For social policy, in addition to the implications for provision of welfare such as the new global economy forcing states to cut social expenditure and to maintain competitiveness (Esping-Andersen, 1996), there are implications for the policy process, such as that issues and agendas will be more and more determined by forces and changes outside the nation-state and which fall beyond the immediate influence of national policy making and governments. The emergence of AIDS has added a particular twist to the global importance of health, as it is a global problem and there are strong arguments that it must be combated at a global level. Similarly, the 1980s and 1990s have seen states view 'problems' such as the supply and transportation of drugs not just as an international problem but as one that requires an international or global response, such as in attempting to tackle the export of drugs from the main producer states.

However, globalisation is not a phenomenon that is universally accepted without question, and some writers have challenged the view that nation-states will continue to see their autonomy reduced. For example, Hirst and Thompson (1995, 1996) question the evidence for a globalised, supranational economic system, and argue that, even within an internationalised world market, nation-states may be able to affect the agenda and make decisions, even if this is as part of an international polity rather than as a national entity; they point out that nation-states retain a large degree of control over their populations. They also note that governing is not the sole preserve of nation-states but can be performed by a variety of public and private, state and non-state, national and international institutions. This is easily illustrated with respect to social policy in the EU, where not only do sub-national and national governments have very significant roles in determining policy and providing welfare, but even within the EU itself responsibility is split between the Commission, the Council of Ministers and other EU agencies.

It is also possible to argue that whilst the agenda may increasingly be set at a global level it remains the case that the nation-state is the most important actor in terms of decision making and implementation. Just because a problem might be seen as international or global does not mean that policy making will take place at that level. Whilst the issues and agendas facing policy makers may be being internationalised, it does not necessarily follow that decision making will converge. Indeed, the 1990s saw an increase in the number of nation-states, primarily through the demise of the Soviet Union and the Eastern bloc. It may also be the case that in some instances, in times of crisis, governments will tend to withdraw from international co-operation and attempt to protect their interests alone.

One of the key questions about globalisation is therefore the extent to which some issues will continue to be primarily local or national problems, whilst others, such as the world economy or the environment, will be seen as global problems.

Conclusion

In addition to the various positions already discussed in this chapter, there are a range of what might be called 'critical' or 'radical' perspectives that can add to our understanding of the exercise of power. For social policy concerns, three of these can be identified that have an immediate importance for our understanding of the subject: gender, race and disability analyses, to which might be added others such as sexuality. These critiques make a variety of points about social policy, including the role of the welfare state and the assumptions about the way that we (should) live our lives (see for example, Williams, 1989). However, for the purposes of examining the social policy process perhaps the most important idea to be drawn from these is that in general they point out that there are a range of institutions – such as the state, the churches, and economic interests – that are more or less linked together in a structure that plays an important role in deciding what issues reach the policy agenda, and which also affects the formulation and implementation of policies. In that respect there are links with Lukes's (1974) third dimension of power. At the same time they can also serve to ensure that we also take account of the danger of underplaying the power relations in society that can shape the lives not only of disabled people, black people, women, and gays and lesbians, but of everyone.

Clearly the concept of power is multi-faceted and can be approached from a variety of different positions, each of which can add to our understanding of the exercise of power in the social policy process, and some of which can also be used in a normative sense, as a description of how the world should be. Taken together they encourage us to focus on a variety of phenomena, from how decisions are made, through the way in which policy aims are set out and achieved, to a consideration of the social, political and economic institutions which shape the way in which we see the world and which may also limit the scope of government's consideration of social problems and their responses to them. The following chapters seek to look at the key features of the social policy process in the UK to which the ideas in this and preceding chapters can be applied.

FURTHER READING

Dunleavy, P (1991) *Democracy, Bureaucracy and Public Choice: Economic Explanations in Political Science* (Hemel Hempstead: Harvester Wheatsheaf).

Hill, M (1997) *The Policy Process in the Modern State* (Hemel Hempstead: Prentice Hall).

Judge, D, Stoker, G and Wolman, H (eds) (1995) *Theories of Urban Politics* (London: Sage).

Rhodes, R A W (1997) *Understanding Governance: Policy Networks, Governance, Reflexivity and Accountability* (Buckingham: Open University Press).

Central Government

CHAPTER OVERVIEW

Central government is arguably the most important determinant of social policy, both through its direct legislative and policy-making functions and through its ability to influence social policy in other ways, both direct, such as fiscal controls, and less direct, such as emphasising particular goals. This chapter discusses the variety of influences upon social policy making at the central government level, including ministers and the executive, the civil service and Parliament and their ability to make and control policy. The increased role of the judiciary and judicial mechanisms in recent years is considered as a developing factor in social policy.

As previous chapters have illustrated, much of the theoretical analysis of the policy process focuses upon the role of central government. From a practical perspective, the significance of central government to social policy is clear. It is the main legislative body within the UK and it remains the most important repository of policy-making powers, as well as possessing a variety of other important means of influencing social policy, as was clear from the significant, largely top-down, reforms of welfare policy introduced under the Conservatives from 1979 to 1997.

Nevertheless, consideration of the role of central government is not always straightforward. For example, there is not always consensus on attempts to define what constitutes 'central government', nor is there any agreement on its precise powers, or even the ways in which power and influence are exercised within central government. Where social policy is concerned it is also true to say that the central state plays little direct part in implementing some key areas of social policy. For example, responsibilities for the delivery of many collective services (including social housing, education, personal social services and health care) are generally allocated to local authorities, health authorities or other bodies. The one major area which is effectively directly provided by central government is income maintenance, with the Department for Work and Pensions being responsible for a whole range of benefits such as retirement pensions, jobseekers allowance, housing benefit, disability living allowance and child benefit. In addition, the role of the Treasury in social policy, both through the collection of taxes (and the allocation of tax credits) and in apportioning resources to 'spending Departments', such as Education and Skills and Health, is important, as perhaps became particularly noticeable during the 1997–2001 Labour government under the Chancellor of the Exchequer, Gordon Brown.

However, for many purposes the importance of central government lies in its role as policy maker and legislator, as it formulates policy and sets the legislative and financial structures for social policy. In addition, as much of the discussion in Chapter 3 highlights, different interpretations of the role of institutions, organisations and individuals, as well as culture, practice and convention, will lead us to understand and explain decisions and their outcomes in different ways.

What is central government?

One of the traditional ways of defining central government in the UK has been in terms of the Whitehall ministries and their outstations, staffed by civil servants – the Department for Education and Skills, Department of Health, Department for Work and Pensions, Office of the Deputy Prime Minister, and so on. However, it is also possible to consider a broader 'central state', which includes other large agencies that respond directly to ministers and to other central policy influences. This would include not only the civil service but also the armed forces and the Metropolitan Police, producing a central state that would be significantly larger in terms of the number of staff and expenditure. Both of these fit closely with the institutionalist approach to analysis discussed in the preceding chapter.

Central government can also be seen as consisting of a number of elements which can be divided in a variety of ways. Whilst there is no one ideal approach, a fairly straightforward analysis can be based loosely around the following: the Prime Minister and Cabinet (which together with some senior civil servants is sometimes called the 'core executive'), ministers, departments and the civil service, and Parliament.

The core executive

In recent years the 'core executive' has been viewed by some as an appropriate model for the conceptualisation of the overlapping and interconnecting networks at the core of central government (for example, Rhodes and Dunleavy, 1995; Smith, 1999). This section will therefore consider the 'core executive', interpreting this as the Prime Minister, the Cabinet and the departments and committees that link them, including in the latter grouping senior civil servants. It will also consider the principal ways in which control of the core executive is often portrayed: by the Prime Minister; by ministers as a group; or by the central bureaucrats. However, it is worth noting briefly that some would point out the frequent common social and educational background of the core executive, and indeed senior members of the judiciary, and argue that this provides some grounds for considering the extent to which there is, if not a ruling elite as outlined in Chapter 3, at least some case for questioning the commonality of interests among this group.

The Prime Minister

Whilst there is no constitutional definition of the role of the Prime Minister, B Jones *et al.* (2001) identify a number of roles:

- Head of the executive – overseeing the work of the civil service and government agencies.
- Head of government policy – having a key influence over the party's election manifesto and the annual Queen's Speech outlining the government's legislative proposals for the coming year; the Prime Minister can also choose which policies they wish to promote or play down, as well as determining the outcome of disagreements between Cabinet ministers.
- Party leader – the Prime Minister is seen by the public as the person who leads and personifies their party; this role is also highlighted by the Prime Minister's role in Parliament and in particularly in the weekly Question Time.
- Head appointing officer – responsible for appointments including the political and executive arms of government, as well as other appointments in the church and other spheres of public life.
- Senior UK representative overseas – with the growth of meetings and summits among governments, Prime Ministers are increasingly required to spend time participating in these activities.

From the 1960s and 1970s, under Prime Ministers of different parties and with differing leadership styles, it has frequently been argued that the UK has been moving towards 'prime ministerial government'. This has been based largely upon the powerful position that British Prime Ministers occupy in the core executive, together with the increasing emphasis on Prime Ministers and party leaders in the media and thus in public perception. Supporters of this view argue that Prime Ministers have the power to choose their Cabinet, to structure agendas and remodel procedures. Cabinet conventions have strengthened the pressures for group solidarity, whilst the growth of the Cabinet Office and the premier's personal staffs has provided additional support. In addition, except in times of personal or political weakness, Prime Ministers can be sure of a majority in both the Cabinet and Parliament for their policies.

The apparent dominance of certain individuals as Prime Minister, such as Harold Wilson and Margaret Thatcher, during the 1970s and 1980s, helped reinforce the impression of prime ministerial government, drawing upon the idea that the powers of the Prime Minister increasingly make the position more like that of a president. From this perspective the Prime Minister and a few close allies dominate decision making, and the Cabinet acts largely as a rubber stamp. This model highlights the powers of the Prime Minister including over:

- the party, as leader of the majority party in the House of Commons;
- Parliament, as leader of the majority party;
- the civil service, though the appointment of the most senior civil servants and through giving leadership over key policy directions;
- the Cabinet, determining membership, chairing meetings, setting the agenda, and deciding membership of Cabinet committees;
- patronage over other appointments including, for example, the creation of peers and appointments to the BBC's Board of Governors;
- determining the date of a general election.

It is worth noting that Margaret Thatcher, widely viewed as a dominant Prime Minister, also made use of other sources of support independent of both the Cabinet and the civil service. During her period in office think-tanks operating outside the formal political institutions were important influences in policy development, not least in social policy. This was reinforced by the close personal links and the interchange of personnel between the Prime Minister's Policy Unit and these think-tanks, such as the Adam Smith Institute, the Institute of Economic Affairs and the Social Affairs Unit. These bodies promoted the virtues of the market, entrepreneurship and self-reliance, and produced ideas and publications on topics including privatisation, deregulation, local management of schools, the underclass and contracting-out of local government services, many of which were reflected in the actions of the Thatcher governments.

Under Tony Blair's first administration many commentators paid greater attention to the strengthening of the machinery at the centre of government, and particularly the growth of the Prime Minister's Office and developments in the Cabinet Office. The former, based in 10 Downing Street, provides support to the Prime Minister. It can be divided into a number of sections: the Private Office, dealing with contact with the government, including documents and official engagements; the Press Office, responsible for liasing with the media; the Policy Unit, providing expert advice and guidance to the Prime Minister on a variety of policy issues; the Political Office, overseeing relations with the party; Appointments and Honours, advising the Prime Minister on range of appointments; and Operations, responsible for daily support from security to computing, cleaning and catering. Under both Conservative and Labour governments, concerns have been expressed from some quarters about the growth and powers of the Prime Minister's Office, sometimes centred around key individuals, including the chiefs of staff, such as Jonathan Powell for Tony Blair, and press secretaries, such as Bernard Ingham for Margaret Thatcher and Alistair Campbell for Tony Blair. Amongst the reasons for this are issues around access to the Prime Minister, both in terms of these people having constant and direct access, and also their control over access for others. At the same time, other concerns have been raised over the growth in the size of the Policy Unit, which contains both civil servants and special advisers. The remit of the Policy Unit includes not only the provision of advice to the Prime Minister but also working with other departments on the implementation of policy and contributing to speeches and publications.

The Cabinet Office has seen some significant changes under Labour, with the creation of a variety of new units within it, including the Performance and Innovation Unit, which has focused on a number of specific topics including adoption, 'active ageing' and child care, and the Social Exclusion Unit, established in 1997 to help reduce social exclusion by producing 'joined-up solutions to joined-up problems'. Following the 2001 election a Delivery Unit was established 'to support the Prime Minister on matters to do with the delivery of public services', together with an Office of Public Sector Reform and a Forward Strategy Unit. Whilst there have been differences of opinion over the efficacy and overlaps in responsibilities of these emerging groups within the Cabinet Office and the Prime Minister's Office, they have widely been seen as further enhancing the power of the Prime Minister at the centre of government, so that Tony Wright, Labour MP and chair of the Public Administration Select Committee, has argued that 'A prime minister's department has been created in all but name, by building up No 10 and annexing the Cabinet Office, but the implications of this for the Cabinet system and for parliamentary accountability have never been openly faced' (*The Guardian*, 22 February 2002, p. 19).

Political leadership

At this stage, before examining the role of the Cabinet, it is worth considering briefly political leadership. In recent decades, media and other concentration on the Prime Minister has meant that the bulk of attention has generally been focused on the leaders of the main political parties, but leadership may also be given by others. Elected politicians may be the most obvious focus, including, for example, individuals who may become leaders of devolved administrations such as the Scottish Parliament, or of local authorities. However, the analysis can also be extended to others who play important roles in influencing policy, including senior civil servants and, at the local level, senior local government officers; as well as leaders of other influential organisations.

Heywood (1997) notes that in some respects the subject of political leadership can be seen to be outdated, as the advent of democratic politics has introduced mechanisms through which leaders can be held publicly accountable. Yet it is also possible to argue that the notion of 'political leadership' has grown in importance as modern means of mass communication (especially television) tend to emphasise personalities as much as policies, and provide leaders with powerful weapons with which to manipulate their public images. Also, 'as society becomes more complex and fragmented people may increasingly look to the personal vision of individual leaders to give coherence and meaning to the world in which they live' (Heywood, 1997, p. 330). Some of the changes made by Labour since 1997 may lead to an even greater emphasis on political leadership, particularly at local level, with the election of a mayor for London (and similar reforms for other parts of local government), whilst perhaps intended to enhance accountability, likely to push local leaders to the fore.

A variety of styles of leadership can be identified (see Exhibit 4.1) including: *laissez faire* with a 'hands-off' approach to political management, allowing leaders

EXHIBIT 4.1   PRIME MINISTERS AS LEADERS

Margaret Thatcher

Margaret Thatcher was clearly in many respects a transformational leader, drawing upon her own strong beliefs and with a certainty that her approach was the right one. She was very formal in her leadership style and aimed to provide strong leadership and to dominate government. This was reflected in most policy areas, particularly social policy, where her ideological views had a major impact. However, even she was forced into pragmatism, for example over the NHS where she not only had to leave it as a service funded from taxation but even to increase public expenditure. She eventually became deeply unpopular with the public and was seen as an electoral liability. It was concern over this among Conservative MPs that led to her political demise in 1990.

John Major

In many respects it was the legacy of Margaret Thatcher's leadership style as well as her policies which led to John Major's election as Conservative leader and consequently Prime Minister. The unpopularity of Thatcher, and to some extent the Conservatives, and the divisions arising from her ideologically led policies meant that Conservative MPs sought to choose a leader who would provide a degree of unity within the party and who would be more pragmatic. To a considerable degree John Major fitted this description. In many respects the Major administration was about coping – with policy problems, with party divisions, and with the public's growing dissatisfaction with the Conservatives. This was very much reflected in social policy, with the general ideological direction of the Thatcher years being maintained, but with less leadership and sense of direction, as well as constant attempts to balance the different factions of the Conservative Party.

Tony Blair

Blair can in some senses be seen as transformational – for example in remoulding the Labour Party, including revising Clause IV of the party's constitution and rebranding it as 'New Labour'. However, he also shows some elements of the 'transactional' style, particularly through the involvement of some of his key advisers, such as Alistair Campbell; and some aspects of his style are almost *laissez faire* in nature, for example he does not often take the strong lead in Cabinet meetings that Margaret Thatcher used to. Focusing on social policy, it is possible to see elements of all three approaches, with some clear sign of a long-term commitment to welfare reform and some apparent willingness to attempt to take on vested interests, although perhaps with less of an ideological emphasis than that of Thatcher. Yet there is also evidence of transactional style, with some interference and hands-on involvement in the remits of other ministers; and also of *laissez faire*, for example in leaving significant power over the economy and large segments of social policy to the Treasury and to Gordon Brown, the Chancellor of the Exchequer.

to concentrate upon key political matters whilst devolving responsibility to subordinates; transactional, with a focus on the unity and cohesion of government and party, with the leader negotiating compromises and attempting to balance different interests and factions; and transformational, where the leader is motivated by strong convictions, and has accompanying strength of character to put their beliefs into practice.

The Cabinet

The Prime Minister heads the Cabinet, a group of the most senior ministers and the main collective body of the political executive. The size of the Cabinet varies but is usually around twenty ministers, with current legislation limiting the number of Cabinet ministers that can be paid a ministerial salary to 22. Most members of the Cabinet are drawn from the House of Commons and are thus accountable to it, but some, most notably, until 2003, the Lord Chancellor, then the highest legal officer in the country, are drawn from the House of Lords and are thus unelected.

Cabinet ministers are normally the political heads of the main government departments and are responsible for both the final determination of major policies and the co-ordination of the work of the various departments. The principle of 'collective responsibility' is widely applied to the Cabinet, so that, whatever their differences, once a decision is made they will present a united front and defend it publicly. However, as Budge *et al.* (2001) point out, in practice from the 1970s the principle appears to be being applied more broadly to all members of the government, apart from backbench MPs, but at the same time more weakly, with some Cabinet ministers managing to voice thinly veiled criticisms of policy and apparently some ministers leaking documents as a means of circumventing collective responsibility. Arguably now the principle of collective responsibility is also applied in Opposition, within the Shadow Cabinet, although the importance and effects there are inevitably less than in government.

Cabinet committees became an important part of the system of government during the crisis time of the Second World War and were maintained and increased as government grew during the post-war years, so that they now make the bulk of decisions, and these have the same status as Cabinet decisions. At one time their existence was secret but, as Prime Minister, John Major decided to take a more open approach and the Cabinet Office now makes their existence and membership public. The creation of Cabinet committees, together with their membership and terms of reference is the responsibility of the Prime Minister. There are two main types of Cabinet committee: standing committees, that deal with more or less permanent policy areas, such as the European Union and local government; and *ad hoc* committees which are established to deal with specific matters, and which therefore usually have a shorter period of existence. In October 2002 there were a variety of committees and sub-committees of clear relevance to social policy, such as the Ministerial Committee on Welfare Reform, chaired by the Prime Minister, the Ministerial Committee on the Criminal Justice

System, chaired by the Home Secretary, the Ministerial Committee on Public Services and Public Expenditure, chaired by the Chancellor of the Exchequer, and Ministerial Sub-Committees on Active Communities and Family Issues, again chaired by the Home Secretary, on Older People (chaired by the Secretary of State for Work and Pensions), Drug Misuse (chaired by the Minister for the Cabinet Office) and on Adult Basic Skills (chaired by the Secretary of State for Education and Skills). There were also others with the potential to influence social policy and the policy process, such as the Ministerial Sub-Committee on Employment, the Ministerial Committee on Local Government and the Ministerial Committee on Constitutional Reform Policy.

The use made of *ad hoc* committees varies with the Prime Minister. Margaret Thatcher made extensive use of them, in part to ensure that she got her own way by choosing their members, whilst John Major was less likely to use *ad hoc* committees and also made them more representative of the Cabinet. In his first government Tony Blair appeared to use *ad hoc* committees for some issues but on others was content for the Cabinet to make decisions. Some people have argued that by making decisions on behalf of the Cabinet these committees erode the authority of the full Cabinet; others that it is only their existence that makes Cabinet government possible, given the volume and complexity of government business.

The Treasury

Whilst the Treasury has always had an impact upon social policy, if only in its role in controlling public expenditure (although for a much fuller consideration see Deakin and Parry, 2000), in recent years its influence has perhaps come under greater scrutiny. One of the features of the first two Blair administrations that has often been remarked upon was the relationship between the Prime Minister and the Chancellor of the Exchequer, not only with regard to the Chancellor's perceived aspiration to be Prime Minister, but also the power wielded by the Chancellor and the Treasury which many commentators perceived to be unusually strong despite the ceding of responsibility for the setting of interest rates to the Bank of England in 1997. There were a number of ways in which this has manifested itself, but in the same manner that the Prime Minister's Office and the Cabinet Office grew from 1997, so did the Treasury. Whilst the Treasury has always played a major role through its overview of government income and expenditure, previously it can be seen as having been limited by 'a particular gap between its wish to intervene on social policy and its ability to do so' (Deakin and Parry, 2000, p. 217), but under Gordon Brown it arguably became more proactive and more collegiate in its relationship with other government departments, and rather than waiting for ideas to be brought forward by others was willing to generate initiatives itself. This has had significant implications for social policy, amongst other areas, with, for example, the introduction of public service agreements for government departments (see Chapter 8) and the move to three-year public spending rounds under the Comprehensive Spending Review strengthening the power of the Treasury over spending departments such as Health and Social Security. At the same time the preference for the use of tax credits, such as Working Families Tax Credit, rather than benefits, has meant that part of the role of the Department of Social Security is now administered through the Inland Revenue. In addition the Treasury has instigated both inter-departmental reviews, including on children at risk and the role of the voluntary sector in delivering services, and independent reviews, such as the Wanless review on the long-term resource requirements for the NHS which resulted in the massive injection of funds promised in the 2002 budget.

Ministers

Whilst it is the relationship between the Prime Minister and the Cabinet that often receives the bulk of attention, there are other ministers in the government, as illustrated for the Department for Education and Skills in Exhibit 4.2. Below the Cabinet comes the second tier of ministers of state. They work within particular departments but normally have responsibility for particular functions and answer for those areas in the House of Commons or the House of Lords. The most junior ministers are usually called parliamentary secretaries or parliamentary under-secretaries. They assist with particular areas of business and are often responsible for helping with the passage of legislation, for example in arguing the government's case on a clause-by-clause basis. There are also parliamentary private secretaries, who assist ministers with parliamentary duties and who can also help them to keep in touch with the views on the backbenches. Although unpaid, this is often seen as being the first step on the career ladder for those seeking ministerial office. Finally there are the 'Whips', who are responsible for the timetabling of government business and ensuring that the government maintains a majority in votes. In total there are therefore over 100 members of the government.

EXHIBIT 4.2 DEPARTMENT FOR EDUCATION AND SKILLS, NOVEMBER 2002

In November 2002 the Department for Education and Skills had the following ministers:

Secretary of State, Charles Clarke MP, who represented the Department in the Cabinet

Minister of State for Lifelong Learning and Higher Education, Margaret Hodge MP

Minister of State for School Standards, David Miliband MP

Parliamentary Under Secretary of State for Sure Start, Early Years and Child Care, Baroness Ashton

Parliamentary Under Secretary of State for Adult Learning Skills, Ivan Lewis MP

Parliamentary Under Secretary of State for Young People and Learning, Steven Twigg MP

Ministerial responsibility

Ministers are accountable to Parliament, and according to convention should take responsibility for failures by their departments, whether or not they were personally responsible. One of the most famous examples of this was the Crichel Down affair of 1954, when Sir Thomas Dugdale, the Minister of Agriculture, resigned over maladministration by his department even though he had not been aware of it. However, despite this example and the existence of the 'convention', over the past two decades there is much greater evidence of ministers remaining in post despite failures by their departments. In practice, it is impossible for ministers to be aware of the bulk of the work of their departments and therefore arguably it may be difficult for them to be held responsible for their actions; and, with the creation of 'Next Steps' agencies which operate with greater independence from ministers, there is further blurring of the line between the administrative failures of agencies and the policy failures of ministers, although the heads of agencies do remain answerable to ministers. Whilst there have been a number of resignations over personal failures or failures in policy areas, in recent governments few ministers have resigned over problems attributed to their department (there have been some exceptions, such as when Estelle Morris resigned as Secretary of State for Education and Skills in October 2002, although even her resignation pointed more at the difficulties of managing a large department than at particular policy failures) and, arguably, the most important factor is whether they retain the confidence of their backbench MPs.

Senior civil servants

British ministers are dependent upon career civil servants to an extent that is unusual in most other western democracies, with only the most partisan of activities normally being outside their remit. The traditional constitutional position has always been that officials advise and that ministers make decisions. This has been underpinned by features such as the permanence of civil servants, who do not change when the political composition of the government changes; anonymity, with ministers being answerable to Parliament and the public, whilst civil servants remain in the background; and neutrality and impartiality, with civil servants being seen as being uninfluenced by their own opinions and carrying out ministers' decisions whether or not they agree with them. Whilst there are few who now accept that view unquestioningly it does provide an important distinction in their roles and also underpins their behaviour. It allows politicians to be seen as decisive and accountable, reflecting their democratic legitimacy, whilst civil servants are seen as neutral advisers on policy.

However, there are critics, from both the political left and right, who argue that in reality the Cabinet and individual ministers have relatively little control, as the majority of policy decisions are effectively made by the way in which issues are processed within the civil service. From the left this has been underpinned by the reported experiences of ministers such as Tony Benn, Barbara Castle and Richard Crossman during the 1960s and 1970s which were perceived by some as the civil service elite blocking radical reforms by Labour governments with the aid of the work of inter-departmental committees, civil service control over the flow of information to ministers and the ability to route potentially difficult issues past 'awkward' ministers, including straight to the Prime Minister. New Right critiques, such as those discussed in Chapters 2 and 3, have also set out to explain why Conservative governments in the 1970s and 1980s failed to achieve major reductions in public expenditure. These have argued that civil servants blocked such initiatives as they sought to maximise their budgets and status. In many respects New Right views of the source of civil service power reflected those of the left, arising from the analysis of the 'failures' of earlier Labour governments, including the control of information and the ability to delay or otherwise diminish radical proposals.

However, as Smith (1999) points out, whilst officials do have very significant resources they do not dominate the policy process, as ministers also have resources, and in particular possess political authority and legitimacy, so that 'Officials and ministers are not in conflict, but are symbiotic' (p. 119). Whilst ministers need the advice and expertise of civil servants, so officials need strong ministers who can gain resources, space in the government's programme for legislation, and inter-departmental support. Policy-network approaches would also highlight that not only is the policy process not as top-down as some analyses might suggest, but also that the variety of actors involved and the complexity of policy making and implementation means that power may be more dispersed across a range of organisations than is implied in simple hierarchical models.

By convention, a department's permanent secretary can refuse to implement a minister's decision if they feel that it is unjustified, either because they view it as a waste of taxpayers' money, or because it is improper. The minister then has to overrule this by issuing a direction instructing officials to carry out the decision. In the last four years of John Major's government this happened on seven occasions, whilst in Tony Blair's first four years it occurred 13 times (Evans, 2001). However, these disagreements are generally over technical issues, and ministers may wish to take a wider view. Evans (2001) notes that in 1999, when it was discovered that errors in the benefits system had led to hundreds of disabled people being paid benefits to which they were not entitled, Alistair Darling, then Secretary of State for Social Security, decided that it was unacceptable that they should be required to repay this money and ordered officials not to recover the overpayments.

A development which was much remarked upon the in 1997–2001 Labour government was the increase in the number of political advisers, not just among the Prime Minister's staff, but across Whitehall, with a rise from 38 under John Major to 74 by 2001. One of the arguments for these advisers is that it can reduce ministers' dependence upon civil servants and can provide a greater range of advice; however this development can also be interpreted as undermining the advisory role of civil servants. Following criticism from the Committee on Standards in Public Life, in 2001 the government introduced a code of conduct for political advisers, including that they should respect the political impartiality of civil servants. However, a public dispute within the Department of Transport in early 2002, over the role of the Secretary of State Stephen Byers's special adviser Jo Moore and the Head of Communications Martin Sixsmith, highlighted continuing strains.

The civil service

Outside the core executive, and below the most senior civil servants who have regular contact with ministers, is the remainder of the civil service. As outlined earlier in this chapter, the traditional view of the policy process at the centre has been that ministers have made policy decisions and that civil servants brief ministers, draw up legislation and implement government policies and legislation. A working definition of civil servants is that they are the staff of all of the central government departments that work for ministers. However, in contrast to the senior civil servants discussed above on the core executive, the vast majority of civil servants do not work in departmental headquarters, are located outside London, and in recent years have become part of 'agencies', as discussed below.

In 2000 there were around 475,000 civil servants (a drop of almost a quarter of a million since 1979) across the government departments, with the largest being the Ministry of Defence followed by the then Department of Social Security and the Treasury. Despite the common perception, and the use of terms such as 'central government' and 'Whitehall', only around 5 per cent of all civil servants work in the London headquarters of their departments; the vast majority are involved in delivering government services and collecting revenue to pay for them, including paying pensions and benefits, running immigration and asylum services, and collecting taxes such as income tax, national insurance and value-added tax (VAT). Traditionally departments have had formal, hierarchical structures, with the most senior civil servant, the permanent secretary, reporting to the minister, and below her or him, deputy under-secretaries, assistant under-secretaries and so on down the ranks. However, more recently many departments have established boards to be responsible for their day-to-day management, as illustrated in Exhibit 4.3.

From the 1980s there have been a series of significant changes affecting the civil service, initially under the Conservatives and latterly under Labour, arguably based at least in part upon the public choice theories discussed in Chapter 3 (note also the discussion of bureaucracies in Chapter 2), with bureaucrats being seen as acting in the interests of themselves and their departments, rather than as governments (and implicitly the public, assuming that those interests coincide) require. These reforms began in 1982 with an emphasis on cost cutting and value for money and the introduction of the Financial Management Initiative, which sought to streamline the bureaucracy and bring business efficiency methods to the civil service (Pilkington, 1999). This was followed by the 'Next Steps' initiative, which originated in 1988 in a report by Sir Robin Ibbs, the head of the Downing Street Efficiency Unit, called *Improving Management in Government: The Next Steps* (Ibbs, 1988). This argued that a greater degree of structural change be introduced and that 'agencies should be established to carry out the executive functions of government within a policy and resources framework set by a department' (Ibbs, 1988, p. 9). The idea of functions being delegated to agencies was not new, with for example the NHS Management Board previously having responsibility for supervision of regional and district health authorities, and the Manpower Services Commission and the Training Agency having played significant roles for the Department of Employment. In addition, these agencies had been given considerable autonomy, including responsibility for

> ### EXHIBIT 4.3   DEPARTMENT OF HEALTH BOARD, NOVEMBER 2002
>
> Nigel Crisp, Chief Executive, combining the role of permanent secretary and NHS chief executive, reporting to the Secretary of State
>
> Sir Liam Donaldson, Chief Medical Officer
>
> Sarah Mullally, Chief Nursing Officer
>
> Denise Platt, Chief Inspector, Social Services Inspectorate
>
> Richard Douglas, Director of Finance
>
> David Fillingham, Director of the Modernisation Agency
>
> Andrew Foster, Director of Human Resources
>
> Professor Chris Ham, Director of Strategy Unit
>
> Sian Jarvis, Director of Communications
>
> Professor Sir John Pattison, Director of Research, Analysis and Information and Head of Genetics
>
> Hugh Taylor, Director of External and Corporate Affairs
>
> John Bacon, Director of Health and Social Care (London)
>
> Ruth Carnall, Director of Health and Social Care (South)
>
> Peter Garland, Director of Health and Social Care (North)
>
> David Nicholson, Director of Health and Social Care (Midlands and the East)

their own budgets and a significant degree of operational freedom, although they had remained constitutionally accountable to ministers. What was new in the Ibbs report was the proposed scale of change, with the argument being that up to 95 per cent of the civil service dealt with executive functions of policy implementation and service delivery and that the bulk of this work could be best done by agencies headed by chief executives who would have considerable managerial freedom and operate at arm's length from their parent department, although they would ultimately remain accountable to that department. Every government department was required to analyse its activities and consider the appropriateness of the creation of agencies, and by 1997 three-quarters of civil servants were operating within agencies, in many instances with departments retaining only small cores of staff at the centre. In the area of social policy the best-known and most widely recognised examples perhaps include the Benefits Agency and the Child Support Agency, but there are many others including the Employment Service, HM Prison Service and the Medicines Control Agency. The Next Steps reforms reflected developments elsewhere in the public sector, with an emphasis on freedom to manage, performance measurement and targets and contracts (see also Chapter 8). Framework agreements for each agency set out their aims and objectives, relationship with the parent department and financial accountabilities.

Whilst the government's initial view was that the creation of agencies had no implications for accountability, as this was to be maintained through the minister of the parent department, early problems, particularly with the Child Support Agency and the Prison Service Agency, showed that this was not the case. These arose to some extent as the agencies were based upon the traditional view that there was a reasonably clear divide between the policy-making role of ministers and the implementation and management role of civil servants. However, in the case of the Child Support Agency in particular, the policies that underlay the creation of the agency were arguably flawed, and the policy failings of ministers thus affected managerial failings in the agency as it failed to meet targets and created large numbers of complaints from the people it was contacting. In addition to questions of accountability there have also been concerns that some agencies' delivery of services may be affected, for example with the pressure of internal targets potentially conflicting with customer needs.

Under John Major the government emphasised its desire to consider privatisation of parts of the civil service through the regular process of agency reviews. This involved consideration of whether an activity should be privatised, contracted out or abolished.

On their return to government in 1997 Labour maintained their commitment to modernisation of government and to the role of the civil service in bringing about changes, particularly in attempts to work across boundaries and to achieve 'joined-up' government. In 1999 a White Paper, *Modernising Government* (Cabinet Office, 1999), was published, with one of the key themes again being 'joined-up government', together with a focus on delivery within government departments to achieve government targets. This has been reflected in the creation of Cabinet sub-committees and ministerial working parties to encourage policy co-ordination across departments, whilst the Cabinet Office has grown, both through its greater co-ordinating role and through the creation of specialist units such as the Social Exclusion Unit and the Women's Unit which have had a particular remit to encourage 'joined-up' policies and implementation (Flinders, 2002). The introduction of units such as the Performance and Innovation Unit within the Cabinet Office was in part an attempt to give a greater sense of direction and an emphasis on results to the civil service through a focus upon particular projects and outcomes (A Gray and Jenkins, 2002).

Parliament

Whilst from a pluralistic perspective it might be anticipated that an elected body such as the House of Commons would be a significant power centre, in reality for most of the past century the executive has been viewed as the dominant body in British government with Parliament (with the emphasis again generally on the House of Commons) not having played a significant role in policy making. Most legislation originates from the executive and emerges more or less intact following its passage through Parliament, although Parliament arguably does provide a forum for debate between the government and its critics, publicising the executive's legislative proposals and its actions. However, strong partisanship, party discipline and the manner of operation of the House of Commons enable government to control debate and maintain a strict legislative timetable. Any private members' bills which might have financial implications are excluded from consideration, at least without government support. Debates and questions to ministers are major activities, but scrutiny of new legislation (largely by standing committees) is disorganised and relatively ineffective. Strong party loyalties mean that there is little sense of a corporate identity of Parliament, and scrutiny of government actions and finances regularly turns into inter-party arguments. The House of Lords' powers are limited by the Parliament Acts of 1911 and 1949 so that it cannot delay or amend a 'money bill' (financial measures), although it can delay any other bill for up to a year.

Nevertheless, Parliament can be seen as playing a variety of roles in relation to social policy. Firstly, some politicians have argued that there are limits to what the democratic polity will tolerate, whether it be levels of unemployment, taxation, public expenditure or central government control over local government, and that this can be regulated through Parliament, and the House of Commons in particular. Secondly, the existence of Parliament serves to legitimise government policies and actions, and issues of legitimacy may act as important constraints on what a government can do, so that political and electoral pragmatism has limited the extent to which reforming governments of both left and right have been able to put their radical policies into practice. Finally, parliamentary institutions act as channels of influence. The impact of this may run in two ways: the use of lobbying tactics by influential groups and interests may be seen as a factor that advances special against mass interests and can therefore be delegitimating; or the capacity of political institutions to enable such lobbying to take place can be seen as a significant factor in preserving sufficient consensus to allow government to continue in an unequal society.

The House of Commons may be a representative institution, but it is far from representative in socio-economic terms, being heavily white, male and middle-class. The post-war years have seen something of a convergence in the socio-economic backgrounds of MPs, with the proportion of Conservatives who have been to state schools and universities other than Oxbridge increasing, whilst on the Labour side the proportion coming from manual occupations has fallen and those who are university-educated and from middle-class professions has grown. The 1997 general election saw a surge in the number of women elected to Parliament, from 60 in 1992 to 120 in 1997, of whom 101 were Labour; and the number of non-white MPs rose to nine, up from six in 1992. In the 2001 election 118 women MPs were returned overall, whilst the number of ethnic minority candidates elected remained very small.

Until the 1999 House of Lords Act, the majority of members of the House of Lords were hereditary peers. One of the major criticisms was that this hereditary component heavily biased control of the House against Labour and towards the Conservatives. The removal of all but 92 of the hereditary peers by the 1999 Act and the increased number of life peers has somewhat redressed the balance, although after the Conservatives the second-largest grouping is the cross-benchers, who remain independent of the party groupings. Life peerages have also had some impact on the socio-economic composition of the Lords, although it remains atypical of the population in terms of class, gender and ethnicity. Supporters of the Lords, however, claim that it is the very experience of its members that both makes them atypical and frequently gives them expertise on important topics.

Scrutiny

Parliament has a variety of opportunities to scrutinise legislation and the actions of the executive. These include examining and debating bills. Every bill has to go through three readings, a committee stage, and, normally, a report stage. The general pattern is outlined in Figure 4.1, although some exceptions are possible.

Figure 4.1   The passage of legislation through Parliament

Stages of legislation	*Where taken*
First reading (formal introduction, no debate)	On the floor of the House
Second reading (debate on the principle)	On the floor of the House
Committee (considered clause by clause; amendments can be made)	In standing committee in the Commons, although some bills are taken on the floor of the House; on the floor of the House in the Lords
Report (bill reported back to the House; amendments can be made)	On the floor of the House
Third reading (final approval; no amendments can be made in the Commons)	On the floor of the House
Lords (or Commons) amendments (consideration of amendments made by other House)	On the floor of the House

Source: Adapted from P Norton, 'The House of Commons' In B Jones, et al., *Politics UK* (Hemel Hempstead: Pearson, 2001), p. 355.

For most bills the main scrutiny in the House of Commons takes place in the standing committee. These are established for each bill and their membership reflects the strength of the parties in the Commons. Standing committees cannot reject bills or make changes that are not in line with the principle that has been approved on second reading; however, they are able to make amendments. Each bill is discussed clause by clause, and any proposed amendments are discussed before a motion is taken that the clause remain part of the bill. However, given that the government normally has a majority on the standing committee and that the progress of legislation is monitored by the party Whips, even though a government may lose the argument, most bills are enacted with few changes other than those desired by the government. In the House of

Lords there is often more time to debate bills in greater detail, making it an important forum for revision of legislation, so that the number of amendments made in the Lords is normally much greater than the number made in the Commons. Arguably one of the key roles of the Lords is therefore as a revising chamber. The great majority of amendments made by the Lords are accepted by the Commons; however, the fact that the unelected Lords can on occasion attempt to reject legislation passed by the Commons remains an issue, as for example happened with the Sexual Offences (Amendment) Bill in 1990, which set out to lower the age of consent for homosexual acts to 16.

Whilst bills are primary legislation, they often contain powers that allow regulations to be made under their authority once they are enacted. This is called delegated legislation and can be made subject to parliamentary approval. However, the procedures for introducing such regulations can vary and whilst the House of Commons undertakes some scrutiny through a Select Committee on Statutory Instruments, there are concerns that time for proper consideration and debate are often extremely limited.

Parliament also has a number of means of scrutinising the actions of government. Perhaps the most obvious to the public are those that occur on the floor of the House of Commons – debates and Question Time. However, these have become increasingly adversarial and are often seen as opportunity for point-scoring, rather than real debates and deliberations. In the House of Commons select committees provide another means of scrutiny. There are a number of types of select committee including 'domestic committees' which advise on the running of the House, 'scrutiny committees' that examine topics such as delegated legislation and European legislation, departmental select committees which monitor the work of the major government departments, and other committees that consider external matters, such as the Public Accounts Committee and the Public Administration Committee.

The current system of departmental select committees was established in 1979 and from 1997 to 2001 included an Education and Employment Committee, Environment, Transport and Regional Affairs Committee, Social Security Committee, Health Committee and Home Affairs Committee. With the restructuring of government departments in 2001 the first three of these were effectively replaced by the Education and Skills Committee, the Transport, Local Government and the Regions Committee (itself replaced in 2002 by the Transport Committee and the Office of the Deputy Prime Minister Committee) and the Work and Pensions Committee. The membership of committees approximately reflects party proportions in the House, although an opposition MP is often elected as chair. Whilst the party Whips had previously played a major role in the selection process, following a backbench revolt against attempts to replace two long-serving Labour chairs in July 2001, the Leader of the House of Commons, Robin Cook, undertook to re-examine the appointments process, holding out the possibility of greater independence for MPs, at least in this regard. Under Labour there were also some other clashes with select committees, including over whether the government's special advisers should give evidence to the committees, with the government consistently maintaining that they should not.

The committees are able to undertake in-depth analysis of government policy and actions and to examine subjects in detail and produce evidence that might not otherwise be available. Normally the committees select topics for inquiry and then collect information, including both oral and written evidence. They are able to question ministers and civil servants and can tackle a wide range of topics, so that in recent years the Health Committee has produced reports on topics including consultants' contracts, access to NHS dentistry, rehabilitation from head injury and the government's provision of information on the safety of breast implants; and the Social Security Committee has reported on pensioner poverty, housing benefit and the social security implications of parental leave on the birth of a baby or adoption of a child. In 2002 the Education and Skills Select Committee produced a damning report on one of the major policy failures of the Labour government up to that date: the introduction and subsequent abolition of Individual Learning Accounts (see Exhibit 4.4). Even those in areas which seem not immediately related to social policy can on occasion step into such territory, as happened with the report of the Select Committee on Science and Technology in 2002 when it criticised the regulation of genetics and embryology, including the Human Fertilisation and Embryology Authority, and called for the 1990 Human Fertilisation and Embryology Act to be revised. However, the scope of their investigations is restricted by time, resources, and the general aims to achieve consensus on reports; for the most part their recommendations are taken up by government only when in line with existing policy; and as they have been unable to interest significant numbers of backbenchers in its work they are therefore dependent upon the media and interest and pressure groups taking up issues if they are to have any real impact on policy. Arguably where the committees can have real value is in their ability to question ministers and civil servants on some potentially key aspects of policy, in making significant amounts of information available, and from time to time in producing authoritative and persuasive reports.

Although frequently criticised for ignoring Parliament, in 2002 Tony Blair did agree to appear twice-yearly before a televised cross-party committee of backbench MPs, leading one expert, Peter Hennessey, to claim that 'At last this closes the accountability gap, whereby the single most important figure in the executive, from Mrs Thatcher onwards, had exempted themselves from the scrutiny of the select committee system' (*Guardian*, 27 April 2002, p. 2).

Influence

Despite the central role of the welfare state in Britain's economic and social life, significant changes in government policy and the interest expressed in opinion polls, only a relatively small number of backbench MPs or peers specialise in social policy issues. There are a variety of methods that they can use to garner information and attempt to influence government. Parliamentary questions in the area of welfare appear to be used largely to request information on issues topical at the time, and in this they appear to be a useful tool (Bochel, 1992). Pressure groups and other lobbying can also help provide information and can encourage MPs and peers to make representations to the government on some

---

EXHIBIT 4.4 A POLICY FAILURE

The Education and Skills Select Committee's report on Individual Learning Accounts

Individual Learning Accounts (ILAs) were one of the key strands of Labour's approach to lifelong learning. They were intended to make a government contribution for some courses for individuals in England seeking to develop their knowledge and skills, with, it was hoped, the full cost being topped up by employers and employees. However, whilst coming into effect on 1 September 2000 and reaching the initial target of one million ILAs by May 2001, almost a year ahead of schedule, ILAs were closed by 23 November 2001 following a perception that their growth had outstripped their anticipated cost to public funds and suspicions of widespread fraud and abuse of the scheme.

May 1997	Labour Party Manifesto
28 July 2000	Learning and Skills Act 2000 received Royal Assent
1 September 2000	Individual Learning Accounts Regulations come into effect
20 October 2000	Department for Education and Skills caps ILAs at £200 – 80 per cent of £250
March 2001	Interim target date for opening half a million ILAs
May 2001	Government announces one millionth ILA
24 October 2001	Secretary of State for Education and Skills announces that ILAs will be closed on 7 December
23 November 2001	Closure of ILAs in England
March 2002	Original target date for one million ILAs

The House of Commons Education and Skills Select Committee identified a whole series of weaknesses with the approach taken by the government (Education and Skills Select Committee, 2002). It concluded that there was a need to provide a system of expanding adult learning, both for individuals and for the nation as a whole, but that any future development would require stronger quality assurance and security mechanisms, a full business model, information on unscrupulous providers and stronger and clearer contract management arrangements with the private sector.

---

issues. However, given party discipline, MPs in particular are not always able to influence government even if they wish to do so, and there is a growing feeling in the House of Commons that lobbying is overdone and that it may therefore even have a negative effect.

At times backbench MPs, either working behind the scenes, or occasionally by threatening to vote against their party, can force the government to re-think its policies, with a notable example from the Thatcher years (but fairly minor in the context of the entirety of social policy) being the Disabled Persons' (Services, Consultation and Representation) Act 1986. This Act was also a successful example of legislation initiated by a backbencher, and illustrates that with the right conditions MPs can introduce and have enacted measures significantly affecting policy and the provision of welfare. Ethical and moral legislation in particular is often left to private members' bills, with major reforms such as the abolition of the death penalty and the legalisation of homosexuality in the 1960s, whilst more recently attempts to legislate on abortion have also come from the backbenches. However, only a small proportion of such bills ever become law. In attempts to influence government measures or in initiating private members' legislation, backbench MPs are helped considerably if there is all-party agreement and/or support from pressure and interest groups and public opinion (Bochel, 1992).

One means by which pressure-group activity and views can be fed into the parliamentary arena is through all-party groups within Parliament. These are unofficial groups consisting of backbench members of both Houses, and tend to cover subjects which are not generally contentious in party political terms, some of which receive administrative and/or financial support from pressure groups. There are a large number of these groups with many in the social policy area, such as the All-Party Parliamentary Childcare Group (in 2001/2 administrative support was provided by the Daycare Trust), the All-Party Parliamentary Disability Group (in 2001/2 research assistance was provided by the Royal Association for Disability and Rehabilitation), the All-Party Parliamentary Group on Homelessness and Housing Need (in 2002/3 a grant of approximately £19,000 per annum was given by the Joseph Rowntree Foundation to the Catholic Housing Aid Society (CHAS) to enable CHAS to cover the administrative costs of the group) and the All-Party Parliamentary Group on Mental Health (which in 2001/2 received research, secretarial and general administrative support from the Royal College of Psychiatrists). Groups' activities typically include meetings and sometimes visits, the issue of occasional publications or newsletters, and the production of briefing papers and suggestions for action in Parliament. These groups represent a channel to MPs and through them to ministers of a more organised nature than might be envisaged from a simple pluralistic perspective in which individual organisations would make their own advances to individual MPs. In turn this could mean that interests around which it is possible to gather all-party support might have an advantage over other welfare interests.

From another perspective, the large increase in the proportion of women MPs at the 1997 general election raised some expectations of change, both in the way in which Parliament operates and in the attention paid to women's issues. However, any anticipation of immediate change was unrealistic; not only were the bulk of these new MPs inexperienced in Parliament but they remained a relatively small group. Dahlerup (1988) has argued that there is a 'critical mass' of around 40 per cent of an elected chamber, when the proportion of women representatives does have a significant impact. In addition, a four-year timescale is relatively short to achieve any major change in the working of an institution such as the House of Commons.

Overall, the extent to which the United Kingdom is a parliamentary state is perhaps diminishing. Not only does Parliament appear weak compared with the executive, but the use by governments of quasi-governmental mechanisms, the growth of influence of the European Union, and devolution within the United

Kingdom are further dispersing power from Parliament. In addition to some of the concerns discussed above, and those implicit in some of the approaches outlined in Chapter 3 (for example, elite theory, Marxist perspectives and New Right critiques), which in some instances question the very nature of parliamentary democracy, these developments raise significant issues about some of the fundamental features of the policy process, including accountability and representation, aspects of which are discussed in Chapters 6 and 7.

The judiciary

While the judiciary is not strictly part of central government – and, indeed, attempts are frequently made to maintain a distinction between it and the executive – it is worth noting that the last two decades have seen an increased role for the judiciary in relation to public policy, including social policy. There have been a number of aspects to this. Firstly, there has been greater use of the courts to try and challenge the actions and decisions of government, including the European Court of Human Rights and the European Court of Justice. Examples of this include criticisms by the former of the UK's censorship of prisoners' correspondence, of corporal punishment in schools, and of immigration rules that discriminated against women. Secondly, there has been a significant increase in the use of judicial review to attempt to challenge decisions. Judicial review is a mechanism through which the courts can be asked to review the legality of actions or decisions either on the grounds that they are outside the powers granted to ministers by the relevant legislation, or on the grounds that they are not in accordance with natural justice. And thirdly, there has been a tendency for governments to use judges to head inquiries into a variety of incidents and issues. Among the most important of these were the use of Lord Scarman in 1981 to look into the causes of riots in Brixton, Lord Justice Taylor's investigation in 1993 into the disaster at the Hillsborough football ground when 93 people were killed and 200 injured, Lord Justice Scott's hearing of evidence in 1994 over the accusation that government ministers broke their own code of conduct by allowing the export of weapons to Iraq, and Lord Nolan's inquiry into standards in public life, which began with an examination of ethical standards in Parliament and which culminated in the establishment of the Committee on Standards in Public Life.

From the perspective of national and local administration, the High Court can be seen as playing the role of a supervisory court, with the purpose of its activities being to ensure that governmental and public authorities follow the proper procedures and fulfil their legal duties and responsibilities. This is effectively carried out by the judicial review process (see Figure 4.2; for a summary of the strengths and weaknesses of this procedure in achieving accountability), which can be initiated by an individual or organisation that is unhappy about the decision of an inferior court, tribunal or administering body. However, there are limits to the power of the courts: as Parliament is sovereign, legislation cannot be ruled to be unconstitutional; and judges can only consider whether actions are lawful, not the merits of the legislation upon which decisions are based. Applications for judicial review can be made upon four grounds: illegality,

Figure 4.2   Judicial review and accountable government

Positive

- It takes place in an environment free from party politics.

- Coercive powers can force the attendance of witnesses and the release of information; decisions can be overturned.

- Applications for judicial review can focus parliamentary attention on an issue.

- Threat of judicial review may act as a counterweight to arbitrary government.

- Procedures for applying for judicial review have been simplified.

- Judicial review may help facilitate 'good administration'.

Negative

- Constitutionally the position of the judiciary is weak, beyond upholding the rule of law.

- The executive can overturn any judicial decision through legislation or remaking the decision following prescribed guidelines.

- It is rarely used as a challenge to central government.

- Applications are rarely against ministerial actions.

- The vast majority of applications fail at the first stage.

- Of those granted leave, the executive wins over 80 per cent of cases.

- Judges remain deferential to Parliament and are unlikely to rule in areas involving economic policy, defence or national security.

- Judges rarely overturn Public Interest Immunity certificates.

- Practical (financial, delays, etc.) and procedural (need to provide 'sufficient interest' and obtain leave) obstacles exist.

- It is a reactive and secondary mechanism of accountability.

- Democratically the judiciary are in a weak position, not being elected or accountable.

- It is a very uncertain and discretion-based process.

Source: M Flinders, 'Mechanisms of Judicial Accountability in British Central Government', *Parliamentary Affairs*, vol. 54 (2001), p. 61.

where a public authority may act beyond its specific powers; procedural impropriety, where the procedures laid down by statute have not been followed; irrationality, where a decision is seen to be unreasonable (for example, in 1997 the courts ruled that regulations introduced by the Secretary of State for Social Security to remove the rights of many asylum seekers to income-related benefits were draconian and should not be contemplated by any civilised nation); and proportionality, where authorities' actions must be proportional to their aims. However, many attempts to use judicial review to affect government policy fail, as was the case in 2002 when the High Court ruled against an attempt by the Society for the Protection of the Unborn Child to ban the morning-after pill. The creation of the devolved administrations in the late 1990s also brought with it implications for judicial activity, with the legislation that created the National Assembly for Wales and the Scottish Parliament laying down the legal process by which the powers and the ways in which those powers can be exercised can be challenged.

At the supranational level the European Court of Justice is the final arbiter on questions relating to the interpretation of European Community treaties. The European Court of Justice makes decisions where there is conflict on the interpretation and application of EU law between member states, between institutions, or between institutions or member states and individuals. Where there is conflict, EU law takes precedence over national law. However, some would argue that if Parliament were to pass an Act that expressly contravened EU law then the doctrine of parliamentary sovereignty implies that British courts should apply the provisions of the Act.

The European Convention on Human Rights was ratified by Britain in 1951, although it was not incorporated into British law as successive British governments refused to take this step, arguing that human rights were already protected under domestic law, and also reflecting the concept of the sovereignty of Parliament. As a result, British citizens who felt that their human rights had been infringed could not appeal to British courts on the basis of the Convention; although they were able to appeal to the European Court of Human Rights in Strasbourg. The Court found against the British government on many occasions, including over the treatment of suspected terrorists in Northern Ireland and the use of different ages of consent for heterosexual and homosexual acts. Although the UK was not bound to comply with the decisions of the Court it consistently did so by introducing changes to UK law to bring it into line with the judgments of the Court. Writing in the early years of the Labour government, and reflecting on developments in the 1990s, Woodhouse (1998) noted that UK judges had been influenced by the role taken by the European Court of Justice on social policy issues, including discrimination and equality; this reflects some of the discussion on Europe in Chapter 5.

With the European Convention on Human Rights (ECHR) having been incorporated into UK law through the 1998 Human Rights Act, it is now possible for the domestic courts to be used by individuals who believe their human rights have been infringed. The Act came into effect in England and Wales on 2 October 2000 and was already having an impact the following year, including upon policy. For example, following a judgment in 2001 on the detention of patients under the Mental Health Act, the Court of Appeal ruled that the onus could no longer be on the patient to demonstrate that they should no longer be detained but that those who are detaining them should have to demonstrate a case. This led to the first fast-track use of the new system of Remedial Orders to propose amendments to legislation incompatible with the ECHR (see Exhibit 4.5).

EXHIBIT 4.5   CHANGING LAW: THE HUMAN RIGHTS ACT AND THE MENTAL HEALTH ACT

On 4 April 2001 the Court of Appeal ruled that sections 72 and 73 of the 1983 Mental Health Act were incompatible with the right to liberty under Article 5 of the European Convention on Human Rights.

On 19 July a proposal for a draft Remedial Order was set before Parliament. The same day the Joint (House of Common and House of Lords) Committee on Human Rights agreed to consult with interested parties on the proposal and to seek answers to a number of questions from the Secretary of State for Health, with responses requested by 15 October. The questions to the Secretary of State included issues about why the Department of Health had decided not to appeal against the ruling, how many patients could be affected by the incompatibility, why the Department had used the non-urgent procedure rather than the urgent procedure, given that the liberty of individuals was affected, and what provision would be made for compensation to people who had been detained in violation of the ECHR.

Following responses from the Health Minister responsible, and others, the Committee wrote again with further questions, receiving a response on 8 November. The non-urgent procedure was then withdrawn and an urgent procedure was then laid before Parliament on 19 November, with the Joint Committee recommending its approval by both Houses, although it did note a number of concerns including the Department of Health's decision to make ex gratia payments to victims of the incompatibility rather than establishing a statutory system. The Remedial Order came into effect on 26 November with both Houses having up to 120 days to make a decision on whether or not to approve it.

Other successful uses of the Act included applications from two women prisoners to the Court of Appeal which ruled that whilst it was acceptable for the Home Secretary to have a policy that children should cease to live with their mothers in prison once they reached the age of 18 months, he or she should be prepared to make exceptions, and that mothers should be given the opportunity to state why the policy should not apply to them. In May 2002 the European Court ruled that the Home Secretary could not keep murderers in jail when the parole board has recommended their release. At the same time some attempts to challenge the law failed, including over the confiscation of drug traffickers' assets and entrapment by police, both of which were ruled not to breach the ECHR.

In more general terms, where social policy is concerned, some have argued that the rights enshrined in the ECHR will have a wider impact. For example, the right to life may mean that police officers who could previously use 'reasonable force' during violent struggles or arrests will be limited to using force which is absolutely necessary. Similarly, the prison service may find that they will be required to take more stringent measures to prevent suicides by inmates in jail. In addition, in contrast to judicial review, where judges have not been allowed to look at the merits of a decision, only whether it was properly and fairly reached, the Human Rights Act does allow an examination of the merits of the case, and the rationing of health care is one area where this might occur. However, with the exception of torture, most of the rights are not absolute, and the state may interfere with most individual rights if this is done in pursuit of a legitimate aim. Perhaps reflecting some continuing ambivalence, whilst on passing the Act the Labour government suggested that it wished to create a culture of rights, with rights becoming acknowledged and maintained with little need for recourse to the courts, it did not follow the example of some other states in establishing a human rights commission, which could have advised public bodies, scrutinised proposed legislation, and advised individuals, perhaps even providing legal representation for test cases, or having the power to investigate suspected human rights abuses.

Conclusion

The use of an analytical approach to central government grounded in the notion of the core executive is appealing, directing attention at some of the key actors in the policy-making process, and reflecting the realities of the relationships between ministers and senior civil servants. That said, it is clear that prime ministers are able to exercise considerable power, as for example Margaret Thatcher did over large realms of social policy, although this may be constrained by their relations with their Cabinet colleagues, and to some extent with their party in Parliament. The extent to which the UK has prime ministerial rather than Cabinet government is therefore not certain, and whether there is a trend towards prime ministerial government remains hard to discern amongst the variety of constantly changing conditions, including the strengths of other members of the Cabinet, the degree of internal party unity or division, the size of a government's majority in the House of Commons, and the salience of particular issues from time to time. As a result the notion of the 'core executive' becomes more attractive as a useful concept for analysing government, bringing with it the recognition that at the centre of decision making there are a number of individuals and organisations that are embedded in a network of relationships between themselves and others in their immediate circles. This extends consideration of the exercise of power away from just the Prime Minister and the Cabinet and towards to the larger network of power relationships that exist within Westminster and Whitehall. The growth in the social policy role of the Treasury since 1997 can therefore be examined in terms of the relationship between the Prime Minister, Tony Blair, and the Chancellor of the Exchequer, Gordon Brown, whilst the confusion over 'fixing' of A-level grades in the autumn of 2002 reflected a lack of clarity in the roles and relationships of ministers, senior civil servants and an executive agency (Tomlinson, 2002).

However – and perhaps of some concern, partly in terms of its representative function, and partly in terms of the relative distribution of power – Parliament is widely seen as currently unable to exercise sufficient scrutiny over the actions of the executive. This arises in part from the control that the parties exert, and in part from the lack of resources available to backbench MPs. For Parliament to be able to scrutinise and even potentially challenge the decisions and actions of the executive, a major problem is the lack of administrative and research support. This is as true for select committees as it is for individual MPs, and whilst unfavourable reports on various aspects of social policy have been produced under successive governments of different parties, it remains easy for the executive to ignore such criticisms.

Under Labour, the government has placed great emphasis on a variety of key concerns around the management of government, and there has been consequent stress on ideas such as the modernisation of government and joined-up government. As a result, Labour have maintained their Conservative predecessors' commitment to managerial change and to improvements in the performance of the civil service, including the continued use of agencies. In addition, particularly through its greater use of special advisers, it too has been accused of politicising the civil service.

Returning to judges and the courts, although they do not always lie at the centre of the policy process in the UK, they can and do play a significant role, in particular through the application of judicial review to constrain some exercise of power by public institutions, and this is increasingly being used in the social arena, with additional impetus arising from legislation such as the Disability Discrimination Act and the Human Rights Act. However, it is important to be aware of the distinction between political decisions and judicial decisions. Political decisions are those that involve choices between alternative courses of action. These should be made by elected politicians and may properly reflect the political outlook of the government of the day. Judicial decisions are procedural or mechanistic decisions based on the laws already laid down by Parliament. They should be concerned with applying the law, not making the law. These should therefore be limited in scope and politically unbiased.

Finally, considering again some of the ideas put forward in the first three chapters of this book, it is important to note that the policy process is much more complex and fragmented than might be seen from a simple reading of this chapter. Approaches such as those on policy networks and policy communities and on regime theory have suggested that much policy making and implementation is developed through the existence of informal networks, with relationships built upon varying degrees of interdependence. In addition, arguments around globalisation and multi-level governance, with power variously being seen as shifting upwards towards multinational corporations or transnational organisations, or downwards towards regional levels of government, also suggest a need to take account of diverse and fragmented sources of power and to emphasise patterns and modes of co-ordination. There are also those who, reflecting elite theory, would suggest that many of the groups covered in this chapter, such as Cabinet ministers, senior civil servants and senior members of the judiciary, often share common background, including social status, school and university education, including many who have attended the major public schools and Oxford and Cambridge, whilst also being overwhelmingly white and male, and that they may therefore possess common values and interests. In some senses, therefore, attempts to develop a comprehension of central government mirror the debates in the early chapters of this book. Much of this chapter essentially takes an institutionalist approach to its topic, seeking to provide a basic understanding through outlining some of the main institutions; but our appreciation can only be further developed through a wider and more diverse approach which takes account of the true nature of the policy process in contemporary society.

FURTHER READING

Griffith, J A G (1997) *The Politics of the Judiciary* (London: Fontana).

Pilkington, C (1999) *The Civil Service in Britain Today* (Manchester: Manchester University Press).

Rhodes, R A W and Dunleavy, P (eds) (1995) *Prime Minister, Cabinet and Core Executive* (London: Macmillan).

Rose, R (2001) *The Prime Minister in a Shrinking World* (Cambridge: Polity).

Smith, M J (1999) *The Core Executive in Britain* (London: Macmillan).

In addition, interesting examples of Select Committee reports that reflect some of the complexities and tensions within central government and difficulties of implementing social policies include: Education and Skills Select Committee (2002) *Third Report – Individual Learning Accounts* (London: House of Commons) and Public Accounts Committee (2002) *The New Deal for Young People* (London: Stationery Office). However, as noted in the discussion of Parliament, their ability to affect government policy and practice remains very limited.

Multi-Level Governance

CHAPTER OVERVIEW

The concept of multi-level governance is one that in some respects is relatively new to the United Kingdom, but which developments over the last two decades have made particularly relevant. This chapter commences with an examination of the role and impact of the European Union on social policy. It then moves on to consider one of the clearest areas of radical change under the 1997 Labour government: the rapid move to devolve power to Scotland and Wales, as well as to Northern Ireland, with potentially significant implications for the future development of social policy. Finally, despite what has been recognised as a continual erosion of local government powers and services since 1979, local government remains important in the planning and provision of many welfare services. This chapter therefore considers the place of local government in social policy and the influences upon it, including the burden of legislation and control imposed by central government, the diminution of the role of local government in the delivery of social policy and the growing involvement of elected members and the role of officers.

Whilst the previous chapter has focused upon central government, it is clear that amongst the major developments affecting the UK polity over recent years has been the addition of new levels of governmental power, in particular the European Union and the devolved administrations of Northern Ireland, Scotland and Wales, whilst local government has also been subject to significant reform. This has encouraged analysts to move away from a focus upon the UK as a unitary state, where, it was often possible to argue, power was relatively centralised. This chapter seeks to explain and analyse these developments and to draw out their possible implications for social policy. Whilst multi-level governance can also be used to take account of the impact of other international, transnational and multinational bodies and organisations, and these should not be discounted as irrelevant for social policy, our interest here is limited to those aspects which have the clearest immediate impact upon social policy in the UK: the growing role of the European Union, the devolved administrations in Northern Ireland, Scotland and Wales, and local government.

It is also worth reconsidering briefly the use of the term 'governance', rather than 'government'. Whilst the former has a variety of meanings, it is increasingly used to imply, for example, a lesser role for government and the state in some areas of policy, the use of a wide variety of mechanisms for the management and delivery of public services, institutional and constitutional reform, and a recognition of the need for policy to be made and implemented through complex networks of groups drawn from public, private and voluntary sectors, as implied by perspectives such as the policy networks and regime theory approaches discussed in Chapter 3.

The European Union

In some respects the placing of the European Union at the head of this chapter is questionable, as it has arguably had a relatively minor immediate impact on social policy, with little European legislation in major fields such as education, health, housing or social care, although there has clearly been some impact in areas such as employees' rights and social security, as well as gender equality. However, the scale of the EU, its impact upon society and the state in general, and its developing role in social policy arguably make its positioning here appropriate. The main EU institutions are:

- The Council of Ministers – the chief legislating body, consisting of a minister from each of the 15 member states, with the membership changing according to the subject. It meets regularly in Brussels or Luxembourg.

- The European Council – the heads of state or heads of government of the member states, with the Prime Minister being the UK's representative. There are twice-yearly 'summits'. The presidency rotates among the member states with each holding it for six months; the state holding the presidency also chairs all meetings of the Council of Ministers and hosts the summit.

- The European Commission (EC) – based in Brussels, the Commission's role is to initiate EU policy, to implement decisions of the Council of Ministers, to act as the guardian of the European treaties and to ensure that European legislation is implemented in the member states. There are 20 commissioners (two nominated by each of the larger states – France, Germany, Italy, Spain and the UK – and one by each of the smaller states) who undertake to act for the Union rather than as representatives of the state from which they come. Whilst social policy had traditionally not figured very significantly in the EU, there are commissioners for employment and social affairs, for health and consumer protection and for education and culture, each with a directorate-general, staffed by the Commission's 'civil servants'.

- The European Parliament – there are 626 Members of the European Parliament (MEPs) of whom 87 are elected from the UK. Despite its name, the European Parliament has had until recently relatively little influence on legislation and its principal roles have arguably been to scrutinise, largely through its committees, proposals from the Commission and the work of the directorates-general, and to approve the appointment of the Commission and the EU budget. However, more recently it has become involved in joint decision making with the Council of Ministers in some areas so that it has the power to reject some proposals.

- The European Court of Justice – the ECJ consists of 15 judges and eight advocates-general who are appointed by the governments of the member states acting together. Membership of the EU carries with it an obligation to accept the ECJ as the ultimate court of appeal on EU law, and EU legislation takes precedence over national legislation, so that one of its functions is therefore to make decisions in disputes between the Commission and national governments. It has made judgments on a wide variety of cases including the freedom of movement of workers and their families, including migrant workers, and on equal pay.

- The European Economic and Social Committee, which comprises 222 representatives of civil society (employers' organisations, trade unions and other groups) and gives opinions on proposals for EU legislation.

- The European Ombudsman, who is appointed by the European Parliament with the brief to investigate complaints of maladministration against EU institutions.

- The European Central Bank, which is the central bank for the euro zone and is responsible for price stability, including interest rates, and the European Investment Bank which facilitates the financing of long-term capital projects.

The 1957 Treaty of Rome which established the then European Economic Community made relatively little allowance for a social dimension, and in the early years the emphasis was primarily on the free movement of workers and the establishment of a common market. The Single European Act gave some greater opening for the development of social policy within the EU, particularly with regard to employment, such as in the areas of health and safety at work, and economic and social cohesion. In recent years the social dimension of the European Union has come rather more to the fore, in part through the emphasis on equal opportunities for men and women and also through attempts to push the viewpoint that economic, employment and social policies can reinforce each other and that they can increase social cohesion. The Maastricht Treaty of 1991 took social policy a step forward, being signed by the then 12 member states, although the UK opted out of the social dimension. The 1997 Treaty of Amsterdam consolidated the mechanisms established under the Maastricht Treaty and gave a sounder grounding for some aspects of social policy, particularly with regard to employment, with the newly elected Labour government signing up to the Treaty, unlike their Conservative predecessors. However, even under the new Treaty, the emphasis of European social policy remains heavily linked with employment, although a non-discrimination clause allows action to combat discrimination on the grounds of sex, racial or ethnic origin, religion, age, disability or sexual orientation. In other areas too there has been some growth of a social dimension, including education, with programmes designed to encourage mobility among younger people such as SOCRATES, TEMPUS and LINGUA, and justice, such as co-operation on both civil and criminal matters, including topics such as asylum, drugs and organised crime.

In general, it is important to recognise that member governments remain the dominant factor in the development (or otherwise) of social policies at the European level. However, as reflected in the title of this chapter, there has been some diffusion of power upwards. Perhaps the most notable area so far where the EU is frequently seen as having been a significant catalyst for the development of policy is equality for women, and in particular working women (see Exhibit 5.1). Whilst this not only indicates the potential for the EU to be a significant policy actor, these developments have also forced a reconsideration of sex equality within national political systems. In addition, they have led to the existence of a new network of organisations (drawing upon groups from the private, voluntary and public sectors) which is involved in the formulation and implementation of sex equality policies at EU levels, in turn creating new policy actors that national governments now have to work with.

EXHIBIT 5.1 THE EU, GENDER EQUALITY AND UK SOCIAL POLICY

Mazey (1998) traces the growth of EU involvement in attempts to achieve greater gender equality to the activities of second-wave feminism in the late 1960s and early 1970s and the emergence of an advocacy coalition (see Chapter 3) which has sought 'to persuade policy makers of the need to address the socio-political causes of sex discrimination against women' (p. 132), basing much of its argument upon Article 119 of the Treaty of Rome which, in theory, provided for equal pay for men and women. Whilst Article 119 had generally been neglected, its existence, together with the institutions of the European Commission and to a lesser extent the European Parliament, provided an alternative policy-making arena for feminists seeking equal pay and equal treatment, whilst EC law and the European Court of Justice gave means of legal redress for sex discrimination. This opportunity was reinforced by other factors, including the desire of many of those working within EC structures to make an impact, as well as a wish to extend the social dimension of the EC, and the more pluralistic and open nature of the EC decision-making process, which allowed greater access to women's groups than was often the case in domestic political systems.

Similarly, Duncan (2002) illustrates how the more corporatist gender-equality model propounded by the EU, particularly after the accession of Finland and Sweden in the mid-1990s, acted against New Labour's tendency towards a more liberal view of the relationship between work and family using the US model as inspiration, and helped ensure that the gendered distribution of work and care moved onto the EU's and thus the UK's social policy agenda.

However, the influence of the EU should not be overstated, for even with regard to this area national governments retain control over many policies which affect women in the labour market (such as child-care provision, taxation and education). The perceived impact of globalisation also has the potential to affect the situation, with member states frequently seeking more flexibility in the labour market, more deregulation and a reduction in the costs of labour, making the policy-making environment much less friendly than during the 1970s when there was a greater general emphasis on welfare.

In terms of the policy process, in the same way as there are concerns about a 'democratic deficit' in the use of quasi-governmental organisations (see Chapter 6), so too have some raised concerns about this at the European level. These tend to be fairly obvious, with the European Parliament, although directly elected, having had very little ability to influence European legislation; and even if the Parliament were to gain substantially greater powers, the lack of Europe-wide parties or clear leaders, as well as means of communication, would arguably still hinder the processes of democratic accountability. At the same time, given the complexity and the degree of networking which takes place at the European level, ideas such as policy networks and the advocacy coalition framework discussed in Chapter 3 are clearly useful tools for analysing decision making, as can be adduced from the examples around equality for women outlined above.

Sub-central government

Whilst some have argued that the existence of the EU and its developing impact upon social policy have seen a shifting of power upwards, away from the UK government, it is equally important to recognise that the last years of the twentieth century and the first years of the twenty-first century saw significant developments in sub-central government in the UK. Following decades of reduction in the power of local authorities and the centralisation of many aspects of social policy decision making, some reversal in this trend appeared to be heralded by the election of a Labour government ostensibly committed to the devolution of power. Among the first actions of the new government were moves to pave the way for the creation of a Scottish Parliament and a National Assembly for Wales; at the same time they continued to follow their Conservative predecessors' blueprint for the creation of a Northern Ireland Assembly with a power-sharing executive. Almost simultaneously the government was publishing discussion documents setting out proposals for the 'modernisation' of local government and the renewal of democracy at local level. Yet one of the most noted tensions within the 1997 Labour government was that between its apparent desire to devolve power and its simultaneous wish to exercise control from the centre, the latter being reflected in a whole range of initiatives which arguably by-passed those whom it claimed to seek to empower. Also, as Stoker (2000a) points out, there have been changing concerns in the study of sub-central politics, reflecting some of the debates outlined in Chapter 1. In particular he notes that:

> a key concern in the study of local politics has become 'governance', which
> can be broadly defined as a concern with governing, achieving collective

action in the realm of public affairs, in conditions where it is not possible to rest on recourse to the authority of the state... Governance recognises the capacity to get things done which does not rest on the power of government to command or use its authority. Governing becomes an interactive process because no single actor has the knowledge and resource capacity to tackle problems unilaterally (Stoker, 2000a, p. 3).

The remainder of this chapter examines the role of sub-central government in social policy, including the devolved governments, local government and other forms of sub-Westminster government in the context of these developments.

Devolution

Devolution is one of the areas where the 1997–2001 Labour government clearly demonstrated a radical dimension to its policies. The Referendum (Scotland and Wales) Bill was the first public bill of the new Parliament, enabling the government to hold referendums on devolution, with the legislation to establish the devolved bodies to follow the referendums. In September 1997 Scots voted overwhelmingly in favour of a Scottish Parliament (74.3 per cent for) and substantially for it to have tax-varying powers (63.5 per cent for) and a week later the Welsh people voted narrowly (50.3 per cent to 49.7 per cent) in favour of a Welsh Assembly. The Scottish Parliament and Welsh Assembly both took power on 1 July 1999. At the same time Labour followed through the Conservatives' approach to the peace process in Northern Ireland with the creation of the Northern Ireland Assembly. Clearly devolution was a major part of Labour's approach to the modernisation of government. For those interested in the policy process and social policy these new decision-making bodies provide a new dimension.

In terms of multi-level governance there is also a significant link between devolution to Northern Ireland, Scotland and Wales and the European Union, as the devolved administrations also seek to influence EU policy making and resource allocation, so that, for example, the Scottish Executive has its own European office in Brussels. Europe's Committee of the Regions has provided one institutional channel for such approaches, although it has frequently been criticised as weak; and Scotland, together with some other regions within Europe, has sought a greater role for regions within the EU (Roller and Sloat, 2002).

The Scottish Parliament

It is important to be aware that whilst the Scottish Parliament may be new, Scotland has long had its own legal system, education system, established church and arrangements for government (particularly through the Scottish Office, created in 1885). What devolution did was introduce a new tier of democratic accountability through the Scottish Parliament, whilst also giving the Parliament power to vary income tax by up to 3 pence on the basic rate set by central government. In addition, the Scottish Parliament is elected using a form of proportional representation – the additional member system – with the result that coalition government is more likely to occur, as was indeed the case following the 1999 and 2003 elections when Labour formed administrations with the Liberal Democrats.

The Scottish Parliament can make laws in relation to devolved matters in Scotland and can amend or repeal existing Acts of UK legislation in relation to devolved matters. It has considerable powers concerning the government of social policy. These relate to health, education, local government, social work, housing, economic development, transport and criminal law. These powers provide the Parliament with the potential to develop policy differently from England and Wales. Such developments might include changes to education at pre-school, primary and secondary levels, changes to higher education policy and funding, the education and training of professionals within the NHS in Scotland, changes to local domestic and non-domestic taxation, local government finance, the designation of enterprise zones and so on. The main social policy powers reserved to the UK Parliament include the fiscal, economic and monetary system (except for the tax-varying powers in Scotland), employment legislation including equal opportunities, and social security and administration including benefits and matters for which the Benefits Agency is responsible. There are also a range of other matters which are reserved, including the control and safety of medicines, reciprocal health agreements, other health matters such as abortion, human fertilisation and embryology, and legislation covering racial, gender and disability discrimination (Scottish Office, 1997).

Whilst in general the early years of the devolved administration saw social policy in Scotland following much the same path as in the rest of the UK (perhaps not surprisingly with Labour being in power in Westminster and Edinburgh), there were some examples where the Scottish Parliament and Executive chose to take a different line to the Westminster Parliament, including in the area of higher education. This happened with the abolition of student tuition fees, and represented an early instance that highlighted the potential not only for social policy change in Scotland but also for conflict with the Westminster Parliament. There is certainly also an argument that this arose not simply as a result of devolution, but also because of the use of proportional representation, as the Liberal Democrats had fought the elections for the Scottish Parliament on a platform of abolishing tuition fees. The need for coalition government in Scotland made this a major issue for the new administration. In a sense therefore, this highlights two ways in which governmental changes have the potential for allowing change in social policy.

Other examples of differential development in social policy can already be seen, for example in Scotland's repeal of 'Section 28', which banned the promotion of homosexuality. This followed a high-profile campaign against the repeal of the section that culminated in a million-strong 'vote' in a privately funded 'referendum' against the plans. In early 2001 came another major divergence with England and Wales when the Scottish Executive decided to accept the recommendation of the Royal Commission on Long Term Care of Older People that long-term social care should be free. In the field of family policy, Wassof and Hill (2002) noted that there had also been some distinctive development so that 'In Scotland since devolution there is evidence of family policies which are more explicit, less normative and more cross-sectoral than hitherto, but tensions nevertheless remain both within Scottish policies and between devolved and reserved policy emphases'. On the other hand the Scottish Executive also experienced some embarrassment with the revelation that it underspent during 1999/2000 (by £435 million, of which £135 million was on health).

However, there remain some questions about the impact of devolution upon social policy. For example, Richard Parry (2002) notes that 'By ranging widely into the poverty and social justice agenda, the [Scottish] Executive has produced some ambitious policy documents combining devolved and reserved powers, but has used the New Labour motif to advance aspirations that run beyond its legislative, policy making and spending resources'. In particular, perhaps, the additional spending commitments – including funding the scrapping of tuition fees, teachers' pay and long-term care – raise questions about the ability of Scotland to afford these policies and the means by which they can be paid for. Whilst this has not yet emerged as a major issue, the potential for a demand for greater fiscal autonomy in the future is clear.

The National Assembly for Wales

Like Scotland, Wales had retained some historical differences with England, particularly over the Welsh language and culture, but these had been far from uniform, attracting much greater support in rural and northern Wales than in urban and south Wales. In addition, there had been a Welsh Office since 1964 and a Welsh Grand Committee to debate Welsh bills, but neither of these had been as powerful as their Scottish counterparts. Like the Parliament in Scotland, the Assembly is elected by the additional member system, giving a degree of proportionality.

The possibilities for distinct social policy developments are limited to a greater extent because the Assembly has considerably weaker powers than the Scottish Parliament. Discussions of its powers often take place in the context of the relative powers of the two. For example, it has no primary legislative and only limited secondary legislative abilities and has no tax-varying power. However, whilst the powers of the National Assembly may be less than those of the Scottish Parliament, they may still be sufficient for Wales to go its own way on many issues.

The Welsh Assembly inherited virtually all of the powers previously exercised by the Secretary of State for Wales. In practice this means that it has responsibility for many aspects of health, education, local government, the environment and economic regeneration amongst others, and control over a small amount of secondary legislation. The latter provides scope to make regulations within the framework established by primary legislation. Thus there is potential for some social policy developments in Wales to be different from other parts of the UK, so that in the years immediately following devolution the Welsh government abolished Key Stage One tests for seven-year-olds and the publication of school league tables, abolished prescription charges for people under 25 and introduced free dental checks for people under 25 and over 60. In addition, in education, groups were already lobbying for the content of the curriculum to be different from that applied in English schools.

However, as is arguably also the case with Scotland, in Wales some potential policy developments have, perhaps inevitably, been limited by the previous patterns of policy making and delivery. For example, with regard to health policy, McLelland (2002) suggested that in the early years of devolution, despite the high levels of deprivation in Wales and the implications of these for a health agenda distinct from that in England, the existing value base which itself is reinforced by existing policy communities, continued to prioritise hospital-based services over attempts to tackle inequalities in health.

Yet, despite some of these limitations, and perhaps demonstrating the extent to which devolution has already become entrenched, in July 2001 the National Assembly launched a review of its internal operation and its relationship with Westminster and Whitehall, and this was followed by a second review into its powers and electoral arrangements which seemed likely also to consider whether, like the Scottish Parliament, primary legislative powers should be available to the Assembly.

The Northern Ireland Assembly

Unlike Scotland and Wales, Northern Ireland did possess its own parliament for much of the twentieth century (from 1921 to 1972), with the Unionists, representing the Protestant community, having a permanent majority and the minority Roman Catholic population being excluded from power and often experiencing discrimination by the government, for example in terms of housing and employment. Following the onset of the 'Troubles', the British government took responsibility initially for law and order and then for all aspects of government, through the Secretary of State. Whilst this arrangement was never intended to be permanent, the obstacles to the re-establishment of devolved government remained too great until the late 1990s. Following the 1997 general election, the Labour government set the target of agreeing a proposal for the government of Northern Ireland and relations with the Republic of Ireland. In April 1998 the Good Friday Agreement was approved by 71.1 per cent of those voting in Northern Ireland, helping clear the way for the Northern Ireland Assembly. The Assembly came into being and an executive was formed in November 1999, but, following disagreements over the failure of proposals for decommissioning arms, the British government suspended the Assembly in February 2000. However, following further discussions, the executive resumed in June 2000, although the nature of the political situation in Northern Ireland continued to threaten a rather on-off existence for the Assembly.

The Assembly's powers are much closer to those of the Scottish Parliament than the Welsh Assembly, including having full legislative and executive authority for devolved matters including education, health and social services. For example, in the period before its suspension in October 2002, the Assembly was discussing legislation to give disabled people in Northern Ireland similar rights to those available in Great Britain through the Disability Rights Commission, through an expansion of the powers of the Equality Commission for Northern Ireland.

Given the so far 'on-off' nature of the Assembly it is difficult to say anything about developments in the government of social policy. However, its powers are such that there is the possibility of distinctive approaches developing, although whether these may be limited or encouraged by the power-sharing arrangements is uncertain.

Other sub-central government

Elements of regional government have existed to a greater or lesser degree for much of the twentieth century, depending upon the fashions of governments. During the 1960s, attempts at economic planning saw the creation of 11 regional boards and councils consisting of employers, trade unionists, academics and local councillors, but by the 1970s such initiatives were out of fashion and they were abolished in 1979. Furthermore, the privatisation of the public utilities of electricity, gas and water during the 1980s further eroded regional administration, ending the existence of water boards, although the National Health Service did continue to operate through regional health authorities.

In 1994 the Conservatives brought together elements of the Departments of Employment, the Environment, Transport and Trade and Industry into ten Government Offices of the Regions headed by regional directors. These have had substantial powers in some areas and have had particular responsibilities for promoting competitiveness of their regions, as well as supporting regeneration and more recently social inclusion.

In addition there have been local and regional quangos and other quasi-governmental organisations such as local public spending bodies (Greer and Hoggett, 2000), the development of which has sometimes been as a substitute for local government. Under the Conservatives this was particularly noticeable in fields such as education, housing, employment training and urban development (see also Chapter 6).

Towards regional government for England?

The idea of regional government for England began to re-emerge on the agenda during the 17 years of Conservative government, fuelled in part by discontent in some areas about one-party dominance and the centralisation of government, the reduction in the autonomy of local government, and by awareness of a growing regional dimension within the European Union, to which England's existing structures could not easily respond. Both democratic and functional arguments were therefore developing over a role for the English regions (for example, Constitution Unit, 1996). Labour's 1997 general election manifesto allowed for some development of regional government in England, asserting that 'The Conservatives have created a tier of regional government in England through quangos and government regional offices' (Labour Party, 1997, p. 34) and included a commitment to build upon this through the creation of regional chambers to co-ordinate planning, economic development, transport and bids for European funding. It also stated that, where there was clear public consent, arrangements could be made for elected regional assemblies, although this is clearly linked to a unitary system of local government rather than the creation of an additional tier of government, and is conditional upon demand being demonstrated. In November 2002 the Queen's Speech announced that the government would put forward proposals for legislation to enable the holding of referendums for this purpose.

In 1999 Labour created nine regional development agencies (RDAs), based on the Government Offices of the Regions, to help co-ordinate regional economic development and encourage competitiveness. It was hoped that they would help reduce the imbalances between the regions. They were also expected to contribute to the development of policies and programmes in areas such as crime prevention, tourism and transport. Although the RDAs are accountable to ministers and to Parliament and their members appointed rather than elected, four of the 13 board members come from local government. In addition, they are expected to consult and work with new regional chambers made up of councillors from local authorities in the region together with representatives from business, education, the voluntary, cultural and environmental protection sectors and trade unions.

Despite the rhetoric of regionalism, Lee (2000) argues, drawing on the example of enterprise policy, that the Labour government has centralised power while decentralising control over policy and resources to the English regions. He notes that mechanisms such as the Comprehensive Spending Review and public service agreements, together with the refusal of Whitehall departments to devolve control to RDAs, have strengthened the centralisation of control over policy and resources.

In some regions there have also been attempts to lobby for further decentralisation and even the establishment of some regional structures. One example of this was 'The Campaign for Yorkshire', launched in March 1999. Its supporters argued that Yorkshire has a bigger population than Wales, that the area has distinctive boundaries and a historical sense of its identity. In addition, a Regional Assembly for Yorkshire and Humberside was formed in July 1996, including representatives from all 22 local authorities in the region. Among the reasons for such developments are fears that regions without decentralised bodies will be disadvantaged in comparison to Scotland and Wales, both in terms of democratic accountability and in the ability to compete for resources at Westminster and Brussels. Those who favour further decentralisation to the regions have frequently cited inequalities to support their arguments and this has arguably been the principal social policy dimension to the debate.

Perhaps the most important step forward came in May 2002 when the Department for Transport, Local Government and the Regions published a White Paper, *Your Region, Your Choice: Revitalising the English Regions*, setting out the possibility for the English regions to choose elected assemblies following regional referendums. This contained a number of arguments for regional government, including recognition of diversity and the desirability of reducing economic and social disparities between the regions, better policy making in the regions and improved effectiveness and accountability through elected assemblies. It was, however, made clear that in any region where an elected assembly were to be established there should be a review of local government aiming to deliver unitary local government structures. The proposed functions of the regional assemblies were primarily strategic but included housing and health improvement as well as areas such as sustainable development, skills and employment and transport. The White Paper suggested that funding would primarily be through a grant from central government, but that there would be the possibility of a precept on the council tax although this would be subject to capping 'to prevent excessive increases' (p. 44).

Interestingly, as well as constituting a significant step in itself, the development of the proposals for regional government also reflected the impact of the EU on the policy process. For example, not only did the White Paper make the point, previously little heard from central government, that England was one of the few parts of the European Union where regions have had little choice of some type of democratic regional governance, but a section was devoted to 'The European Dimension to English Regional Governance'.

Local government

In the United Kingdom, local government derives its powers from central government. It is effectively an offshoot of central government that has some power to govern over a range of services and responsibilities at the local level. However, local authorities have no independent right to exist and their role and responsibility can be changed by Parliament. In addition, local government can only undertake activities that have been authorised by Parliament. This is different from the position in some other countries where local government can take responsibility for any affairs that are not explicitly ruled out by central government. The weak constitutional position of local government has also been reflected in the fact that it was subject to two major reorganisations in less than three decades.

As Stewart (2000a) notes, one of the key characteristics of local government is that it is part of a substantial network of institutions including other local authorities and many other public sector bodies such as police authorities, health authorities and regional development agencies as well as the variety of voluntary and private organisations that undertake functions on behalf of government. If one of the key roles of local government is to play a leading role in the social, economic and environmental well-being of its area, then its relationships with these other organisations will be crucial. One of the key issues for social policy is that for many years local government was an important provider of many welfare services, such as education, housing and the personal social services, and as such was useful to central government and at the same time was frequently in direct contact with large sections of the public. However, under the Conservative governments from 1979 to 1997, many of the powers of local government were eroded. For example, the government introduced limits on the ability of local government to raise income through local taxation (initially property rates, later the poll tax and finally the council tax), instituted a requirement to contract out some services, applied stricter central government guidance and other requirements. For social policy, some of the most obvious implications of these changes were a lessening of involvement of local government in the direct provision of services, as a result of reforms such as the selling-off of council housing and reductions in the scale of provision of local authority residential care for older people; and a more general shift to a role as enablers rather than providers of services.

Cochrane (1993) described the 'rise of the local welfare state' as occurring in two main periods. Firstly there was a period of consolidation and expansion up to the early 1960s. Whilst local government actually lost many powers and responsibilities during this period (poor relief in 1934, trunk roads in 1936, administration of supplementary benefits in 1940, hospitals in 1946, electricity in 1947 and gas in 1948), with the centralisation of many functions and the growth of the welfare state, these were counter-balanced by the expansion of responsibilities in social policy and related fields, and notably in relation to education and housing which came to dominate local authority budgets. In addition, local government was arguably increasing in importance in people's everyday lives: the 1944 Education Act expanded the role for local authorities in school-age education, and the Town and Country Planning Act 1947 meant that new development proposals had to pass through a local authority based planning system. There was also a steady growth of local authority based personal social services, as part of the 'cradle to the grave' coverage of the welfare state. Councils were therefore increasingly responsible for the management of a local welfare state which required face-to-face 'professional style' involvement with people variously defined as clients, parents, tenants, and so on, whilst more straightforwardly rational-bureaucratic activities, such as the distribution of social security benefits, were allocated to the national level. The NHS, with the professional power of doctors taken for granted, was also effectively removed from direct democratic accountability. Local government was therefore the home for what Lipsky (1980) called the 'street-level bureaucrats' (see Chapter 2), who on some occasions have considerable autonomy and discretion and who therefore can have a significant impact upon the implementation of policy.

The second phase in the development of local government had its origins in the complexity and variety of council structures. A number of reports appeared in the late 1960s and early 1970s which stressed the need for improving managerial efficiency and streamlining decision making within larger authorities, for example the Redcliffe-Maude (1969) and Bains (1972) reports. In 1970 the White Paper *Reform of Local Government in England* (Ministry of Housing and Local Government, 1970) set out the framework for reform which led to the rationalisation of local government in England and Wales in the 1972 Local Government Act, with the resultant creation of fewer but larger authorities in 1974. A parallel restructuring took place in Scotland. One of the aims of these changes was to introduce a new, more managerial, style, with strategic planning that would operate in a framework more conducive to rational decision making. It was at this time (from 1970 but particularly with reorganisation in 1974) that recognisable social services departments came into being, with the amalgamation of a range of social care functions that had previously been spread among children's, welfare, housing and health departments.

The period up to the early 1960s was therefore one of expansion and consolidation, whilst from the early 1960s to the mid-1970s the emphasis was on attempts to modernise local government as part of a more extensive strategy of state-backed social and economic modernisation (shared by governments of both major parties), whilst retaining split responsibilities for welfare between central and local government, along the lines of those underpinning Cawson and Saunders's dual state thesis identified in Chapter 3. However, as with other areas of the welfare state, local government came to be affected by ideas and thinking relating to the notion of 'crisis' from the mid-1970s. The late 1970s to the late 1990s can therefore be seen as a third period that could be summed up using Rhodes's (1981) characterisation of the relationship between central and local government as including 'direction', 'abolition' and 'revolution'. The consequences, such as erosion of powers and changes in role, have already been referred to above and are discussed at greater length in the course of this chapter.

The structure of local government

For a considerable part of the twentieth century, the structure of local government remained virtually unchanged despite the increasing range of functions and responsibilities being laid upon it. As indicated above, in the first half of the 1970s significant reforms of local government took place throughout the UK. The Local Government Act 1972 introduced a new pattern of authorities for England and Wales, and the Local Government (Northern Ireland) Act 1972 and the Local Government (Scotland) Act 1973 new, but very different, structures in Northern Ireland and Scotland. However, barely a decade later, the Conservatives' Local Government Act 1985 abolished the Greater London Council and six metropolitan counties in England and left a structure of local government in England that consisted of a mix of two-tier (39 county councils, 296 district councils (these were three-tier if parish councils are included)) and unitary structures (36 metropolitan districts, 32 London boroughs and the City of London). This remained in place until 1995.

In Wales the situation remained unchanged from the 1975 reorganisation up to the mid-1990s, with a two-tier system of eight counties and 37 districts, with the options of community councils (the equivalent of England's parish councils) taken up in some areas. Similarly, in Scotland the structure introduced by the 1975 reorganisation remained in place: this consisted of two tiers of nine regional councils and 53 district councils, and three all-purpose islands authorities created for the island areas (the Western Isles, and the Orkney and Shetland Islands).

At this stage the broad social policy responsibilities of the different forms of local government could be delineated roughly as:

- county councils/regional councils – structure planning, education, social services;
- district councils – environmental health, refuse collection, housing;
- metropolitan districts – environmental health, refuse collection, housing, education, social services;
- London boroughs – environmental health, refuse collection, housing, education, social services.

Clearly, these included a significant role in the administration and supply of welfare services, with local government remaining responsible for the provision of the bulk of school-age education, a significant proportion of the nation's housing stock and the delivery of social care, particularly for older people. For a few issues, such as some aspects of planning and transport, responsibility was shared between two tiers of local government. Where the police were concerned, the reorganisation of the early 1970s made the police the responsibility of the police authorities in England and Wales and the regions in Scotland, with the Metropolitan Police remaining under the control of the Home Secretary. However, constitutionally the police have a significant degree of independence so that decisions about operational policing can only be taken by the police themselves, and local authority police committees were restricted to the provision of resources and to discussions of a general nature.

The position in Northern Ireland was rather different, in part reflecting the smaller population, with 26 unitary district councils responsible for a very limited range of services such as refuse collection, cemeteries and recreation and tourism. In addition there has been a system of regional boards (for example, the four health and social services boards and the five education and libraries boards), which have consisted of appointed members, although up to 40 per cent of these have been nominated by the district councils.

In the early 1990s the Conservatives were again turning their attention to the structure of local government in England, Scotland and Wales. In 1991 the Secretary of State for the Environment, Michael Heseltine, proposed a commission to review local government arrangements in England. The Local Government Commission was officially established with a remit to try to clarify in the minds of the public the responsibilities of local government, since the two-tier system which existed outside London and the metropolitan districts was seen by many as confusing. In addition, there was often considered to be some overlap in services and provision between the tiers. The review had clear implications for social policy in terms of the effectiveness of service delivery and the numbers of people for whom services could be provided. The Conservative government believed that to do away with the existing structure and put in its place a single all-purpose tier of local government would not only clarify the issue of accountability but also make services more cost efficient and effective, resulting in direct benefits to the consumer. Thus the government of the day were keen that the outcome of the review should be a unitary pattern of government wherever possible.

Under the chairmanship of Sir John Banham (former director-general of the CBI), the Commission was thus asked to observe two principles: to produce, wherever possible, a pattern of unitary government, where people would get services from a single council; and to take account of local opinion. However, despite the strong steer towards unitary authorities, the Commission finally recommended that the status quo be retained in 14 areas, that there be 46 unitary authorities and that 20 areas adopt a 'hybrid model' (a mixture of unitary status in some parts of the county combined with two-tier status in the remainder of the area). The result was that the structure in England was left as 115 unitary authorities (the 36 metropolitan district councils, 46 unitary councils, 32 London boroughs and the City of London Corporation) and a two-tier system in other areas comprising the 34 non-metropolitan county councils with 238 non-metropolitan district councils below them. Thus the outcome was not uniform local government structure, and the problem of confusion that the review was aimed at solving was not resolved.

In Scotland and Wales the Conservatives had also decided to reform the structure of local government, but in these countries there were no equivalent Commissions established, nor was there any significant consultation. Instead the Local Government Act 1992 led to the creation of 21 unitary authorities in Wales, whilst the Local Government (Scotland) Act 1994 established 29 new unitary councils in Scotland and retained the three Island councils. However, even in these areas the aim of 'simplification' was arguably not met for, as Wilson and Game (1998) point out, 'In the [former] Strathclyde Region... there are now more bodies responsible for fewer services than there were previously... [and] significantly fewer of them are directly elected' (p. 63).

As indicated earlier, following the election of the Labour government in 1997 the pressures for change in local government continued but the only immediate structural alteration was the introduction of an elected mayor for London and the establishment of a Greater London Authority following a London-wide referendum in May 1998. In Scotland, Wales and Northern Ireland the new devolved Parliament and Assemblies discussed earlier in this chapter were given responsibility for the organisation of local government.

The internal organisation of local government

However, whilst the new Labour government did not introduce any further structural changes to local government, it did have a number of concerns about the democratic accountability and effectiveness of local government and believed that the existing decision-making processes within the traditional structures of the full council and its committees and sub-committees could lead 'to inefficient and opaque decision making' (Department of the Environment, Transport and the Regions, 1998, p. 25). In their view, in order to modernise local government it was desirable to introduce new political management structures, and by the late 1990s local authorities had begun to adopt new structures based upon the models put forward by central government.

Essentially Labour proposed three models for decision making: a directly elected mayor with a cabinet; a cabinet with a leader; and a directly elected mayor and council manager. Under the first model 'the mayor would be the political leader for the community, proposing policy for approval by the council and steering implementation by the cabinet through council officers' (Department of the Environment, Transport and the Regions, 1998, p. 27). This clearly followed the pattern of local government in the United States and that adopted by the new government for Greater London, with a focus upon a powerful mayor who would be clearly and directly accountable to the electorate.

In the second paradigm the leader is elected by the council and the cabinet can comprise councillors either appointed by the leader or elected by the council. The main difference from the first model is that the leader's authority, unlike that of the mayor, is derived from the council members and not the electorate, and he or she can thus be replaced by the council. This highlights a power difference between the leader and the directly elected mayor. Whilst they may both have similar executive powers, where the leader is not directly elected 'there is no direct mandate from the electorate for the leader's programme' (Department of the Environment, Transport, and the Regions, 1998, p. 27) and he or she cannot claim the same level of legitimacy as their directly elected counterpart.

The third model saw the mayor as being directly elected by the public, with the clear implication that he or she would have a strong mandate which would be distinct from that of the councillors; although in this instance the government still envisaged the primary role of the mayor as 'one of influence, guidance and leadership rather than direct decision taking' (Department of the Environment, Transport and the Regions, 1988, p. 27). He or she would therefore provide political leadership and propose a broad policy framework whilst responsibility for day-to-day decision making and strategic policy would be delegated to an officer or 'manager' – the chief executive of the council.

Whilst the government proposed three models of political management, it rapidly became clear that most local authorities were moving to adopt a cabinet (or executive) with a leader (Local Government Association, 2000), although there were a variety of differences in how these would be operationalised, including whether they would only be made up of members of the majority party or whether they would include members representing other parties, and whether members of the executive would have specific portfolios of responsibility. For example, during 1999 Kingston upon Hull City Council decided to adopt a version of this model. Nine councillors, including a leader and deputy, were elected by members of the Council to form the City's first Cabinet, although this was later expanded to 13. Two cross-party scrutiny committees were also set up with the remit of questioning and challenging policy decisions made by the Cabinet Committee. In addition there was an attempt to encourage greater public involvement in local decision making through the creation of seven 'area' committees, with the intention that they be devolved certain powers. In contrast to the relative enthusiasm to adopt this model, it was not until July 2001 that the first local authority in England other than London (Watford) held a successful local referendum to demonstrate support for an elected mayor. By April 2002 eight further authorities had approved the idea through referendums, although in 15 others there had been 'no' votes.

Of course, one issue about such changes is whether they result in the intended improvements in decision making and accountability, a matter which so far remains unresolved. Another, important for this book, is whether changes in political management structures have any implications for social policy and if so what these might be. Clearly, despite the reduction in the powers and responsibilities of local government since the 1970s, the way in which local authorities operate continues to have a direct impact on the resources allocated to services and the way in which those resources are used, including significant aspects of services such as education, housing and personal social services. If, as the Labour government argued, under the traditional committee structures councils are inefficient, then it follows that this impacts on the level and quality of service delivered to the consumer. It is this that New Labour aimed to address through the introduction of the new political structures. The separation of executive and backbench councillors under the new political structures was intended to enable councillors to have specific roles. Executive councillors (members of the cabinet) were expected to take responsibility for implementing policies under the political guidance of the leader (or mayor in a few cases) and to take delegated executive decisions either as a group or as individuals. Backbench councillors would spend less time in meetings and more time addressing the concerns of their constituents and building up a more detailed knowledge of the communities they represent. It was hoped that this would enable them to be more aware of the needs of people in those communities and to be in a better position to argue their case in the debate over the allocation of resources to particular service areas. The government thus hoped to provide more efficient, transparent and accountable local government and that 'councils everywhere will have greater scope to design a system of governance which is best suited to local circumstances' (Department of the Environment, Transport and the Regions, 1998, p. 31).

To some extent it is possible to compare the approach of Labour with that of the preceding Conservative governments. Whilst both were clearly unhappy with many aspects of the role and operation of local government, the response of the Conservatives was to attempt to hive-off local authority services and responsibilities and to encourage accountability to consumers through mechanisms such as charters and parental choice of school. Labour sought to maintain traditional notions of democratic accountability to the electorate through councillors, but to improve the political decision making process whilst remaining fairly neutral about whether services were best provided by local government or by the private and not-for-profit sectors.

Running parallel to local authorities' political decision making structures are those of their departments. These vary significantly across authorities, in part depending on the type of authority and its responsibilities, although for some types of council certain committees are mandatory, with social services being an example in the English counties, metropolitan districts, unitary councils and London boroughs. Most councils have a chief executive or manager who is the most senior officer of the authority and who normally takes responsibility for corporate activities. The chief executive's department, itself comprising various elements, heads and generally co-ordinates this structure, below which there are a variety of departments which may or may not be hierarchically organised depending on the particular local authority structure. Each department is headed by a chief officer or director and staffed by specialist and generalist officers. Many have a long history, with for example, the term 'local education authority' dating back to before 1902 (Stewart, 2000a). Others are more recent, with social services departments coming into being following the Seebohm report (1968) and the reorganisation of local government in the mid-1970s. Some departments, such as education, housing and social services, provide services directly to the public, whilst others provide services and support to other departments within the authority. The role of departments and the officers within them is to implement the decisions and policies determined by the elected members of the council.

Within departments the role of the chief officer is a key one and has traditionally been defined by the services for which his or her department is responsible. This has set parameters for the relationship with the elected councillor responsible for chairing the corresponding council committee. The committee system has arguably encouraged the development of strong alliances between the member chairing the committee and the chief officer of the department for which it was responsible, as 'the chair needs the chief officer to give advice and action and the chief officer needs the chair to give legitimacy and to win political support' (Stewart, 2000a). Whilst the professional role and judgement of the chief officer can affect the relationship, the electoral legitimacy of the committee chair can also be a powerful tool, so that whilst chief officers do possess some delegated powers and committee chairs have no formal authority, few chief officers would be willing to exercise those delegated powers in any new significant way without consulting the chair.

The relationship between chief officers and committee chairs has undergone significant change over the past two decades. The rise of political partisanship, increasing financial constraints on local authorities, and the growing assertiveness of elected members has resulted in elected councillors being more willing to challenge officers. The traditional view, referred to above, that members are responsible for the formulation of policy and officers for its implementation has generally been replaced by an awareness that formulation and implementation are inextricably linked and that there is a significant role for officers in the making of policy and for members in carrying it out. One view of decision making in local government is that there is a 'joint elite', comprising chief officers, their deputies and committee chairs and vice-chairs (Stoker, 1991), but the reality varies widely from authority to authority. In addition, further down the hierarchy, many of the employees of local authorities do have a significant degree of discretion, as is clearly the case with social workers and teachers who can therefore have a considerable impact upon the way in which policies are actually implemented and delivered to users.

Whilst departments are the key building blocks in the council structure, there has always been significant variation in departmental structure, and recent years have seen this amply illustrated with regard to welfare provision which, in addition to the traditional departmental arrangement, can be found in other models including merged social services and housing departments, and some merging of education and social services. There are a variety of reasons for these developments including a new emphasis on multi-disciplinarity in service provision and an awareness of the need to work across existing professional and departmental boundaries.

Like the civil service and parts of the NHS, local authorities are in many cases large-scale bureaucracies, and many of the perspectives from Chapter 2 can usefully be applied to them. The fact that parts of local authority provision have been largely professionalised, including social work and to some extent housing management, brings strengths in terms of training and knowledge, together with a recognition of expertise and professional qualifications, but can also sometimes be accused of encouraging uniformity and rigidity of provision and resistance to change (Stewart, 2000a).

Functions of local government

As already indicated, traditionally local authorities have played and continue to play a substantial role in governing locally, whether through the direct provision of services or through ensuring that provision is made by the private and not-for-profit sectors. Indeed, their origins lay with the introduction of measures designed to improve sanitation, public health, housing and highways. Since then they have had a wide range of responsibilities including housing, education, social services, refuse collection, environmental health, local planning, transport, leisure and fire and police services. By the 1960s local authorities had a central role in the community, based in large part upon their delivery of such services. However, from the 1980s the function of local authorities has changed dramatically. In general, whilst they remain providers of services, that part of their role has diminished significantly whilst their responsibility as service enablers has grown. This stemmed in large part from changes introduced by the Conservative governments of the 1980s and 1990s (encouraged by right-wing think-tanks such as the Adam Smith Institute and the Institute of Economic Affairs), which sought to diminish the size and scope of local government and to encourage the private and not-for-profit sectors as service providers. Examples of this included the sale of council houses, compulsory competitive tendering for a variety of services and the obligation to encourage private and voluntary-sector provision in community care. Schools were enabled to opt out of local authority control and a number of new schools (City Technology Colleges) were established, again outside council control. Local government also lost powers to new quangos, non-departmental bodies and corporations. For example, employer-led training and enterprise councils took on much of the role previously undertaken by local authorities in further education for employment training. Sixth-form colleges and institutions of further education became corporate institutions in their own right, following the previous incorporation of polytechnics and colleges of higher education; and responsibility for urban regeneration and development in many areas was removed from local authorities to bodies such as urban development corporations and housing action trusts.

The Conservatives thus sought to promote a role for local authorities in overseeing (or 'enabling') service provision, whilst handing over much of the direct delivery of services to outside organisations. These changes have arguably resulted not only in the lessening of their day-to-day involvement in the delivery of services but also in reducing the importance of local authorities to their publics and in further eroding their power and influence.

Following their return to power in 1997, Labour produced a plethora of documents and policies dealing not only with the modernisation of local government but also with many of the services for which they are responsible. For example, the White Paper *Modern Local Government: In Touch with the People* (Department of the Environment, Transport and the Regions, 1998) attempted to set out a new role for local government in England and Wales in promoting the economic, social and environmental well-being of communities. In addition, local authorities were affected by many other initiatives in areas such as education and social care, as well as with issues ranging from tackling social exclusion to housing asylum-seekers and attempts to tackle crime by greater regulation of drinking in public places and the introduction of child curfews. Although these developments were wide-ranging and varied, it is possible to identify a number of themes running across many of them. These include a continued stress on the role of local authorities as enablers, although perhaps with less of an 'anti-public sector as provider' emphasis than had been the case under the Conservatives; considerable emphasis on partnerships, across public, private and voluntary sectors; and continued use of inspection and performance-measurement mechanisms, including school league tables and the work of the Audit Commission, emphasising the government's approach to issues such as standards and quality. The emphasis on the strategic role rather than a close direct involvement in the provision of services is illustrated by the government's view of the role of local education authorities set out in Exhibit 5.2.

In the newly re-created Greater London, the Mayor of London was given the power to initiate policy, set budgets and make appointments. Where social policy is concerned, the Mayor and the Assembly have little power, with the emphasis being on strategic economic and to some extent transport policy and the environment. Nevertheless, it seems unlikely that in the medium to long term any mayor could avoid some involvement in social policy issues, such as on homelessness, race or the health service in London, particularly given the emphasis on the representative function of the post and the often populist nature of equivalent positions in countries such as France and the United States. However, the local government responsibility for social policy issues remains largely with the London boroughs.

Best Value

One of the changes introduced under Labour was the replacement of Compulsory Competitive Tendering (CCT) with Best Value from January 2000, following a period of piloting in 16 local authorities in England from April 1998 (there was also a parallel pilot scheme in Wales). Although presented by Labour as quite distinct from CCT from some perspectives, this was seen by some as a continuation of the policies implemented under previous Conservative governments and in some respects could be argued to be an incremental change. However, Labour argued strongly that Best Value was about much more than the cost of a service:

> A modern council – or authority – which puts people first will seek to provide services which bear comparison with the best. Not just with the best that other authorities provide but with the best that is on offer from both the public and private sectors. Continuous improvements in both the quality and cost of services will therefore be the hallmark of a modern council, and the test of best value (Department of the Environment, Transport and the Regions, 1998, p. 64).

Unlike CCT, Best Value removes the requirement that contracts should go to the lowest bidder in all but exceptional cases. Rather than being based upon

EXHIBIT 5.2   THE ROLE OF THE LOCAL EDUCATION AUTHORITY

Special educational needs

- ensuring that individual children's needs are identified and matched by appropriate provision;
- running education psychology and support teaching services;
- developing partnerships with health and social services to provide a co-ordinated service to children and their families.

Access and school transport

- making sure there are enough school and pre-school places;
- securing fair school admissions policies;
- enforcing school attendance;
- managing major spending on schools and co-ordinating the provision of networked information and communications technology across schools;
- arranging suitable transport for children who need it.

School improvement and tackling failure

- monitoring the performance of all schools;
- focusing school improvement services in schools that need challenge and further support to secure improvement, and intervening where a school is failing its pupils;
- drawing together education authority and school targets in an education development plan.

Educating excluded pupils and pupil welfare

- ensuring that suitable education is provided for excluded pupils;
- providing education other than at school for children who are unable to attend;
- ensuring that children return to school when ready to do so;
- ensuring suitable provision for pupils with behavioural difficulties;
- producing a behaviour support plan setting out what will be done for children with behavioural difficulties.

Strategic management

- ensuring provision of factual information and advice to schools and school governors and supporting parent governors;
- auditing school spending;
- allocating spending to schools locally, taking account of the overall funding made available by government and rules governing the distribution of funds across schools.

Summarised from Department for Education and Employment, *The Role of the Local Education Authority in School Education*, (DfEE: London, 2000).

cost it is intended to be a comprehensive system encouraging the improvement of services. Best Value requires local authorities to set standards covering both cost and quality for all the services for which they are responsible and to establish targets for continual improvement. However, in areas where the government has key commitments and responsibilities, such as education and social services, it sets national standards which councils will need to take into account when setting local standards. If a council is deemed to be failing in its duty to secure Best Value, the Secretary of State can intervene and this could mean the authority losing the ability to provide a service and an outside provider being imposed.

Another significant difference, which distinguishes Best Value from CCT, is its emphasis on public involvement. In particular it requires public consultation and obliges local authorities to demonstrate to their public that they have achieved best value, including a consideration of both quality and cost.

In line with the general atmosphere of audit and inspection (see Chapter 8) the Audit Commission was given additional powers to audit local authorities' plans for improvement and to undertake inspections of local services 'to assess their quality and cost effectiveness and how likely they are to improve in future', the results of which are published on its Inspection Services web site.

It is still relatively early in the life of the initiative to make firm judgements on both the extent to which Best Value will actually differ from CCT in practice and on the relative emphasis placed on quality and cost. As Taylor (2000) points out, whilst there may be real advantages in the Best Value approach, much will depend upon the ability of local government to ensure that provision is based upon quality as well as efficiency, and the reality may be that local authority services will reflect 'better' rather than 'best' value.

Beacon Councils

In 1999 the government designated 42 authorities as 'Beacon Councils' in a scheme that aimed to identify 'excellence' in local government and to encourage authorities to share such experience. Reflecting the continued importance of local government in welfare provision, the themes for selection included education, housing and social services, as well as service delivery, community safety, planning and sustainable development. Beacon Councils were expected to be strong overall and to be excellent in the service for which Beacon status was to be awarded, not only in terms of performance but also in the processes associated with that. Since this system only became operational in 2000 it is early to make any judgements about the success of the initiative, but Stewart (2000b) has pointed out that some aspects may be likely to prove problematic, including whether the information available to those identifying Beacon Councils is adequate, and whether the few authorities selected will actually differ significantly from the majority of others. He also notes the possible view that 'most authorities and even particular services contain and provide a mixture of excellent, good, fair and even poor activities' (p. 207).

Paying for local government

Up to the 1980s one of the strengths of local government was its ability to raise local revenues through the 'rates', effectively a form of local taxation based on the value of property, although it was only property owners who paid rates directly. Rates enabled local government to raise a substantial part of its income whilst the bulk of the remainder came from central government (the rate support grant) and a small amount derived from charges for services. However, in the post-war years the proportion of local government income that came from central government grew significantly, thus increasing councils' financial dependence on the centre. By the 1970s governments were looking for alternative methods of financing local government, and the Conservative governments from 1979 to 1997 introduced a number of major changes. In 1980 they replaced the rate support grant with a system of grant-related expenditure. This allowed central government to set spending targets and cut their grants to local authorities if the latter overspent. However, many authorities simply increased their rates in order to raise expenditure, particularly in the Labour-controlled large cities that at the time were coming increasingly into conflict with the Conservative government. The Conservatives responded by introducing 'rate-capping', which meant that, if a local authority were to overspend, central government would reduce its contribution in order to keep its income to a certain level. This effectively gave central government the ability to control local government expenditure.

However, the Conservatives' reforms of local government finance did not end there. Fearing the political impact of rate revaluations on domestic rate-payers, they decided to replace the system of rates with a flat-rate charge for every resident of a council, with some reductions for poor people. The result of this was the community charge (or the poll tax as it was better known). This meant that owners of large, valuable properties paid the same as occupants of poor quality or cheap housing. It also meant that many millions who had not previously paid rates now had to pay substantial sums for the new tax. At the same time the Conservatives took control of the non-domestic (business) rates away from local authorities and gave the responsibility for setting, collecting and distributing them to central government. They also simplified the grants system, using standard spending assessments (SSAs), as the basis for calculating local authority grants.

The poll tax was implemented in Scotland on 1 April 1989 and a year later in England and Wales. Its introduction has since widely been seen as one of the greatest British policy failures of the twentieth century: the costs of administration and collection of the tax were enormous, large numbers of people simply refused to pay, more than one million potential voters disappeared from the electoral register, and the costs to those who paid the tax were increased due to late or non-payment by others (see Wilson and Game, 1998).

The failure of the poll tax contributed to the fall of Margaret Thatcher and when John Major succeeded her as Prime Minister he made its replacement a priority. The current system is based upon the council tax and the uniform business rate. Under the council tax each property is rated according to a band (from A to H), with the tax falling on the occupant of the property. The council tax has been far less controversial than its predecessor and has been easier and cheaper to administer. However, many local authorities have remained critical of the SSAs, which they have seen as allowing central government to criticise 'overspenders' and to control council budgets.

On coming to power, Labour seemed more favourable to the idea of shifting the balance of local revenue towards locally raised taxes but, despite an apparent commitment to increasing the role of local government, has remained cautious and has failed to relax significantly the controls that were imposed under the Conservatives. Whilst apparently controversial, it is worth noting that council tax accounts for only around 4 per cent of total tax receipts.

For social policy the funding of local government remains important as, despite significant change over the past two decades, councils continue to play an important role not only in the planning and enabling of services, but also in direct provision, particularly in education and social services. Levels of funding, together with the ring-fencing that has occurred in some areas, inevitably impact upon the quality and quantity of services provided. The methods of funding also have other social policy impacts. The poll tax being a regressive tax had a greater impact upon poor people, whilst the council tax has some mildly progressive elements but is linked to the value of a property rather than the ability to pay. The source of local government funding can also be seen as having relevance to issues of democracy, accountability and control of local government, and upon central–local relations.

Central–local relations

The relationships between central and local government are of crucial importance for a number of reasons, including the impact upon the social policies implemented through local authorities and the level of resources available to them. The period since 1979 has included a number of phases in the relationship between central and local government. Up to 1983, central government's primary concern was arguably to reduce public expenditure, and this was inevitably reflected in its attempt to control local government expenditure through the introduction of the range of measures described earlier that restricted local authorities' powers and activities. These included changes to local government finance and the encouragement of the sale of council homes through the 1980 Housing Act. In this period central government's approach could also be characterised as more directive and less consultative than had previously been the case.

The period from 1983 to 1987 saw the Conservatives' abolition of the Greater London Council and the metropolitan county councils, all of which were Labour controlled and many of which were viewed by the government as high-spending, bureaucratic and extreme. From 1987 the Conservatives' approach to local authorities (as with their approach to social policy) became more radical. They abandoned further attempts to control local government and attempted to pass control to consumers using mechanisms such as the market and consumer charters. They also set about removing powers from councils through legislation such as the 1988 Education Reform Act which gave schools the opportunity to opt out of local education authority control, and imposed the National Curriculum. The 1990 NHS and Community Care Act did give local authorities lead responsibility for community care but little by way of additional powers of funding, whilst also requiring them to reduce their own levels of provision and instead to make greater use of the private and voluntary sectors.

Under John Major the erosion of local government powers and services continued, but with a greater emphasis on co-operation and partnership with the private sector. Reflecting the government's emphasis on enabling rather than providing authorities, Stewart and Stoker (1995a) refer to 'the creation of a system of 'local governance' in which local authorities find themselves increasingly working alongside a range of other agencies in their localities' (p. 194). It is also worth noting that this emphasis was linked closely to other Conservative concerns, such as notions of efficiency, effectiveness and accountability. In addition, the establishment of the Local Government Commission and the subsequent abolition of large Labour-controlled authorities such as Avon and Humberside, and the restructuring of local government in Scotland and Wales, also reflected the approach of the mid-1980s.

The return of the Labour government in 1997 appeared to herald a somewhat more promising period for local government. Publications such as the White Paper *Modern Local Government: In Touch with the People* (Department of the Environment, Transport and the Regions, 1998) suggested that the government was seeking a more positive relationship with local authorities, referring to partnership between central and local government and the important role for local government in empowering citizens, service provision and responsibility for a large proportion of public expenditure. Other central departments also stressed the need for partnerships with other bodies (for example, in the provision of social services (Department of Health, 1998) and over collaboration with voluntary organisations (Home Office, 1998; see also Chapter 7)). At the same time the DETR White Paper set out proposals for the modernisation of local government including public participation, electoral accountability, new political structures, local financial accountability, improving local services and promoting the well-being of local communities. Nevertheless, the Labour government's actions and approach to local government also implied a degree of conditionality, with the potential of greater freedom for local authorities depending upon their acting in a manner that central government found appropriate. Similarly, parts of New Labour's approach, including Best Value, appeared to remain firmly based in central government's auditing and inspection of local authorities, together with the possibility of intervention if councils are perceived to be 'failing', as happened in Leeds City Council's education service in 2000. Nevertheless, by early 2001 some authorities were piloting the use of public service agreements, where councils could potentially achieve greater freedom and financial awards for meeting agreed targets. However, the potential fragility of central–local relations was amply illustrated by the decision of the Labour MP Ken Livingstone to contest the 2000 election for the Mayor of London as an independent, ultimately defeating the official Labour candidate as well as Conservative and Liberal Democrat opponents.

A number of Labour's initiatives also highlighted the government's desire for partnership between public, private and voluntary sectors, such as education action zones, employment zones, health action zones and Excellence in Cities. These focused on particular geographic areas and were intended to tackle inequalities in some of the worst-off areas of the country. They have emphasised partnership and have targeted resources at certain areas, with additional funding coming from central government but frequently conditional on attracting contributions from the private sector.

The start of the second Labour term appeared to feature a degree of continuity of approach from the centre, but with a somewhat greater emphasis on outcomes rather than processes as measures of performance, with the extension of local public service agreements an important feature of this. Audit and inspection were likely to figure prominently both in terms of the performance of individual services, such as the star ratings given to social services departments in England in 2002, and to the overall performance of authorities. In addition to this the White Paper *Strong Local Leadership: Quality Public Services* (Department for Transport, Local Government and the Regions, 2001) continued to promise greater freedom for local authorities, but conditionally on achieving the government's aims, with 'failing' authorities implicitly likely to be subject to greater intervention.

In general, there is an argument that New Labour's approach to local government reflects an interest in some aspects of a communitarian approach to social policy, with the emphasis on responsibility as well as rights, self-reliance rather than welfare provision, and the renewal of communities rather than urban regeneration (Salmon, 1995). Stewart (1999) has also pointed out that, whilst there are some positive aspects of Labour's proposals for the modernisation of government, there are a number of areas where processes could be extended. For example, whilst there is an emphasis on listening to people through a variety of devices such as citizens' juries and focus groups, there is relatively little on empowering and involving people through democratic practices. Similarly, whilst local authorities and their partners are expected to develop community strategies to meet local need, there has been little consideration of the implications of these for central government, so that the potential value of a bottom-up approach may be undermined.

Models of central–local relations

As was implicit in some of the discussion in Chapter 3, the role and relationships of local government, including with central government, have been a fertile area for theorists, with, for example, the dual state thesis, the policy communities and policy networks approaches, and regime theory owing at least part of their emergence to the analysis of this policy area. Until recently, models of central–local government relations have tended to fall into two broad groups: one representing a relationship based on partnership and the other a more traditional view based on a power relationship in which central government has the upper hand and in which local government is seen as its agent (Rhodes, 1981; Wilson, 1995; Chandler, 1996). However there are a variety of ways in which these relationships can be conceptualised (for example, Wilson and Game, 1998). Three views are presented here.

The traditional view

The traditional view, or agency model as it is sometimes referred to, with its emphasis on the power of the centre, has been seen to be particularly relevant since the mid-1970s. Reflecting the top-down approach to policy making outlined in Chapter 2, from this perspective local authorities are seen to have little discretion and exist primarily to implement the policies of central government. Where they fail to do so, central government has a variety of methods available to it to control them. For example, central government's financial support and control gives it significant power as well as providing local authorities with a strong incentive to toe the government line. Central government can also organise systems of inspection, for example into schools and other local authority services; it can also initiate inquiries into the conduct of local authority business. Ultimately, of course, it can reform and restructure local government.

One of the weaknesses with this model is that it fails to recognise the interdependence of central and local government, and in particular central government's need for co-operation from local government for the successful implementation of many of its policies, for example, in community care and in education. An alternative way of viewing the relationship between central and local government is to consider the policy networks model developed by Rhodes.

Policy network approaches

Discussed in greater detail in Chapter 3, these approaches emphasise the complexity of relationships, whether they be based upon personal relationships between policy makers and administrators who operate within a common framework and who are frequently in contact with each other, or upon the structural relationships between the organisations responsible for policy making and implementation. Supporters of this perspective argue that it reveals the complexities of policy making and reflects the significant changes that have occurred in British government with the shift from a unitary state to a position where power and the policy process are fragmented. Policy networks have therefore become an important part of the policy process, for example, consisting of systems of (vertical) linkages between professionals (and associated councillors) and civil servants responsible for policy within departments of central government, together with perhaps others from the voluntary or private sectors. In terms of central–local relations, each side of the network is dependent on the other: at local level officers are dependent for finance from the centre, and at national level civil servants (and ministers) are dependent on the local tier for implementation.

The policy network approach therefore provides a useful tool with which to approach the analysis of some aspects of central–local government relations. However, it is not without its critics. Some authors contend that it is not appropriate for policy areas where there is a large degree of conflict and opposition. For example, Leach (1996) cites the example of the Local Government Review for which he argues policy networks would be an inappropriate tool for analysis, since in this case many of the key actors may have had very little direct contact or influence. Pemberton (2000) notes that it can be criticised, as only the two ends of the continuum – policy communities and issue networks – are normally considered, so that the very idea of the continuum can be questioned. Perhaps the most significant criticism, however, is that the model would tend to suggest that policy networks promote continuity and stability, and that it is therefore difficult to explain why change occurs.

Stewardship

Chandler (1996) argues that central–local government relationships in Britain cannot be seen purely in terms of structures and power. He believes that underlying the local government system are attitudes and values that have gradually shaped local government over centuries. Whilst central government is recognised as having the greater power, it nevertheless delegates significant authority to local government. He describes this attitude as one of stewardship.

> The policy makers in central government, whether party politicians or bureaucrats, use local authorities as their steward in much the same way as the aristocratic owner of a large eighteenth-century estate would have employed a steward to manage his country estates... within central government, there is a pervasive ethos that perceives local government to be a generally useful but subordinate arm of a national political system that is controlled by Whitehall and Westminster. Local authorities are of value because they take from the centre the tedious and detailed task... On occasion, the government will consult with local authorities and even defer to their opinions... However, the centre may often refuse to take local advice and will certainly discipline or *in extremis* remove local units that oppose central interest (Chandler, 1996, pp. 118–19).

From this perspective, stewardship is an attitude entrenched within central government that places local authorities in a subordinate role in policy making. Such a view provides a rather different perspective than either the agency/traditional model or the policy networks model. Whilst these models can be useful in directing our attention to the different emphases of the relationship, as Stewart (2000a) rightly notes:

> no simple metaphor can describe the relationship... Sometimes and in some places, the relationship can be one of 'conflict' or one of 'co-operation'. At times, central government will be acting as 'judge' between different bids or as 'arbitrator' between different local authorities or between local authorities and other bodies, and central government and local authorities can have a 'learning' relationship when central government learns from the initiative of local authorities and local authorities draw upon the expertise of central government. The relationship can take many forms and use many instruments (Stewart, 2000a, p. 90).

'Partnership'

At this stage it is perhaps worth while directing some attention explicitly at one of the concepts that has come to prominence in policy making, and perhaps particularly in policy implementation and service delivery under Labour since 1997. Under the Conservatives there was some attention paid to partnership between the public and private sectors, particularly in areas such as urban regeneration and crime prevention, for Labour the notion of 'partnership' has been at the heart of much of New Labour's vision for social policy, and, as Newman (2001) notes, 'on partnership as a way of governing' (p. 105). Whilst under Labour the term has been applied to all tiers of government, the importance of the idea has been most evident in some of the initiatives pursued at sub-central level. However, this conception of partnership is very different from that implied from such perspectives as corporatism, discussed in Chapter 3. As Jones and Bird put it:

> The range of partners is greater, its organisational arrangements more flexible; its accent falls on decentralisation rather than central administration; on inter-agency working rather than departmentalism; innovation rather than the rule-following characteristic of bodies established in the corporatist period. (Jones and Bird, 2000, p. 492)

One approach to this has been the use of partnerships in attempts to tackle the complexities of particular social 'problems', including area-focused initiatives, as embodied in 'action zones', such as for education and health, which also reflected Labour's desire to achieve 'joined-up government', with better collaboration between agencies. Whereas under the Conservatives much of the emphasis in social policy was placed upon the role of the market, under Labour 'partnership' has largely been conceived of as a mechanism for utilising the perceived strengths of the market for benign social ends and for recognising the complexity of contemporary society. It has also been linked with the emphasis on 'what works', discussed further in Chapter 8. However, in relation to education action zones (EAZs), Jones and Bird (2000) have noted that the range of agencies involved tends to have excluded more informally organised community interests, or any substantial representation of teacher's organisations, other than a nominal level, and that it is important to recognise that, whilst the organisations brought together in the zones may share a general adherence to an education agenda, the range of interests represented is limited and this in turn restricts the possibilities for debate over wider agendas which might fit less well with the EAZ project. Similar misgivings have been aired by Drakeford and Vanstone (2000), who have pointed out that with respect to criminal justice partnerships, and in particular those envisaged in the Crime and Disorder Act 1998, 'are the partnerships of the powerful – the police, the local authorities and other outposts of government' (p. 377).

Where the often difficult relationship between health and social care is concerned, Hudson and Henwood (2002) noted that when Labour returned to power in 1997 ministers clearly believed that the quasi-market approach introduced by the Conservatives had failed and that the best way of ensuring the effective planning and delivery of services lay in the form of 'partnerships'. There followed a raft of initiatives aimed at encouraging collaboration, including the 1999 Health Act which gave greater flexibility over the transfer of funding between NHS and local authorities. However, almost immediately *The NHS Plan* (Department of Health, 2000) set out proposals for structural reforms, including compulsory 'partnerships', including Care Trusts in areas where local authorities and the NHS 'have failed to establish effective joint partnerships' (p. 73) or where inspections show services to be failing. This perhaps reflects the need of politicians sometimes to achieve rapid change in order to satisfy imperatives other than just the successful delivery of services.

Public–Private Partnership

Another way in which the term 'partnership' has become important under Labour since 1997 is through the significant emphasis placed upon the role of public–private partnerships (PPPs) in improving the quality of public services. This has arguably sought to take a middle road between those who have supported a privatised view of the funding and provision of public services and those who have supported a public sector monopoly of public services. The Commission on Public Private Partnerships (2001) argued that there is a need to 'manage a diverse public sector effectively so that it enhances social equity by improving the quality of, and commitment to, publicly funded services' (p 2) through: reasserting the case for publicly funded universal services; distinguishing between the funding and provision of public services; being open minded about public authorities entering into partnerships; and having clear criteria for assessing whether PPPs are the right approach. However, whilst supporting the need for PPPs, the Commission criticised some aspects of the government's approach, including: the creation of unrealistic expectations; the impression that partnerships are punishment for failure, as seen in threats from government that 'failing' public bodies, such as schools and local education authorities, would be punished by being replaced by the private sector; the patchy performance of many Private Finance Initiative projects; the rigidity of the government's approach and the adherence to particular models of PPP; and the potential links between PPPs and partial or full privatisation of public services.

One of the most controversial aspects of the partnerships approach has been the Private Finance Initiative (PFI), opposed for example by many trade unions. This involved private sector organisations designing, building, financing and operating a provision which is then leased to a public sector body, with ownership reverting to the public sector after a given period of time (Butcher, 2002). Although introduced under John Major's Conservative government, the PFI came to the fore under Labour, being used to build new hospitals, which were then leased to the NHS. Critics claimed that the cost of these arrangements to the public sector was often significantly greater than it would have been if the developments had been wholly undertaken by the public sector. The PFI has also been used within local government, particularly to provide new schools, as well as other services such as housing and some aspects of the personal social services.

The growth of public–private partnerships under Labour has accentuated some concerns over accountability, for example through further blurring the lines between operational issues delegated to private bodies and policy decisions made by ministers, and legitimacy, where non-public bodies might be responsible for spending public funds. However, supporters of PPPs claim that these are merely extensions or different expressions of accountability problems that already exist and that these criticisms can be answered through transparency, responsibility and responsiveness on the part of organisations involved in PPPs (Commission on Public Private Partnerships, 2001).

Conclusion

As is clear from this chapter, the scale of change in terms of multi-level governance has been great in recent years, although the implications for the making of social policy and the provision of services may take much longer to unfold fully. Whilst its scope for intervention in social affairs remains limited, the EU, both directly and indirectly, is having an effect on social policy in the UK, as outlined in this chapter and also in the consideration of the role of the judiciary in Chapter 4.

Sub-central government has undergone very significant changes in each decade since the 1970s: the 1970s saw a major reorganisation of local government throughout the UK; during the 1980s some large (Labour-controlled) local authorities were abolished and there was the start of the Conservatives' attempts to recreate councils as 'enablers' rather than providers of services. The 1990s saw the continued erosion of the powers and responsibilities of local authorities and yet more changes to the structure of local government in England, Scotland and Wales under the Conservatives, and, with the return of the Labour government in 1997, the pursuit of devolution in Scotland and Wales, as well as in Northern Ireland. In addition there has been the introduction of a mayor for London and the Greater London Assembly, with the increased scope for more diversification in both policy making and implementation that these have brought with them.

Yet, despite all these changes, local government has remained a significant actor in the policy process, due in part to it having some degree of democratic legitimacy and also the continuing need of central government to have agencies responsible for strategic planning at a lower level and, in some instances, for ensuring the actual delivery of services. As discussed earlier in the chapter, the relationship between central and local government is a complex one that is continually evolving, and in practice it is often difficult to analyse through the application of a single model, yet the use of models can help to facilitate a greater understanding of this relationship.

Despite the changes introduced during Labour's first term of government, the historic tension between central and sub-central government remained obvious, with much of central government's rhetoric supportive of local government and decentralisation to the regions, whilst at the same time many initiatives reinforced central control. Equally, as Prachett (2002) has pointed out, a simple commitment to democratic renewal is not enough, as it also requires changes in the culture and approaches of local politicians, officers and citizens, and altering these and the informal practices of local government may take much longer to achieve.

In contrast, the early years of devolution clearly created new dynamics in the social policy process and immediately demonstrated the possibilities for increasing the differential development of social policy, particularly in Scotland where the abolition of tuition fees for university students and the promise of free social care for older people deviated significantly from the position in England and Wales. Whilst the developments associated with devolution have not yet led to significant tensions between the devolved administrations and with Westminster, this is unlikely to continue to be the case in the long term, particularly when different political parties come to control the various assemblies.

Where partnership is concerned, Ling's (2000) arguments about health care also hold true for much of the rest of the public sector. He argued that whilst 'partnership' may continue to be a vague concept, it is important as it reflects some of the shortcomings of the managerialist approaches of the 1980s and 1990s and seeks to address problems through bringing together partner organisations and using 'joined-up' government to achieve goals. This illustrates an acceptance by government that the public sector is not always able to deliver, and that the private sector may sometimes achieve things that the public sector might not (although, like others, Ling points out that the problems of the Private Finance Initiative suggest that this form of partnership also has practical limits). It may also reflect a shift in paradigm whereby the problems of 'using the existing NHS structures to deliver the values of equity, efficiency, effectiveness and responsiveness has prompted a search for new techniques' (p. 100).

Returning briefly to some of the themes introduced in the early chapters of this book, the development of multi-level governance suggests that top-down, centralised, models of policy making and implementation are less likely to be appropriate now than they may previously have been, whilst approaches such as regime theory and policy networks, which emphasise complexity and fragmentation, together with the need to build co-operation, partnership and trust to implement policies successfully, may provide useful pointers for the analysis of social policy.

Given the very significant changes that have occurred in many aspects of multi-level governance in recent decades, the future development of social policy at these levels may be likely to see further change in the coming years.

FURTHER READING

For general reading see: Newman, J (2001) *Modernising Governance: New Labour, Policy and Society* (London: Sage); Richards, D and Smith, M (2002) *Governance and Public Policy in the UK* (Oxford: Oxford University Press); Stoker, G (ed.) (2000) *The New Politics of*

British Local Governance (London: Macmillan); Wilson, D and Game, C (2002) *Local Government in the United Kingdom* (Basingstoke: Palgrave Macmillan).

And for an early analysis of the impact of the relationship between pre- and post-devolution see: Parry, R (2002) 'Delivery Structures and Policy Development in Post-Devolution Scotland', *Social Policy and Society*, vol. 1, pp. 315–24.

6

Quasi-Government

CHAPTER OVERVIEW

Quasi-government is important for social policy because it is responsible for delivering many welfare services – National Health Service trusts, much of health education, housing through housing associations, education through grant-maintained schools, benefits through the Benefits Agency, the Child Support Agency, and so on – as well as having a major role in areas such as urban regeneration and employment through organisations such as training and enterprise councils and urban development corporations. The role of quasi-government in social policy arguably increased significantly under the Conservative administrations of 1979–97 and continues to have a major role under the Labour government. But what is quasi-government and does it have implications for social policy? This chapter considers the role and rationale for quasi-government, together with a range of important associated issues such as accountability, control, scrutiny and the politicisation of quasi-government.

An understanding of quasi-government and the issues surrounding it is important for those interested in social policy because many of the bodies that deliver welfare services, such as registered housing associations, grant-maintained schools, learning and skills councils, further and higher education corporations such as colleges and universities, and the Qualifications and Curriculum Authority, either are or can be better understood as quasi-governmental agencies.

From the 1970s quasi-government has increasingly been recognised as important for a number of reasons. These include the unelected status of those responsible for making what are often important decisions, and the extent to which this can be seen as effectively 'by-passing' representative government; other issues relate to democracy, accountability and the proportion of public expenditure for which quasi-government is now responsible.

What is quasi-government?

When examining the public sector in the UK it soon becomes apparent that much of the public sector does not fall easily into the category of either central or local government, but that there are a wide variety of other organisations that undertake the work of government. These can be important in the policy making and implementation process and range from large organisations such as the NHS and the BBC to bodies such as the Disability Rights Commission, the Commission for Racial Equality, the Criminal Cases Review Commission, and the Student Loan Company, and to individual NHS trusts and other small bodies with specific responsibilities.

Their very utility for government and the consequent diversity also complicates our attempts to understand them. The position is further confused by the variety of terminology and definitions that are applied to a very loose category of organisations. Perhaps most obvious is the use of various terms such as 'quasi-government', 'quasi-autonomous non-governmental organisations' (quangos), 'non-departmental public bodies', 'fringe bodies', 'semi-autonomous authorities' and 'extra governmental organisations', sometimes interchangeably, but also to apply to what may often be very similar types of body. Indeed, the academic literature reveals that there is no agreed definition of quasi-government and Doig's (1979) view that 'that there is no one characteristic, or lack of characteristic, that distinguishes quangos or non-departmental public bodies from other organisations in the structure of government' (p. 311) remains entirely apposite, whilst Hogwood (1995) points out the many pitfalls in attempting to define quangos. Nevertheless, for our purposes, and to attempt to understand their importance for social policy, the emphasis should perhaps be on the 'arms-length' nature of the relationship with government, with organisations constituting 'quasi-government' having some or all of the following characteristics:

- undertaking some of the functions of government;
- being funded entirely or to a large extent by government;
- the appointment of leading officers likely to be under the control of a minister or department;
- a degree of independence from ministers and departments, particularly in their day-to-day operations;
- often being less subject to the scrutiny of Parliament than are government departments.

When Margaret Thatcher first came to power in 1979 she announced her intention to reduce the cost and size of quasi-government and asked Sir Leo Pliatzky (1980) to undertake a review of government agencies. For this he adopted the Whitehall term 'non-departmental public body' and within this he identified three categories: executive, advisory and tribunals.

More recent official government definitions and statistics have built upon this but have included bodies such as NHS trusts, as does, for example, the

Cabinet Office's current term 'public bodies'. Others, such as Weir and Hall (1994), who prefer to use the term 'extra-government organisations', argue that what they call 'non-recognised' executive bodies should also be included in statistics relating to quasi-government, and this interpretation brings to our attention the greater range of other bodies that exist, including many at local level.

Nevertheless, as for current purposes there is no real need to go beyond the characteristics outlined above, or to make distinctions between the different types of quasi-government, in this chapter the terms quango and quasi-government will be used interchangeably.

Classifying quasi-government

Pliatzky's (1980) categorisation remains useful and the following provides an indication of the range of bodies:

- Executive – those which are direct instruments of government policy, for example, in terms of education (such as higher education corporations, the Higher Education Funding Council for England, and the Scottish Higher Education Funding Council), housing (the Housing Corporation, registered housing associations and registered social landlords), health (NHS public bodies including NHS trusts), inner-city regeneration (local enterprise companies) and environmental protection (the Environment Agency). One of the main developments of the 1980s and 1990s was the significant growth in the number of executive bodies at the local level.

- Advisory – described by Hall and Weir (1996) as 'a near invisible layer of government, even though they shape government decisions of vital importance which touch people's lives where they are most vulnerable' (p. 4). These are perhaps most obvious in the fields of food and health and include the Food Advisory Committee, which oversees the safety of the food we eat; the Committee on the Safety of Medicines which oversees the medicines we are prescribed; and the Advisory Committee on NHS Drugs. Other advisory quangos can influence government decisions in the areas of environmental pollution, the toxicity of chemicals in food, medical aspects of food policy, welfare benefits, and so on. Again, these came more to public attention in the late 1980s and 1990s as a result of a series of food and public health scares.

- Tribunals – having a licensing or appeals function based in a specific area of law, such as industrial tribunals, disability appeals tribunals, the special educational needs tribunal, and children's panels in Scotland, and boards of visitors of prisons.

The actual number of quasi-governmental organisations in existence is an ongoing debate. With the definitional problems discussed above, and the constantly changing picture arising from mergers, abolition of some bodies and the establishment of others, it is almost impossible to give an agreed figure. Perhaps the two most widely accepted figures are those based upon the government's official definition of 'executive non-departmental public bodies' which would have given a tally of 301 in 1996 (although the revised broader official definition recognised around 1000 'public bodies' by 2000), and that calculated by Hall and Weir (1996) which results in more than 6400 (Table 6.1). Weir and Hall break executive quangos down as follows: 266 at national level; 318 at regional level and 5166 at local level. The vast difference in the number of organisations is accounted for mainly by those executive bodies that operate at local level which are included by Weir and Hall but not in the official definitions. This difference is important for social policy as over 1800 of Weir and Hall's quangos were involved in the direct provision of education (grant-maintained schools) and over 2500 in the provision of housing (such as registered housing associations).

From 1997 the Labour government began to be somewhat more open about quasi-government and also started to accept some of the extra-governmental organisations identified by Weir and Hall and others. In *Public Bodies 1998* (Cabinet Office, 1998a), the government therefore not only provided the numbers of non-departmental public bodies (Table 6.2) but estimated the number of

Table 6.1   Executive and advisory quangos, 1996

Executive

Non-departmental public bodies	301
NHS bodies	788
'Non-recognised' Northern Ireland NDPBs	8
'Non-recognised' local quangos	4653
Total executive	5750

Advisory

Non-departmental public bodies	674
Total	6424

Source: W Hall and S Weir, *The Untouchables: Power and Accountability in the Quango State* (London: Democratic Audit/Scarman Trust, 1996), p. 5.

Table 6.2   Non-departmental public bodies, 1998

Executive	304
Advisory	563
Tribunals	67
Boards of Visitors	137
Total	1071

Source: Cabinet Office, *Public Bodies 1998* (London: TSO, 1998).

non-recognised 'local public spending bodies' as 4650, with a total of 69,693 board members. In 1998, of the board members of the organisations included in *Public Bodies*, 32 per cent were female (with the proportion of women among those appointed by ministers being slightly higher at 34 per cent) whilst only 4 per cent of appointees came from ethnic minorities, and by 2001 these proportions had risen slightly to 34 per cent and 5 per cent.

Quasi-government, in its different forms (see Exhibit 6.1 for examples), is responsible for a considerable proportion of public expenditure. For example, in 1994/5, the figure for officially recognised executive quangos was £20.8 billion, but using Hall and Weir's wider definition of non-elected executive bodies this rises to £60.4 billion (Hall and Weir, 1996).

The government's own figures for 1998 produce over 1900 bodies involved in the direct provision of education and over 2600 registered social landlords or registered housing associations.

Finally, to reiterate the scale and importance of quasi-government, even given the definitional problems discussed above, by 2000 Rhodes was able to write that 'There are now 5,521 special-purpose bodies spending at least £39 billion a year and to which ministers make 70,000 patronage appointments. This sector is larger than local government!' (Rhodes, 2000, p. 156). Given these developments it is perhaps appropriate to note that this in itself contributes to the complexity and fragmentation of policy making and implementation mechanisms, lending further credence to approaches such as policy networks which emphasise this and which move away from simplistic top-down models of the policy process.

The origins and growth of quangos

Despite the attention devoted to it by politicians, academics and the media from the 1970s, quasi-government is not new. The Crown Agents date from the mid-nineteenth century and the Horserace Totaliser Board (the Tote) was established in 1928. Even during one of the main periods of government growth, the Fulton Committee (1968), reporting on the civil service, recommended that further consideration should be given to the possibility of hiving-off functions to non-departmental organisations. However, it is arguably now the scope and scale of quasi-government that is different.

Skelcher (1998) identifies three phases of growth in quangos in the twentieth century. Up to the 1950s appointed bodies were generally used to manage public enterprise in the form of public corporations, such as the BBC and the Forestry Commission. In the 1960s and 1970s this model was extended to incorporate 'key interests' into tripartite boards involving government, employers and unions, reflecting the shift towards a corporatist model of decision making. For the Conservative governments of the 1980s and 1990s this approach was less acceptable, and a business model emerged which not only reflected the idea of public managerialism at arm's length but also saw an influx of business representatives onto the boards of many organisations.

By the 1970s the perceived growth in the number and scope of quasi-governmental organisations was giving cause for concern and was highlighted

EXHIBIT 6.1   EXAMPLES OF QUASI-GOVERNMENTAL AGENCIES

Commission for Racial Equality (CRE) – created in 1977 – exists to tackle racial discrimination and promote racial equality, including providing advice and information to individuals, working with other organisations to promote equal treatment for all, raising awareness of race issues and ensuring that new laws take account of the Race Relations Act. The Board consists of 14 members (nine male, five female in 2001) appointed by the Home Secretary. Its expenditure was £17.1 million in 2000/1, of which £16.7 million came from the government. It reports to the Home Office. The CRE employed 196 people in 2001.

Addenbrooke's NHS Trust – created in 1993 – is a major teaching hospital, the district hospital for the population of Cambridge and the surrounding area and a focus for significant medical research. The Trust employs more than 6000 staff and has well over 1000 in-patient beds. The Board consists of the Chair and five non-executive directors appointed by the NHS Appointments Commission, and five executive directors (of whom two were women in 2002). In 2001/2 it had a total expenditure of £239 million. It reports to the NHS executive and the Secretary of State for Health.

Learning and Teaching Scotland was established in 2000 through the merger of the Scottish Consultative Council on the Curriculum and the Scottish Council for Educational Technology. Its aim is to develop and provide high-quality advice to Scottish ministers and, where appropriate, others on the pre-school and school curriculum, and on the use of information and communications technology in learning. It has a Board of 11 members (8 male and 3 female in 2001), appointed by the Scottish Executive. In 2000/1 it had a total expenditure of £12 million and employed 195 people. It reports to the Scottish Executive's Education Department.

The Housing Corporation was created in 1964. Its role is to fund and regulate registered social landlords in England. The Corporation's Board is appointed by the Deputy Prime Minister. It consists of 13 people, of whom in 2000/1 five were female and eight male. In 2000/1 it spent £1010.3 million of which £1004.2 million came from the government, and employed 593 people. It reports to the Office of the Deputy Prime Minister.

The Human Genetics Commission was established in 1999 to provide ministers with strategic advice on human genetics, with a particular emphasis on social and ethical issues. It has 18 members (eight of whom were women in 2002), together with representatives from each of the four UK Chief Medical Officers. It reports to the Department of Health.

The Quality Assurance Agency for Higher Education is a rather different body from those described above, being a limited company. However, it is included here to illustrate the wide range of bodies that affect social policy. The QAA was established

> **EXHIBIT 6.1   EXAMPLES OF QUASI-GOVERNMENTAL AGENCIES (cont'd)**
>
> in 1997 to provide an integrated quality assurance service for higher education institutions throughout the UK and its main business is to review the performance of universities and colleges of higher education. The Board consists of 14 members, four appointed by representative bodies of heads of higher education institutions, four appointed by the funding bodies in higher education and six are independent directors appointed by the Board itself. In 2002 seven members of the Board were female and seven male; that year the QAA spent £10.3 million and employed, on average, 102 people.

in academic work, by politicians and in the media. As noted earlier, soon after her election Margaret Thatcher made clear her intention to reduce the numbers, power and costs of quangos. However, the trends in the usage of quasi-government over the past two decades are far from clear, partly due to the definitional and classificatory difficulties discussed above, so that it was possible for the Conservative government to argue that it had reduced the number of non-departmental public bodies whilst simultaneously its critics argued that the number of quangos had increased. In addition, Hall and Weir (1996) use expenditure by executive quangos to highlight the growth in their role, noting that this increased from £41.6 billion in 1978/9 to £60.4 billion in 1994/5, an increase of 45 per cent in real terms, to a figure which represents more than one-third of central government expenditure (local government spent £73.4 billion in 1994/5). In contrast the officially defined 'non-departmental public bodies' spent £20.8 billion in 1994/5. Another measure would be the membership numbers of quangos, and Skelcher (1998) points out that by the late 1990s there were more than twice as many members of local appointed executive bodies as there were local authority councillors.

The types of activities undertaken by quasi-governmental agencies have changed dramatically, so that with the demise of nationalised industries and the reduction in direct government intervention in the economy, activity in this field has arguably been significantly reduced, whilst changes in education, health and housing have meant that the numbers and activities of quasi-governmental bodies in these areas have dramatically increased.

There are a number of explanations which can be put forward for this growth in the role and scope of quasi-government, some of which are particularly important for social policy. One is that the Conservative governments had identified the growth of the state as a problem and believed that there were too many tasks for government to be able to undertake. One of their solutions to this was to shift from 'government' towards 'governance' by retaining core functions as government responsibilities and hiving-off what they perceived of as 'non-essential' tasks to private, voluntary and 'third sector' organisations who had the specialist expertise to undertake these functions. This meant that in theory government could get on with the task of policy formulation, what has sometimes been defined as 'steering', whilst other organisations would be able get on with policy implementation and service delivery or 'rowing' (Peters, 1997). In practice, this, together with the Conservatives' questioning of the role of the welfare state, manifested itself in a new culture whereby the welfare state was no longer seen as sacred, and the market rather than the state became prominent in the governance of the state and the economy. Based on selected aspects of public choice theory and New Right ideology, new economic policy instruments were introduced, including the privatisation of state assets, internal markets, deregulation, contracting-out of local authority services and so on.

These new policy instruments had consequences for social policy in that organisations and services previously run and controlled by the state were now independent organisations requiring some form of regulation. For example, the privatisation of services such as gas, water, telephones and council housing required that regulatory bodies be set up to monitor the operation and standards of these previously state-run services. The resulting bodies such as OFGAS (Office of Gas Supply) OFWAT and OFTEL are all quasi-governmental agencies. In housing the shift of state funding of social housing away from local authorities towards housing associations meant an increased role for these bodies and for the channels of finance, such as the Housing Corporation and Scottish Homes. Similarly, the pressure on local authorities to reduce their provision of residential care for older people meant that whilst these were privatised in some areas, in others new organisations came into being which were quasi-governmental in nature. Similar developments can be identified in health, with the establishment of NHS trusts, and in education with the encouragement of schools to opt out of local authority control and to become self-managed.

A second explanation is that, as had been the case with previous governments, the Conservatives also used quangos as a mechanism to by-pass local government, reflecting the top-down approach to policy implementation frequently taken by central government, as outlined in Chapter 2. Local authorities, particularly those controlled by Labour councils, were often seen as, and frequently were, hostile to the Conservatives' plans, and the creation of different forms of quasi-government arguably enabled the Conservative governments to put their policies into practice without having to encounter direct opposition. As their tenure in office grew longer, their base in local government grew weaker and indeed the incentive, or even the need, for government to use quasi-governmental bodies to implement its policies increased. This incentive was further reinforced by the New Right's critique which saw local authorities as bureaucratic, inefficient and wasteful. The creation of many organisations such as locally managed schools, economic development agencies and housing associations therefore arguably enabled Conservative governments to keep a tighter rein over both expenditure and policy direction, because instead of these services being funded and provided by local authorities they were directly funded by central government. In addition, as Gleeson and Shain (1999) discuss in relation to further education, the influence of board members from business and industry has also impacted upon the cultural ethos, bringing a greater emphasis upon economic and business competitiveness rather than pedagogy.

At the local level Stewart (1995) noted three broad trends under the Conservatives, which both separately and together had the potential for impact upon social policy:

- the removal of local authority representatives from boards on which they once sat, such as district health authorities;
- the removal of responsibilities from local authorities to an appointed board, such as further education colleges and grant-maintained schools;
- the separation off and redistribution amongst newly created agencies of activities previously under the control of a single organisation, such as occurred with the establishment of NHS trusts.

However, one of the issues arising from these shifts is that the actual process of governing becomes more complex because of the number of organisations involved. This proliferation not only raises many of the issues discussed in the arguments for and against quasi-government (see below): it can also lead to difficulties such as 'implementation deficit', where attempts to put policy into practice can be hindered even by relatively small differences in focus among a number of organisations responsible for it. This could certainly be said to be the case in relation to welfare provision in which a huge range of organisations are involved, many of which are of a quasi-governmental nature.

In other areas the Conservatives were criticised for the degree of control retained by ministers. For example, the new police authorities established by the Police and Magistrates' Court Act 1994 are criticised by Hall and Weir (1996) for the extent of the Home Secretary's power over them – he appointed five of the 17 members, had the power to set standard spending assessments, provided half of their budget directly, approved capital projects and set nationally determined 'key objectives' for the forces.

The uses and abuses of quasi-government

Cogent arguments can be deployed both in support of and against the use of quasi-government in policy making and implementation (see Figure 6.1). Indeed, both Labour and Conservative parties have criticised them, but also made use of them when it suited them. As Hogwood (1995) points out, our perspective on quasi-government tends to vary with the issue, so that some who opposed the very idea of housing action trusts to regenerate run-down council estates would have supported wages councils as a means of maintaining wage levels for low-paid groups, and vice versa.

Whatever the debates are about quasi-government, it remains the case that it is an important feature of British government and that at the start of the twenty-first century it has significant influence over social policy, and in particular over some areas of food and medicine safety and the delivery of local services. It is

Figure 6.1   Arguments for and against the use of quasi-government

Arguments for quasi-government

- It allows particular expertise to be brought into government.
- Judgements about the application and interpretation of policy can be made by individuals who are independent of government.
- Single-purpose boards offer potential for focus on specific policies, and tasks which may be inappropriate for political control, such as the BBC.
- It can allow stakeholders to be brought onto the board in a way that may not be possible in representative government.
- Policy implementation may be enhanced where those who are responsible are sympathetic to the policies.
- Delegation of authority reduces demands on centres of elected decision making.
- It can allow large numbers of people to take part in public life, with the great majority being unpaid volunteers.

Arguments against quasi-government

- It allows representative government to be by-passed.
- It places functions in the hands of unelected, sometimes unaccountable, individuals.
- The democratic deficit undermines the legitimacy of elected tiers of government.
- The role of elected politicians is constrained by distancing themselves from some fields of governmental decision making;
- It allows politicians to distance themselves from potentially unpopular decisions;
- There is a frequent lack of rationale for the allocation of executive functions between elected and appointed bodies;
- The number of bodies can cause problems of co-ordination, strategic and joined-up government;
- Claims of independence can be undermined by the potential for political bias in appointments;
- Certain groups may dominate and others may lose out among patronage posts.

Source: Adapted from C Skelcher, *The Appointed State* (Buckingham: Open University Press, 1998) p. 179.

also the case that, despite many of the criticisms outlined in this chapter, there are some significant arguments in favour of at least some quasi-government.

For analysts of social policy, concern about secrecy in quasi-government runs further even than the concerns over democracy and accountability. As Hall and Weir (1996) point out, should anyone in the mid-1990s have wished to investigate the impact of Housing Corporation decisions and practices on the black community, or the decisions that the Funding Agency for Schools made over 'failing' schools, they might have been unable to make any real progress. At local level the picture is mixed, with higher education corporations, including universities, being required to publish the agendas and minutes of their meetings and a register of their members' interests. Housing associations are required only to publish the latter, and career service companies, which are responsible for the careers services previously provided by local councils, need do none of these. Nevertheless, many quasi-governmental bodies have, to a greater or lesser extent, attempted to achieve a degree of openness that goes beyond the minimum required of them; but for many of the critics of quangos it is the lack of rights available to the public that is the key issue. In contrast, all local councils are subject to appeals to the ombudsman, have to open council and committee meetings to the public, publish agendas, background papers and minutes and maintain registers of members' interests.

In recent years criticisms of quasi-government have tended to focus around three main (sometimes inter-related) areas located around the notion of the 'democratic deficit', these being accountability, membership and patronage, and performance, to which Skelcher (1998) usefully adds governance.

The democratic deficit

One of the key concerns over the growth of quasi-government is the extent to which the 'appointed state' (Skelcher, 1998) is accountable and subject to democratic control. This is frequently referred to as the 'democratic deficit'. Even in 1979 it was observed that:

> the growth of fringe bodies is a retreat from the simple democratic principle evolved in the nineteenth century that those who perform a public duty should be fully responsible to the electorate – by way either of a minister responsible to Parliament or of a locally elected council. The essence of the fringe body is that it is not so responsible for some or all of its actions (Chester, 1979, p. 54).

With the Conservatives' use of quasi-government frequently linked with the marketisation of services (including internal markets and increased competition), and particularly welfare services, criticisms became even more pointed so that Clive Gray (1994) argued that 'We have unfettered market institutions protected by authoritarian, unaccountable, quasi-governmental apparatus', whilst one Labour MP, Tony Wright, contended that the growth of quangos since 1979:

> is part of a whole consumerist approach to public services and to government itself. Accountability has been redefined away from politics and towards the market... It is a world in which nobody is responsible for anything any more, with individual consumers left to claim their 'rights' in an irresponsible public market place of quangos, contractors, providers and purchasers (Wright, 1994, p. 22).

There have been many criticisms directed at the public accountability of quasi-governmental bodies. These have been usefully highlighted by, among others, Weir and Hall in their *Democratic Audit* (1994) and *The Untouchables* (Hall and

Weir, 1996), and to some extent reinforced by the House of Commons' Public Accounts Committee (1994) and the Committee on Standards in Public Life (1996) in its report on local public spending bodies. It is certainly the case that, taken as a whole, there are a variety of mechanisms for regulating and holding accountable quasi-government, including their contractual agreements and obligations, investigations by parliamentary select committees and by individual MPs, auditors, ombudsmen and the courts. In addition the media sometimes take up issues associated with either particular quangos or quasi-government as a whole. Nevertheless, among the main criticisms have been: that whilst there may exist a variety of mechanisms for ensuring the accountability of quasi-governmental agencies, these are not applied rigorously or consistently, for example when compared to the position of local government; there is frequently a lack of local accountability for non-elected bodies which provide local public services; and that public access and direct accountability are often poor.

The response of the Conservative governments to such criticism was to suggest that its reform programme was different not only in content but also in nature. They argued that people should now be seen as customers and consumers of services provided by organisations such as opted-out schools, NHS trusts and contracted-out local authority services. From this perspective they suggested that not only did previous methods of accountability continue to function, but that in fact there had been a 'democratic gain', new formal lines of accountability having been created from agencies to their customers and to individual citizens. One example of this was the introduction of the Citizen's Charter in 1991, aiming to raise standards in public services and to provide the public with information about the standards of service that they could expect and some means of redress should these not materialise. However, there were criticisms that agencies often set standards that were relatively low and that they were likely to be able to meet and that in reality there was little redress for the consumer when things did go wrong.

Issues of patronage have also been a focus for critics of quasi-government, Hall and Weir (1996) estimating that there are at least 66,000 appointments to the variety of quangos. External scrutiny of these appointments, by Parliament and others, is very limited and rarely do they have to be accounted for, let alone on performance grounds. One view is that this gives ministers enormous scope for taking into account political factors and making appointments of people with politically similar views, and that it affords the opportunity for government by co-option rather than by election or by appointment through merit. During the 1980s and 1990s there was considerable criticism of the high level of Conservative sympathisers being appointed to quangos. However, as Skelcher (1998) points out, ministers are only responsible for around half of the appointments to executive quangos, with most of the remainder being made by the bodies themselves, an arrangement which perhaps raises even more fundamental questions about the appointments process, accountability and representativeness, and the extent to which these bodies and the appointments mechanisms serve to replicate and even reinforce existing social inequalities. For example, among the boards of non-departmental public bodies, women and black people are under-represented whilst business people are over-represented, including as chairs of boards. Quango members are also a highly educated group (see Skelcher, 1998).

By the mid-1990s there were some signs of change in the procedures for appointments to quasi-governmental agencies, with increasing use of public advertisements inviting applications and the use of search committees to identify potential members. Yet the situation remains at best blurred and, in addition to the issues of accountability discussed earlier, there are perhaps three fundamental questions which are relevant to appointments to quangos: does patronage result in the best people being appointed; does it give ministers too much power to influence supposedly independent organisations; and does it enable particular groups to dominate the appointed state?

During the 1980s and 1990s the debate about the role of quasi-government became closely related to that about the performance of public agencies and services more generally. The Conservative governments' use of mechanisms such as NHS trusts and grant-maintained schools was mirrored by the introduction of Next Steps agencies in the civil service, whilst the introduction of performance measures has been seen across large swathes of the public sector. Under the Conservatives the model of quasi-government based upon a small board free from the encumbrance of party politics (perhaps particularly where local politics was dominated by other political parties) also appeared to fit well with the introduction of markets into the public sector and the shift towards a new public management approach.

However, there are significant methodological problems in attempting to measure performance (see Chapter 8). Skelcher (1998) pulls together a range of evidence on three types of quango – urban development corporations, training and enterprise councils and grant-maintained schools. He argues that the evidence suggests that the performance of local education authority schools and grant-maintained schools is very similar, and that in the absence of competitors it is hard to draw conclusions about relative performance, although both types of body appear to have been significantly affected by their interdependence on other agencies and processes, and in particular on the performance of the economy. He also cites Pollitt *et al.* (1997) who studied the impact of self-management in education, health care and housing, and concluded that self-management often correlated with increasing activity levels, but that it was hard to know whether this resulted from better management or other pressures.

Skelcher (1998) highlights an additional and often neglected aspect of quasi-government that is of considerable relevance to this book – its internal governance, the process by which decisions are made and the interactions within the organisation and with stakeholders and other interests. He explores three aspects of this: the personal contribution of individual board members in terms of their views and expertise, the internal governance of the organisation and the external relationships with users and stakeholders. He points out that there is considerable variety across the three aspects, but notes that in terms of interaction with users, newer and community-based bodies appear to be more ready to engage in exercises designed to involve users and local interests, citing housing action trusts and City Challenge organisations as examples, and contrasting them with the urban development corporations that preceded them. Greer and Hoggett (2000) suggest that the boards of 'local public spending bodies' have failed to exercise significant influence over managers and that there is a need to ensure greater representation of stakeholders on boards, together with a willingness to recognise that the differing perspectives that this might create might lead to conflict, but that this could be constructive.

Next Steps agencies

The growth in the use of Next Steps agencies under the Conservative governments was briefly referred to in the previous section (see also Chapter 4). Although these do not fit entirely comfortably with the characteristics of quasi-government outlined earlier in this chapter – for example they remain part of the government department in which they originated – they do share some common ground with quasi-government, and an analysis from this perspective can be useful.

One of the recommendations of the Pliatzky report on non-departmental public bodies (1980) was that the degree of satisfaction with hived-off bodies was

> sufficient to justify recourse to the non-Departmental method in further cases on a selective basis, but there have also been enough problems to give ministers pause before creating new chosen instruments... Generally speaking the moral indicated is, not so much that we should set about turning the clock back, but that we should not think in terms of a further considerable extension of 'hiving off' as an instrument for securing improved efficiency and economy across a wide range of public activities (p. 19).

However, in 1988 the Efficiency Unit produced a report, *Improving Management in Government: The Next Steps* (Ibbs, 1988), as part of a general review of management reform. The report recommended that 'agencies' should be established to carry out the executive functions of government within a policy and resources framework set by a department. An 'agency' of this kind might be part of government and the public service, or it might be more effective outside government. In making the possibility of the creation of agencies outside government an option, the report ran completely counter to the Pliatzky report and to the thinking that had led up to it. To have pursued such a policy might have involved the Conservative government in a significant policy U-turn. However this was avoided by the decision that such agencies would generally remain within the civil service and that their staff would continue to be civil servants. Yet the resulting agencies are not dissimilar to some forms of quasi-government and both types of organisation raise similar questions around the delegation of functions, the arm's-length approach, and problems of accountability and control. Many of these agencies have a direct responsibility for significant parts of social policy, including the Social Security Benefits Agency, the Child Support Agency and the Social Security Resettlement Agency. Indeed, Foster and Plowden (1996), referring to issues of independence, argue that 'in a general sense all quangos and executive agencies are agencies. And, indeed, comparable functions may be carried out by quangos and agencies... From the point of view of improving efficiency, quangos and executive agencies raise similar issues' (p. 149).

Where performance is concerned, James (2001) argues that agencies have partly met the expectations of reformers, with improvements in economy as measured by falls in administrative costs after 1996. However, with regard to efficiency and effectiveness, he suggests that the picture is less clear, with, for example, the Benefits Agency having problems with inaccurate payments (on average amounting to 7 per cent of the payments budget which itself was 90 per cent of the Agency's total spend). Indeed he notes that:

> problems with effectiveness meant that the efficiency of the body was compromised in key areas. There was further indirect ineffectiveness by bodies depending on joint working with the Agency, especially local authorities in the administration of Housing Benefit, where problems with inaccurate information contributed to the outcome of 7 per cent of expenditure being paid out inaccurately (p. 45).

Reforming quasi-government

Whilst there is criticism of quasi-government from many sources, including the major political parties, together with a whole raft of proposals for reform from across the political spectrum, radical change has not yet occurred. In 1979 the Thatcher government promised a 'bonfire of the quangos', with the Pliatzky report intended to underpin this, but the Conservatives then found a number of reasons for continuing to use quasi-government, with considerable growth particularly in the area of social policy. Then, by the mid-1990s, allegations of 'sleaze' in politics had embraced quango appointments and accountability as well as the behaviour of politicians, the two being linked together for some commentators by the perceived propensity for Conservative supporters to be placed in positions of influence in quasi-government. In one instance the House of Commons Public Accounts Committee (1994) believed that poor financial control in the Welsh Development Agency and the Wessex and West Midlands Health Authorities had led to inadequate stewardship of public money and that there were poor standards in public conduct in many areas.

One of the results of these concerns was the creation of the Committee on Standards in Public Life. The Committee's first report (1995), whilst not concerned primarily with quasi-government, set out seven principles of public life (selflessness, integrity, objectivity, accountability, openness, honesty and leadership) and included a chapter on quangos, making a number of recommendations, particularly about the appointments process, some of which were implemented under the Conservatives. Perhaps the most important in some respects was the appointment of a Public Appointments Commissioner to monitor, regulate and approve departmental procedures, together with the recommendation that all public appointments should be governed by the overriding principle of appointment on merit. The first Commissioner for Public Appointments, Sir Leonard Peach, was appointed in 1995. The Committee's second report (1996) was concerned exclusively with 'local public spending bodies', including universities and colleges of higher and further education, grant-maintained schools, registered housing associations and training and enterprise councils. Again the concern was largely with accountability and appointments. Amongst its recommendations the Committee advocated the retention of the principle of unpaid voluntary service by board members and moves towards greater local accountability.

In addition think-tanks, academics and politicians have all added their thoughts on the possibilities for reforming quasi-government. There are essentially two types of approach: the first involves changes to the existing system to improve perceived weaknesses such as the appointments systems and accountability, the second is a more general 'democratisation' of many of the functions and duties currently performed by quasi-government.

Proposals to reform the current system of quasi-government can arguably be grouped under three headings: the appointment of members; the accountability and internal governance of quasi-government; and the regulation of quasi-government.

Appointing members

Amongst the proposals relating to appointments is the introduction of registers of members of boards which would include information such as contact details, level of payment, and political affiliation, if any. There could also be clear procedures for making appointments, such as requirements to advertise vacancies, job descriptions, application forms and requirements to interview and to observe equal opportunities practices. These would all be publicly available. Some would like to see appointments scrutinised before they are confirmed, either by an independent body or by a committee of the appropriate tier of representative government. Since 1997 the government has taken some further steps in these directions.

A variety of codes were introduced during the 1990s for board members of some quasi-governmental organisations including NHS trust boards, boards of public bodies and advisory non-departmental public bodies. These cover topics such as accountability, integrity and openness.

Improving accountability and internal governance

A similar approach could be taken to ensure the accountability of quasi-governmental organisations, a code of conduct or set of rules setting out the appropriate requirements, such as public access to meetings and to minutes, coverage by ombudsmen, declarations of interests and requirements for independent audit. Stewart (1995) also suggests that local government might be given either the power or a duty to scrutinise the activities of appointed boards operating at the local level. Whilst this would not strictly mean that they could be held to account, it would bring their activities to public view.

The Committee on Standards in Public Life (1995) (itself an advisory body) was concerned about the variety of audit measures applied to quangos and the apparently *ad hoc* nature of these. Where financial control is concerned it might also be appropriate for the position of board members and senior managers to be brought into line with local councillors who are liable to be surcharged if expenditure is incurred *ultra vires* or through wilful misconduct. There is already a code of conduct for staff of executive non-departmental public bodies, which includes accountability, conflicts of interest and staff concerns about improper conduct.

Regulating quasi-government

From the 1970s there have been proposals that the House of Commons should have a greater ability to monitor quasi-governmental bodies and to hold them to account. The Public Accounts Committee can undertake some investigations as can the relevant departmental select committee, but there is no mechanism to enable Parliament to take a strategic view of the development and actions of quangos across the UK. Some critics of quangos have proposed the importation of practice from some of the states in the USA, whereby bodies are created for a fixed term and automatically abolished at the end of that term unless there is a clear decision to renew them. On occasion select committees have commented on the role of particular quangos, as happened in 2002 when the select committee on Science and Technology responded to a comment by the former Chair of the Human Fertilisation and Embryology Authority that the HFEA protected MPs from a direct involvement in such ethical deliberations. In its report the Committee argued that 'Parliament does not need protecting and democracy is not served by unelected quangos taking decisions on behalf of parliament' (Science and Technology Select Committee, 2002, para. 26). In this particular instance the Committee also highlighted the tension between the 'expert' role often assigned to quangos and the demands of representative democracy for involvement in decision making.

Democratisation

The more radical approach proposed by some would involve a shift in the style of government away from quasi-governmental agencies towards organisations that afford greater democratic control. However, as this would mean that some of the 'advantages' associated with quasi-government would be lost, the arguments for democratisation are sometimes seen to be stronger where policy decisions are made on the basis of values, rather than technical or scientific considerations.

There could, of course, be different approaches to bringing quasi-government under democratic control, particularly at the local level. In some instances the duties could simply be handed over to local authorities, for example by returning grant-maintained schools to local authority control or by making local authorities responsible for the running of local health services; whilst in others there might be a stronger case for electing the members of the board overseeing a particular function. However, whilst arguably more overtly democratic and accountable than the existing system, these suggestions inevitably raise issues about the representative process itself, particularly at local level where electoral turnout is often poor.

The devolution which took place during the 1990s has brought with it greater scope for the development of different models and approaches to quasi-government in different parts of the UK, since the Scottish Parliament and the National Assembly for Wales have the potential to make their own decisions about many aspects of policy making and implementation, as well as having control over many existing quasi-governmental organisations. Indeed, Hirst (1995) sees advantages in decentralisation and democratisation to the regional level for the rest of the UK, pointing out that a regional tier would be more able than local government to take on the major functions of government, would be in a position to bring themselves to the attention of the electorate, and would be less likely to be dominated by one party, particularly if elected by proportional representation.

Labour and quasi-government

Labour's 1997 manifesto (Labour Party, 1997) had little of a direct nature to say about quasi-government, but there were some areas which clearly drew upon the debates of preceding years and in particular on standards in public life, freedom of information and devolution, which had the potential for significant impact on quangos. As we have seen in Chapter 5, the manifesto committed the new government to devolving power within the UK, including, for example in the case of the Welsh Assembly, being 'specifically empowered to reform and democratise the quango state' (p. 33). It also pledged a more open style of government, including a Freedom of Information Act, and to clean up politics.

In *Quangos: Opening the Doors* (Cabinet Office, 1998b), the new government undertook to keep the number of quangos to a minimum and to make those that remain more open, accountable and effective. Among the proposals, many were aimed at encouraging a greater degree of openness and providing more access to information, although there was rather less attention to issues of accountability. It set out a commitment to establishing new non-departmental public bodies only where it could be demonstrated that this would be the most cost-effective and appropriate means of carrying out a given function. And it stated that financial management and policy reviews of these bodies would take place at least every five years to establish whether their functions were still required. The annual edition of *Public Bodies* has since contained some further information, such as the terms of reference and the names of the chair and chief executive of each body included within it. In general it is the case that at least some additional information is now available on a wide variety of quasi-governmental bodies than was previously the case, even if there is no immediate evidence of any significant changes to the organisations themselves.

However, Labour, like other governments, have found that quasi-governmental bodies can often be useful and that their abolition is not always easy or, from the government's perspective, desirable. This reflects some of the advantages of quasi-government discussed earlier in the chapter, including the expertise of those on the boards of quangos, as well as the relative ease of policy direction of these organisations. Furthermore, there remains the question of whether alternatives to quasi-government would work effectively and economically. Labour's approach since 1997 might therefore be characterised as not having been concerned with abolishing quasi-governmental bodies but rather with some attempts to open them up to more scrutiny. To this end they have been using a variety of mechanisms, including passing responsibilities to the new devolved governments, exerting greater pressure on organisations themselves to be open and transparent and at least rhetorically encouraging scrutiny by the public and Parliament.

At the same time, Labour's enthusiasm for the establishment of taskforces to examine and advise on a variety of issues led to the creation of over 200 such bodies by the end of 2000, including the National Skills Taskforce (Department for Education and Employment), the NHS Taskforce on Staff Involvement (Department of Health), the Advisory Group on Marriage and Relationship Support (Lord Chancellor's Department) and the Treasury Taskforce to support Private Finance Initiative activities. Whilst most of these have a finite lifetime they can nevertheless be seen as another development in this area. Labour maintained the position of the Commissioner for Public Appointments, with Dame Rennie Fritchie succeeding Sir Leonard Peach, and themselves received some criticisms, with for example, the 2002 report (Office of the Commissioner for Public Appointments, 2002) noting that the proportion of women being appointed to the boards of public bodies had remained at around 38 or 39 per cent for five consecutive years, although the same report noted that the numbers of people appointed from ethnic minority backgrounds had remained 'proportionately high' at around 9 per cent. The report also noted shortcomings among a number of departments, with for example, the Treasury, the Scottish Executive and the Department for Culture, Media and Sport being criticised for having poor systems to assess the performance of individuals being reappointed; and the Treasury was also criticised for a minister requesting that a particular candidate who had not applied for a post be added to those shortlisted for interview.

Under Labour, the devolved administrations in Scotland, Wales and Northern Ireland were given substantial powers over many aspects of quasi-government in their territories. This brings with it the possibility of alternative approaches to quangos in different parts of the UK. Richard Parry's (1999) view of the situation in Scotland was that 'Organisational failure is more difficult to conceal, but the pool of advice and appointments is smaller. The Scottish Parliament is certain to make scrutiny more intense and require each quango to justify its governance and performance' (p. 24). However, at the same time there is the possibility that devolution may lead to some duplication of quasi-governmental bodies, as, where one may have sufficed previously, now separate bodies might be required to undertake somewhat different roles in the various component parts of the UK. The evidence so far is that the Scottish Executive have sought to reduce the number of quangos, but that some of this is rationalisation of numbers, rather than activities, with, for example, the 43 separate health boards and trusts being brought together into only 15 new boards. As a result it seems likely that over time the structures and functions of quasi-government may develop distinctive identities within the different components of the UK, with the consequent scope for both diversity and for new models to emerge.

Conclusion

Quasi-governmental organisations remain an important consideration in social policy, primarily because such bodies are frequently responsible for policies and provision which impact on people's lives, such as much social housing, health care and education. In addition, others play important advisory roles including over the safety of food and medicines, whilst for some, although relatively few, the tribunal role can be an important last resort.

Under the Conservatives there were accusations that the use of quasi-government was contributing to the centralisation of power as well as acting as a tool for the furtherance of the introduction of markets and the new managerialism into the public sector. In the face of such criticism many Conservatives argued that the new bodies that they had created were misunderstood and that they were actually designed to give power to the citizen by removing power from bureaucrats and giving citizens greater opportunity to exercise power for themselves, particularly acting as consumers in the market. However, when combined with accusations of a Conservative and business bias in the appointment of board members and criticisms of secrecy and lack of accountability, the 'democratic deficit' became a significant issue in the mid-1990s: issues which did not disappear under the Labour governments, despite some greater degree of openness about quasi-governmental organisations.

Whatever the reasons for it, the continued widespread use of quasi-governmental mechanisms lends support to views that the policy process in contemporary society has become increasingly complex, and can best be understood using a combination of analytical models. For example, the existence of quasi-governmental bodies has implications for pluralistic perspectives, simultaneously creating additional power centres whilst at the same time arguably diverting power away from representative institutions. Also, in order to understand fully the position and role of these organisations it is helpful to draw upon both institutional approaches to the policy process and those which emphasise the complexity of decision making and implementation, such as policy networks, whilst for some of the larger bodies, or those with responsibilities for service delivery, we may benefit from an analysis which considers the nature and power of bureaucratic institutions and street-level bureaucrats. There are also additional risks in the use and growth of quasi-government, including the reduction of opposition through co-option, and thus of disguising what may be genuine and well-founded dissent, or of using such mechanisms to keep issues away from the mainstream agenda, whilst from another perspective too much incorporation of some groups into the policy making and implementation process may mean that other, frequently less powerful or disadvantaged groups may be excluded.

Yet there is undoubtedly a case for the continuation of quasi-government in social policy. There remain a number of advantages of such an approach, including the possibilities of bringing expertise to bear on particular areas of policy. Advisory quangos in particular may have a particular role to play where technical and scientific knowledge is required, such as the safety of food or medicines. In addition, the ability to create particular balances on quango boards can have advantages for bringing a range of interests and expertise into the decision-making process, as has happened in some areas of urban regeneration. Those who often miss out on representation, such as young people or ethnic minorities, may be included by such a method and this may lead to both better and more consensual outcomes than if decisions were left to elected politicians alone.

The arm's-length function of quasi-government also brings potential benefits, with the argument that members can be more 'objective' than elected representatives. This role is particularly important in the quasi-judicial role played by tribunals, although tribunal members may find themselves in a position of conflict between their decisions and the government that appoints them. Similarly, there is an argument that quasi-government can reduce the demands on elected tiers of government, with politicians making strategic decisions whilst detailed implementation is left to specialist bodies. However, this implies discretion on the part of quasi-government which may lead to different outcomes from those desired by the politicians on whose behalf they are supposed to be acting. Patronage may be one response to this, but this in turn compromises the arm's-length approach itself.

However, the problems summarised in the 'democratic deficit' remain strong criticisms of quasi-government. It has weaker standards of accountability, audit and internal governance than do elected bodies. For many critics this was exacerbated in the 1980s and 1990s by the withdrawal of government from provision of some services, together with the emphasis on managerialism and markets, with the view of the public as 'consumers' taking precedence over that as 'citizens'. If quasi-government is to succeed and have a useful role in the social policy process it may be necessary, as Hirst (1995) points out, to achieve a new settlement between state, citizen and the intermediate institutions of civil society. Certainly a minimum requirement will be for a greater willingness to engage in debate about openness, accountability and participation that goes beyond the often cursory consultative exercises of many existing bodies, together with the development of some public vision of the policy agenda.

FURTHER READING

Hall, W and Weir, S (1996) *The Untouchables: Power and Accountability in the Quango State* (London: Democratic Audit/Scarman Trust).

Skelcher, C (1998) *The Appointed State: Quasi-Governmental Organisations and Democracy* (Buckingham: Open University Press).

For a case study see: Gleeson, D and Shain, F (1999) 'By Appointment: Governance, Markets and Managerialism in Further Education', *British Educational Research Journal*, vol. 25, pp. 545–61.

The latest edition of *Public Bodies*, published by the Cabinet Office, will provide information on a wide range of quasi-governmental bodies, together with some overall details of appointments and expenditure.

Participation

7

CHAPTER OVERVIEW

This chapter addresses 'participation' in a broad sense. Concepts such as participation, involvement and empowerment have been important social policy issues for some time and are likely to remain so. This chapter examines the processes and pitfalls for participation for individuals and groups as well as the mechanisms by which government and social policy agencies attempt to encourage or reduce participation. The modes of participation for users, citizens and groups will be examined, together with their impact upon the processes of policy making and implementation.

The notion of 'participation' has, in one form or another, been an important feature that has underpinned many developments in social policy over the past thirty years. At the level of individual users of services this has perhaps been reflected in the shift away from a pattern of welfare provision where professionals were largely seen as knowing what was best for their 'clients', to perspectives that have recognised the desirability of individuals having greater control over decisions that affect them, even viewing them as 'consumers' or 'customers' of agencies. This growth in emphasis on the centrality of individual participation can be identified, whether underpinned by the New Right perspective that stresses individual freedom and choice, or the view from the left that is based much more on the concept of individuals having social rights. To some extent this concern with involvement and participation has been echoed over the past decade in the much more widespread use of the concepts of social exclusion and inclusion to aid our understanding of social policy and its outcomes, with the greater emphasis on exclusion through lack of a voice and the role of processes in reinforcing or challenging exclusion. Lister (1990), for example, has noted that the exclusion of poor people from debates and decision making about poverty serves to reinforce their exclusion from full citizenship. It is this view, with the recognition of the ways in which people can be included or excluded in the policy process and the implications that can have for individuals, communities and society, that underpins the consideration of participation in this book.

The accent on public participation was bolstered by developments in public policy and management under the Conservatives, and in particular by attempts to make services more responsive to users and more accountable to them, including through market mechanisms. Newman (2001) identifies the growth of consumerism as a key influence, linked with changes such as the importation of private-sector techniques into public management, government reforms such as the Citizen's Charter and the involvement of parents on school governing bodies, and the rise of user movements. However, as Deakin and Wright (1990) recognise, there is an important difference between consumers and citizens, and increasing accountability to citizens as a whole is very different from increasing accountability to or participation of the users of services; indeed the two groups may have very divergent views and interests.

Under Labour the importance of participation has been repeatedly emphasised by government. For example, in *Modern Local Government: In Touch with the People* (Department of the Environment, Transport and the Regions, 1998), the government emphasised the need for greater public say in key decisions affecting the services provided by local authorities, and stated its wish to see 'consultation and participation embedded in the culture of all councils' (p. 39). Authorities have responded using the range of mechanisms noted above. Some have even sought to test local opinion over their plans for spending and the local taxation needed to support them, although with varying results.

A wide variety of mechanisms now exist that are used to encourage and enable participation by bodies responsible for the planning and provision of welfare services, particularly at the local level. These include the use of a variety of techniques associated with market research, such as focus groups and opinion polls, citizens' juries, and local referendums. Rao (2000) was able to note that:

> Councils have developed their own mix of strategies to reflect the diversity of local needs and political preferences. Developments in communications technology may extend these experiments to enable larger numbers of people to comment on matters of common concern. Telephone phone-ins have become popular for the media, the publication of email addresses is now more common, video conferencing possibilities have been explored, while interactive television provides radical possibilities for the future (Rao, 2000, p. 140).

Similarly, a report for the Scottish Executive identified 22 different consultation techniques being used by public sector bodies (Scottish Executive Central Research Unit, 2000).

At the central government level there has also been some recognition of the problems that can arise from top-down implementation and the need to enable participation, so that, for example, the Social Exclusion Unit (1998) report on neighbourhood renewal stressed the importance of 'involving communities, not parachuting in solutions' (p. 10). However, the extent to which this message has spread across government remains questionable.

There has also been debate about e-government and the possibilities of encouraging participation through the use of the Internet, although in reality this has generally been much more concerned with the delivery of information and services than with citizens' input. In November 1996 the Green Paper *government.direct* (Cabinet Office, 1996) was published, providing a prospectus for the electronic delivery of government services. It envisaged the introduction of direct, electronic one-stop access to public services, to be available 24 hours a day, seven days a week, in the manner of 'direct' banking or insurance services. This was embraced by the incoming Labour government, and the White Paper on government reform *Modernising Government* (Cabinet Office, 1999) confirmed the central place of electronic government in the government's plans and promised that all government services would be available electronically by 2008. This target was later revised to 2005. However, there continue to be major issues around the use of e-government to run/deliver welfare services. Amongst the most obvious issues for social policy is that of inequality of access to information technology (for example, Silcock, 2001), which is likely to mirror existing social inequalities. The government's approach to this is to develop the widest possible range of distribution channels for electronic public services, including those that will continue to provide telephone or face-to-face contact. Much effort is also being devoted to introducing as many people as possible to new information technology including linking up schools and colleges to the Internet and providing low-income families with discounted computers. At local level too there are attempts to develop participation through information and communications technology (see, for example, Exhibit 7.1). However, there is as yet little evidence on how successful this will be in evening-out access. In addition, there are significant

---

EXHIBIT 7.1   HIGHLAND YOUTH VOICE

The Highland Youth Voice is one example of how public sector bodies have sought to consult and involve young people, a group who are often seen as not amenable to traditional methods of involvement. It is an elected parliament of young people drawn from across Highland, with elections being held in every secondary school and additional local fora for those who have left school.

Highland Youth Voice has been developed as a representative organisation that can give young people a voice in decision making, including, for example, having been involved on the multi-agency Joint Committee on Children and Young People, and has also instigated debates such as over drugs and alcohol.

At the same time Highland Youth Voice has reflected interest in the use of information technology and has sought to use this to facilitate communication among members and to extend opportunities for participation to young people across the large geographic area covered by Highland Council. It is possible not only to access information through its web pages, much of which is provided by members of Youth Voice, but also to contribute to online debates and even for schools to vote online. It therefore seeks to combine participation with some of the tools of e-government and e-democracy.

questions over the security and privacy of data, whilst there remains the potential major difficulty of making the leap from the provision of information to a limited number of individuals to achieving the genuine participation of large sections of the community.

This emphasis on participation can be seen as occurring at a number of levels including: the involvement of individual users in decisions that affect them; a desire to achieve more user and public representation in decision-making processes; and a concern with the very legitimacy of the representative democratic process itself, with low and/or falling turnout in elections to most tiers of government. In addition, concerns have also been expressed about the future of the voluntary sector, in terms of both the quantity and form of citizen involvement. Finally, some would argue that greater public involvement in decision-making is not only a good thing in its own right, reinforcing democracy and the civic culture, as well as contributing to the development of social capital, and potentially leading to better policy making, but can also serve to justify and legitimise significant decisions such as higher taxes or cuts in the level or quality of services, depending upon the outcomes of participatory processes.

Approaches to participation

It is possible to identify two very different approaches to public participation: 'consumerist' and 'democratic'. The consumerist view is founded in the role of the market and from the 1980s has often been associated with the politics of the New Right, including their analysis of the motivations and operation of welfare bureaucracies (as outlined in Chapter 2), and public choice (see Chapter 3). As it was applied to welfare services during the 1980s and 1990s it coincided with the expansion of 'independent' provision and political pressure for a mixed economy of welfare. With its emphasis on identifying the preferences of individuals, the users of services were increasingly viewed as consumers. From this perspective, participation is therefore overlaid with the language of consumerism and the concerns of the market, whilst challenging the perceived dominance of bureaucrats and professionals in large areas of welfare. It has as its basis the idea of buying goods and services rather than making collective provision, and issues of whether individuals have or may receive the resources to use a service are thus relegated to a minor role. It is underpinned by giving priority to the wants and needs of the consumer, and commodifying their needs so that the market can deal with meeting them.

The democratic view is linked to people's roles as citizens and taxpayers, and rights and responsibilities relating to these. It has often been associated with a view of public services that are provided as part of the state's commitment to enable its citizens to participate in social and public life. In recent years it has also been connected with the emergence of self-advocacy and organisations that have sought to speak for users themselves, rather than having other groups speaking on their behalf, and often with the notions of civil rights and equality of opportunity. One example of this can be seen in the disability movement's concern for the achievement of anti-discrimination legislation, a freedom of information act and the adequate funding and resourcing of organisations of disabled people. Underpinning the democratic approach, therefore, are a belief that participation is a key element in ensuring a healthy democracy and society, and a recognition that the full range of interests in society should be represented in the decision-making process.

Lupton *et al.* (1998) highlight the significant differences between consumerist and democratic approaches in relation to accountability so that:

> Whereas in the democratic model accountability lies essentially with the individual representative, in the consumerist approach it rests with those who instigate the various forms of public consultation or involvement. In the democratic model, moreover, the notion of public representation is fundamental to effective political decision making, whereas in the consumerist model it may play only a very small part in the wider process of performance management (Lupton *et al.*, 1998, p. 54).

Richardson (1983) notes that there is also an important distinction between direct and indirect participation. Direct participation is where people come face-to-face with decision makers, for example in the context of statutory or *ad hoc* meetings. Indirect participation covers other activities where people attempt to influence the policy process, such as through voting in elections or involvement in political party or pressure group activity. However, Lupton *et al.* (1998) usefully add a third type of participation: 'mediated' representation, when citizens' views are represented to decision makers by others. They identify four forms of mediated representation: 'elected representation, professional representation or advocacy, provider representation within managed markets and statistical representation' (Lupton *et al.*, 1998, p. 52). Elected representation is that established for national and local governments through regular elections based upon geographic constituencies, and generally linked with the policies of a particular political party. Professional representation and advocacy occur where professionals seek to represent the interests of service users, either as individuals or collectively. This is widely used in social policy and particularly in health and social care. It is closely linked with provider representation, where those providing services argue for the provision of resources based upon information that is often derived from consumerist methods of public involvement. Statistical representation is based upon the use of surveys and opinion polls using representative samples of a particular population to carry out research.

The concept of power and the manner in which it is exercised is clearly crucial in any consideration of the impact of participation. Yet, as Chapter 3 has shown, it can be very difficult to analyse the existence or sources of power and influence. With regard to participation, perhaps the best-known models are Hirschman's (1970) conceptualisation of involvement through 'exit', 'voice' and 'loyalty' and Arnstein's (1969) ladder (Figure 7.1) of citizen participation. Hirschman saw individuals exercising control within a market system not as citizens who use their voice through complaints and consultation mechanisms, but as consumers who are able to exit by moving to another supplier, assuming that there is an accessible alternative. However, he recognised that factors such as convenience and commitment to a product (loyalty) could ensure that consumers continue

Figure 7.1   Arnstein's ladder of citizen participation

8	Citizen control	⎫
7	Delegated power	⎬ Degrees of citizen power
6	Partnership	⎭
5	Placation	⎫
4	Consultation	⎬ Degrees of tokenism
3	Informing	⎭
2	Therapy	⎫ Non-participation
1	Manipulation	⎭

Source: Adapted from S Arnstein, 'A Ladder of Citizen Participation', *Journal of the American Institute of Planners*, vol. 35 (1969), p. 217. Reprinted by permission of the Journal of the American Planning Association.

to use it even if they are not completely satisfied. At the same time, these activities are all inter-related: for example, consumers who are vulnerable and with limited access to alternatives may be unwilling to express discontent, whilst providers may be more likely to listen to their consumers if there is a realistic danger that they may lose them.

Arnstein (1969) identified a variety of different types of participation which can be formulated into a 'ladder'. She recognised that public participation can be subject to the effects of other influences upon the exercise of power, which in some cases can distort or frustrate the desired outcomes, and these affect the presentation of the 'ladder' in terms of who has power and the extent of influence involved. The lower rungs are those forms of 'participation' that she argues are designed primarily to give people a feeling of involvement, with few possibilities for real influence. These would include consultation exercises where the key decisions have already been taken, or consumer surveys that are mainly public relations exercises, rather than being designed to guide change. Progressing up the ladder are the provision of information, consultation – which involves listening to views before decisions are made, and ideally a commitment to acting on those views that are expressed – and placation, which enables a very limited degree of decision making within the wider framework. Towards the top of the ladder are the forms of participatory activity which Arnstein suggests give the public 'decision-making clout' (p. 217), and which bring with them some commitment to the continuity of such processes and to the integration of participants' views into the wider decision-making process.

Many attempts to achieve participation have so far been primarily consumerist in nature, or have viewed participation as consultative and marginal to their 'real' aims, rather than attempting to open up major issues such as important priorities or large budgets to public involvement. Initiatives such as education action zones or health action zones, whilst often having a remit of public involvement, have perhaps unsurprisingly focused primarily upon the delivery of services and on meeting targets. Schemes aimed at encouraging participation have rarely challenged the exclusions faced by women, black people and other groups, and as a result 'participatory' schemes have tended to mirror divisions in society, with the average participant being a middle-class, middle-aged, able-bodied white man. Such participation is likely to reinforce existing biases.

In addition, efforts designed to increase participation have been seen as creating their own problems. For example, participation may involve delay in taking action, as decision making has to wait for people's involvement; this can be extended further if there is a need to establish new groups or organisational structures prior to feeding into decision-making mechanisms. There are also dangers of incorporation and co-option, with individuals and groups being drawn into participatory arrangements which could limit and divert their options for action and opposition to decisions. Such involvement can also lead to inappropriate perceptions, with involvement giving the appearance of consent and thus providing legitimation for decisions. And there may be dangers of tokenism, for example through encouraging the minority involvement of oppressed or powerless groups without the real transfer of power.

Lupton *et al.* (1998) link Arnstein's ladder to the three dimensions of power identified by Lukes (1974) (see Chapter 3) so that:

> forms of public participation may be established which appear to give people influence when viewed in terms of a single-dimension explanation of power, but which are actually used to prevent certain issues from being discussed. By channelling interaction to a limited agenda, attention can be diverted from areas of potential conflict that those with power wish to avoid. Seen in this way, participatory mechanisms can serve as a means of social control by preventing challenges to the status quo. By engaging people and giving them responsibility in a particular area of policy or service, moreover, the process of public participation may also serve to contain criticism and unrest by helping the public to appreciate the realities of government and/or by implying public support for the actions taken (Lupton *et al.*, 1998, p. 48).

For social policy Newman (2001) provides a useful summary of the debate around 'equality, diversity and the politics of difference' and its implications for democracy. In terms of representative democracy, she notes that the notion of citizenship upon which formal equality is based is both gendered and racialised; that formal political equality has not sufficiently redressed social inequalities, and that elected bodies remain very 'unrepresentative' of the population, for example in terms of race and gender. In addition, for participatory democracy to be successful, she argues that 'there is a need to recognise the multiplicity of sites in which dialogue is conducted and interests and identities shaped' (p. 136) so that attempts to achieve 'representativeness' may be less important than the use of a variety of methods of participation and accepting challenges to dominant norms and discourses. Of course, any real attempt to go beyond consultation and progress towards the higher rungs of Arnstein's ladder is likely to have to reflect on the nature of power and the way in which it can be exercised, including issues such as social exclusion and inclusion as well as the importance of agenda-setting and even the mobilisation of bias. However, it is also possible to argue that public participation can have more positive consequences in improving the quality of decision-making processes and the policies that emerge from them, and perhaps even more fundamentally, that

> in a complex, modern society such as Britain, the active involvement of citizens has to be an essential part of democratic life. If the price of liberty is eternal vigilance, the price of democracy is, to put it at its least demanding, a willingness to participate (G Parry *et al.*, 1992).

In this regard it is possible to link an initiative, such as the Labour government's introduction of citizenship into the National Curriculum, not only with concerns about rights and responsibilities, but also with encouraging an understanding of and involvement in the political and decision-making context, and with what the then Home Secretary called 'a major expansion in volunteering – in getting people involved in their communities' (Straw, 2000).

User involvement

For social policy perhaps the most obvious arena in which participation has come to the fore has been in relation to the involvement of 'users' in public services. In the early 1990s Croft and Beresford (1992) noted three overlapping developments that had been working to encourage an emphasis on participation:

- Public participation in land-use planning – this gained momentum in the late 1960s and early 1970s with large-scale urban redevelopment and a desire by central government to reduce the number of appeals by involving the public in planning and devolving objections to local public inquiries; however, planning was still seen as a 'professional' activity and, as it was limited to planning issues rather than extending to include social issues, the extent of public participation remained limited.

- Community development, which developed in Britain during the 1960s, with an emphasis on collective rather than individual action. Whilst the overall concern was with bringing about change and involving people in the process, arguably there were three overlapping models for this:
  1. Community development – creating and servicing community organisations and bringing people together to identify their needs and work on meeting them;
  2. Community and political action – a more class-based approach, seeking to link working-class organisations and campaigns;
  3. Social planning – promoting joint action between voluntary and community organisations and the local state to change and improve services;

- User-involvement – the 1980s saw a new focus on participation, with pressures for a shift away from service-led or provider-led services towards more user-centred services. These demands have been for different, better and more responsive services and have in general been underpinned by the idea of user involvement at all stages, from planning to evaluation.

In addition to these it is possible to identify a number of broader developments that led to this interest in more user-centred services:

- The rise of the political right in the late 1970s and early 1980s and the election of four consecutive Conservative governments with their dislike of the 'nanny welfare state', objections to government provision and preference for a greater role for the market.
- A realisation by some on the political left that the welfare state was not always working as had been expected. Particularly relevant to social policy was the view that state services could be alienating for consumers, with both planning and services often being viewed as being run in the interests of the providers rather than those in need. This linked with public disquiet about poor quality, paternalistic and unresponsive state (especially welfare) services.
- The increase in interest in welfare pluralism, which frequently aimed at the decentralisation of services and an increase in voluntarism, with an increased involvement in both planning and providing services.
- The growth of consumerism outside welfare.
- The emergence of organisations and movements of users of welfare services who were not happy with the services that they received and wanted something different.
- The increasing evidence of unequal access, opportunities and provision for women, black people and members of other minority groups.
- Progressive professionals and other service workers who were concerned about the oppressive nature and lack of accountability of services and agencies.
- The appearance of new kinds of support services (such as rape crisis lines, women's refuges and black women's refuges and advocacy schemes) which often established different relationships between service users and providers, met needs that had previously been ignored, and emphasised the deficiencies of the old services.
- The emergence of new philosophies, such as 'normalisation' which gave greater force and focus to ideas of involvement.
- The development of a new politics of disability based on a redefinition of disability, a critique of existing services and an attempt to create an alternative structure controlled by disabled people.

(Adapted from Croft and Beresford, 1992).

The differing underlying philosophies of consumerist and democratic approaches are reflected in their approaches to empowerment of individuals, with the former drawing upon market approaches to imply individuals' needs for information, choice and redress and the latter on the notion of social rights for citizens and a commitment to the welfare state to meet needs.

The 1980s and 1990s saw significant emphasis on empowerment in welfare services across all tiers of government, whether for users of health or personal services, social housing tenants or other groups (see Exhibit 7.2 for a brief consideration of public involvement in the purchasing of health care). This was largely founded in the Conservative governments' commitment to individual 'freedom' and 'choice' and the value of the market as the best way of providing and distributing goods and services, but was also reinforced by the commitment of many professionals to empowerment of service users. The period therefore saw a range of policies intended to provide and extend choice, including sales of council homes, 'parental choice' of children's schools, greater freedom for people to choose their GPs and the introduction of individual assessment in community care. Other initiatives such as the Citizen's Charter and the creation and publication of performance measures and 'league tables', such as those in education and health care, were designed to encourage competition and to provide information for consumers as a stimulus to improvement.

EXHIBIT 7.2   PUBLIC INVOLVEMENT IN THE PURCHASING OF HEALTH CARE

Lupton et al. (1998) examined attempts to involve the public in health, and in particular in the purchasing of health care, and noted that, with a few exceptions (the establishment of community health councils in the mid-1970s, and the establishment of complaints procedures), there were few attempts to encourage public involvement until the 1980s. However, from the late 1980s and 1990s there was an increase in activity from the user movement, a simultaneous growth of interest in consumerism from within the NHS, and concerns over quality and accountability, all of which encouraged consultation with the users of services. They suggest that a variety of methods emerged including the provision of information to users and the public, the use of panels of people with supported access to health authority information, needs assessment, and the gathering of feedback on services. However, they argue that a variety of problems existed due in part to a lack of clarity about the reasons for public involvement and the tension that arose from trying to reconcile consumerist and democratic approaches.

However, there are some problems with the notion of 'choice' and the way in which it can be interpreted by governments. For example, choice requires adequate public knowledge of alternatives and the opportunity to choose between them. Yet the information made available to the public, including measures of quality, may be misleading. Among the best-known instances are the use of tests in school-age education, which are likely to reflect the quality of student intake rather than the quality of schooling, whilst average hospital waiting times, or case clearance rates in social security administration, may measure the extent to which resources are focused on the simplest cases (see also Chapter 8). In some areas, such as medicine and the personal social services, the consumer may not be a good judge of his or her own need, or indeed in a few cases may be unable to express a preference, and must then rely on the decisions of a professional, such as a GP or case manager. As exemplified by Hirschman's (1970) conceptualisation of 'exit' discussed above, choice also implies the ability to choose between alternatives, but for some groups, there may not be a range of options available. For example, Arnold *et al.* (1993) noted that as the mixed economy of community care developed there emerged a wide variety of forms of accommodation for people with 'special needs', but that the choice available to any individual user was often extremely limited. This is most obvious in relation to the most vulnerable groups of users, such as those patients or school students who are least mobile or least skilled in self-advocacy, or tenants who are unable to buy their homes. In the past this problem has been further compounded by the resulting incentives for providers, wherever possible, to accept less problematic cases and to discriminate against unattractive consumers who may appear to contribute to higher costs or less 'efficient' performance. Examples are GPs who face targets for the delivery of immunisations and who may therefore seek to drop 'difficult' individuals or families from their lists, or schools who face publicity in league tables and who may therefore seek to select 'better' pupils (themselves perhaps more likely to be drawn from better-off homes). Beresford and Croft (1993) have also noted the need for adequate training, of both providers and users, if attempts to increase the impact of user involvement are to be successful, yet, whilst there are examples of good practice, this is far from institutionalised across the systems of welfare provision.

Under the Labour governments since 1997, approaches to 'choice' have remained broadly similar to those promulgated by the Conservatives, although there has perhaps been some additional concern with the quality of provision generally, driven by a shift of emphasis in mechanisms such as inspection and audit, together with the introduction of Best Value in local government, rather than upon individuals making choices in market situations. However, the arena of social housing provides an example of where governments of both parties have sought to link some degree of choice and participation with a key strand of policy, the attempt to transfer the bulk of council housing stock to housing associations. The mechanism that has been used in this case has been collective decision making, so that, regardless of how individual tenants vote, it has been the result of the overall vote that has determined whether the transfer of entire estates takes place. There has been some success with this approach, generally linked to the greater borrowing capacity of housing associations and thus to promises of improvements to the housing stock, perhaps most notably in Glasgow where in 2002 tenants did vote for the transfer of the city's housing stock to Glasgow Housing Association. But there have also been some notable setbacks, particularly in urban English authorities, including Birmingham, the largest council landlord in the UK. Local authorities have also increasingly begun consulting their publics over plans for public spending. For example, in 2000 Birmingham established a panel of 1000 people and ran a poster campaign encouraging the public at large to add their contributions. Some councils have used referendums as consultative mechanisms, which have also been designed to provide legitimacy for decisions, so that in early 2000 the Labour-controlled council in Bristol held a referendum linking proposals for increases in council tax with a threat to cut expenditure on education. On a 40 per cent turnout, 54 per cent of voters voted for no increase in the tax. In Croydon in 2001 and 2002, although a zero increase was not offered as an option, voters opted for the lowest level of increases presented by the council. However, a referendum in Milton Keynes in 1999 resulted in local council taxpayers opting for a 10 per cent increase in taxes.

Political parties

Despite the apparent importance of political parties there is relatively little written about their impact upon social policy, perhaps because their role appears so obvious. However, the role and influence of parties is worth consideration here. For present purposes, parties may perhaps be seen as having four main functions:

1. Integration and mobilisation – parties are concerned to organise and express the choices of citizens who share common ideals and interests (in some cases this has included a unifying ideology) and to establish grass-roots organisations that will help to mobilise electoral support.
2. Influencing voting – although there have been exceptions, for the past century the only real hope of being elected to Parliament is to stand for a political party and to represent the party label. To a considerable extent, electoral behaviour is dictated by voters' support for particular parties and not by the personalities of candidates. Therefore, in order to win political power it is necessary for individuals to have the backing of a party. Of course parties can influence voters in both a positive way (being attractive in the sense of having 'popular' policies, leaders, and so on) and a negative sense (being unattractive and unpopular – as perhaps Labour was for much of the 1980s and the Conservatives for at least the second half of the 1990s).
3. Elaboration of policies – generally political parties present themselves as potential 'parties of office': they aspire to power, currently exercise it or have done so in the past. To gain power they must put forward programmes and policies (normally in a manifesto, as well as the variety of other means of promoting themselves, particularly through the media) to voters and undertake to implement them if they accede to government. Parties therefore develop a whole range of policy proposals that they set before the electorate. However, both the formulation and implementation of policies is conditioned by the wider environment, including the range of influences discussed throughout this book. Most parties' aspirations are limited by these and their awareness of and relations with other powerful influences – pressure groups, big business, trade unions, the media, civil servants and so on, as well as by the economic circumstances and international affairs. Despite this, parties do play a significant role in policy development through the channelling and expressing of demands. They also help to fulfil a 'feedback' function, establishing channels of communication between citizens and government and thereby helping to temper and modify government policies.
4. Recruitment of political personnel – finally, parties are the main means by which political personnel emerge, particularly at central level with virtually

all MPs since the war coming from political parties (see also Chapter 4). At the level of local government there are more independent councillors, particularly in rural areas, although their numbers have been steadily diminishing. In the UK the vast majority of government ministers are MPs, and even those who are drawn from the House of Lords are only called upon because of their links with and support for parties. In addition, the parties also often influence or control appointments to other parts of the state, for example through appointments to quangos, as discussed in Chapter 6.

One of the key issues around the role of parties has been the attention focused on turnout at elections, particularly for local government, and consequent concerns over democracy, accountability and even legitimacy. As a result a number of schemes have been piloted to attempt to encourage participation in elections, including greater use of postal ballots, mobile polling stations, polling booths in supermarkets, and spreading voting across additional days, as well as the changes to political decision making mechanisms in local government discussed in Chapter 5. Despite the decline in electoral turnout evident at recent general elections, with a drop from 78 per cent in 1992 (the highest since February 1974) to 71 per cent in 1997 and 59 per cent in 2001, political parties continue to play a central role in the development of social policy, perhaps most obviously in the development and articulation of new and existing policies. They also act not only as catalysts for the views of their members and supporters but as channels of communication more generally. In addition, their role in mobilisation serves to provide legitimation for the actions of governments, at central and sub-central levels. It is therefore useful for analysts of social policy to be able to recognise and account for the position of parties in the policy process.

The voluntary sector

Another form of participation is that which might be loosely termed as 'through the voluntary sector'. With the creation of the post-war welfare state there was a widespread assumption that over time the need for voluntary activity would reduce as the welfare state developed, either reducing need or providing services. However, by the 1960s there was a growing awareness that the welfare state was not always successful and not only was not meeting some needs but was also often poor at responding to those who required its services. Some argued that one answer to the 'failure of the state' could be a significantly enlarged role for the voluntary sector (Hinton and Hyde, 1981). The 1960s and 1970s saw a significant growth in voluntary bodies, either seeking to campaign for better state provision for particular groups, or in some instances attempting to meet those needs themselves. One of the most obvious examples of this was the growth of the 'poverty lobby' (Whiteley and Winyard, 1984), comprising organisations that sought to influence the income maintenance policies of the government in favour of the poor, with both longstanding organisations and the emergence of new groups such as Help the Aged, Shelter and Child Poverty Action Group.

Voluntarism

It is possible therefore to identify at least two types of activity: volunteering and lobbying. The latter of these is perhaps the most important in the context of this book, but voluntarism is worthy of some discussion (for some alternative perspectives see Whelan, 1999). Under the Conservatives from 1979 to 1997 there were a number of occasions when the government sought to emphasise a significant role for voluntarism and the voluntary sector. The primary mechanism for developing this was through the encouragement of the market and welfare pluralism, but there were also calls from ministers such as Douglas Hurd and John Major for a greater role for their conception of 'active citizenship' – essentially volunteering – whilst initiatives such as community care effectively sought to combine the two approaches. These initiatives involved a greater role for the private and voluntary sectors in the provision of many services, whilst also stressing the role of informal carers in the community, although frequently conveniently omitting the implication that this generally meant unpaid care by women.

Despite government rhetoric, however, in some respects perhaps the most important development since the 1980s was the establishment in 1995 of the Independent Commission on the Future of the Voluntary Sector in England (ICFVSE) (and an equivalent in Scotland). This was intended to outline a future agenda for the voluntary sector. In its report, the Commission (ICFVSE, 1996) saw the diversity of voluntary organisations as a major strength, both in terms of the support and provision they offer and as a backbone of civil society. The report identified social care, and accommodation and housing, as the most substantial areas of activity for the voluntary sector and argued that in many respects the sector was very healthy. Nevertheless a number of areas of concern were identified including: the relationships with government, central and local, and in particular the need for appropriate, specific policy and funding arrangements; the legal context within which voluntary organisations operate; and questions over 'governance' such as the role of values for organisations and concerns over objectives such as efficiency and accountability.

When Labour came to power in the 1990s its emphasis on partnership, and Tony Blair's rejection of the division between 'public' and 'private', appeared to align well with much of the Commission's report, although the Chair of the Commission noted elsewhere (Deakin, 2000) that there were concerns about the emphasis on partnership, in particular through the danger that the voluntary sector might be drawn into acting as an arm of the state. Wyatt (2002) reinforces this point, whilst also arguing that the increasing government emphasis on ensuring effective collaboration between NHS bodies and local authorities (see also the discussion in Chapter 5 on 'partnership') risks making partnership with voluntary organisations peripheral. However, from a different perspective, Atkinson (2000), reviewing urban policy, notes the attempts under Labour to join up, through linking urban policy with mainstream economic and social policy, but also that, for the government, partnership appeared to have achieved an almost mythical status as the panacea for all problems, whilst denying conflicts of interests between partners and whilst 'the private, community and voluntary sectors have all been allocated increased roles at the expense of the public sector' (p. 228).

As with the Conservatives, under Labour there has been some attempt to encourage volunteering through the establishment of an Active Community Unit and the Active Communities Challenge (encouraging employers to give employees paid time to undertake voluntary or community work), and also the decision to establish 'citizenship' as part of the National Curriculum, including some emphasis on engagement with and participation in community activities and the wider world. However, some of these activities, and in particular the Active Community Unit, were criticised by some parts of the voluntary sector for promoting volunteering rather than developing the skills and capacity of the sector. Perhaps more fundamentally, the Home Office's own evidence (Home Office, 2002) has suggested that people in the least deprived neighbourhoods are less likely to be involved in volunteering (and are also less likely to participate in other community activities) and, whilst there is an argument that people become good citizens through active participation, if the poor are excluded from such voluntary involvement because they lack skills or resources, then they potentially become further excluded from mainstream civil society (B Jordan, 1998). Yet for many policy makers, the notion of active citizens remains appealing, particularly when linked with the notion of social capital and the view that communities with high levels of social capital (where citizens trust each other and are involved in a variety of networks of civic engagement, including organisations such as self-help and mutual aid bodies (Wann, 1995)) are more likely to have better health, higher educational achievement and lower crime rates, at the same time as promoting electoral participation and thus legitimation of decisions.

Pressure groups

Underpinning much of the notion of a pluralist society, as outlined in Chapter 3, including through representing individuals and groups in society and in competing for access to power, the role of pressure groups and the extent of their involvement in contemporary social policy can be illustrated by reference to recent campaigns on a wide variety of issues such as cuts in disability benefits, opposition to genetically modified crops and demonstrations by globalisation protestors against multinational companies such as McDonalds and Starbucks, as well as the sheer number of organisations campaigning on welfare issues. The place of pressure groups in society is also considered in the discussion of pluralism in Chapter 3.

Pressure groups can be described as organisations that are concerned with influencing government either to produce changes desired by the group or to prevent changes which might be undesirable to them. Unlike political parties they do not seek to enter government themselves. They may range in size from national bodies that represent large numbers of members to local organisations representing a few people. As discussed in Chapter 3, pluralists see the lobbying activity of pressure groups as crucial factors in strengthening civil society and maintaining an effective democracy. In recent years the numbers of people who have been members of pressure groups has far outstripped those who join political parties, although the numbers who actually participate in elections through voting is much greater still. Pressure groups are therefore a major means of participation and representation, including, importantly, in the period between elections. However, critics have argued that they can undermine democracy as they campaign for specific sectional interests whose aims may not coincide with those of society as a whole.

Pressure groups are frequently categorised in different ways, but for the purposes of this book that used will be 'sectional' and 'cause' groups.

- Sectional – these groups seek to represent the interests of particular groups in society. Examples include trade unions, professional organisations such as the British Medical Association, the Police Federation and the British Association of Social Workers.

- Cause – these groups promote causes based on shared values and beliefs, which may not be directly related to the interests of their members. Examples include Action on Smoking and Health, Child Poverty Action Group, Shelter, the Society for the Protection of the Unborn Child, the National Association for the Howard League for Penal Reform and Amnesty International. This category would also include *ad hoc* groups such as those that might be formed to oppose the closure of a local school or hospital.

Groups can also be categorised as 'insider' or 'outsider', with insider groups being those that are 'regarded as legitimate by government and are consulted on a regular basis' (Grant, 1995, p. 15), whilst outsider groups 'either do not wish to become enmeshed in a consultative relationship with officials, or are unable to gain recognition' (Grant, 1995, p. 15). Whilst the status of an insider group may appear more favourable, it is also likely to require some acceptance of constraints, such as a willingness to compromise, and a preference for discussion and evidence rather than threats and direct action.

In terms of their position in the policy process, pressure groups have the opportunity to play a significant role at a number of stages (see Exhibit 7.3). Taking a view grounded in the process through which legislation passes, as outlined in Chapter 4, they are clearly concerned to ensure that issues reach the policy agenda, whether through direct influence over policy makers such as Cabinet ministers or MPs, or indirect influence through the media; when governments issue discussion papers, consultative documents or proposals for legislation (including Green and White Papers) groups are frequently involved in lobbying MPs and civil servants; and as legislation passes through Parliament they are likely to maintain pressure. Whilst Parliament is not as important as it once was, nevertheless it remains an important access point for many groups. From another perspective, given the concentration of power in the core executive as outlined in Chapter 4, it becomes a primary target for pressure group activity. However, the bulk of contacts are likely to take place at the level of junior ministers and junior civil servants.

Some groups also seek to influence policy decisions through public opinion, with notable campaigns including those which led to the abolition of the poll tax, the banning of handguns, and that opposing genetically modified crops. The policy network approach (see Chapters 3 and 5) suggests further opportunities for pressure groups as part of the 'policy communities' or 'issue networks' that may be involved in policy formulation in particular areas. These analyses are also generally applicable to pressure group activity at sub-central levels. Indeed, some of the mechanisms by which local authorities have sought to encourage consultation and participation, such as public meetings and community forums, may themselves give a greater role to pressure groups. The emphasis by government on partnership, including public, private and voluntary sectors, may also give a greater role to some groups.

EXHIBIT 7.3   PRESSURE GROUPS AND PUBLIC HEALTH

Baggott (2000) considers the role of pressure groups in public health:

- The public health lobby is fragmented into single-issue groups, environmental pressure groups and professional organisations; the UK Public Health Alliance, seeking to act as an umbrella organisation, was finally formed in 1999.

- There is a mixture of insider and outsider groups, the former having higher status and greater opportunity to comment to government, but the latter can also mobilise public opinion and on occasion use direct action.

- There is scope for joint campaigning.

- The greatest impact is when these groups are more or less united in one direction.

- There are concerns about the potential dominance of the medical profession and an emphasis on care and cure rather than prevention.

- And, perhaps crucially, 'the policy networks that determine public health policy remain relatively closed' (p. 253).

It is also worth noting the growth of pressure group activity at the European level. Whilst agricultural groups have long had an interest in attempting to influence policy, the extension of the EU's involvement in national affairs has increased activity in the new policy areas, including the environment, consumer issues and employment and trade union interests. Chapter 4 briefly outlined some of the developments that have occurred in terms of gender equality. Coxall (2001) suggests that the main foci for pressure groups at this level are the European Commission, the Council of Ministers, the European Parliament and the European Court of Justice.

In addition there have arguably been three other significant developments in recent years. Firstly there has been the rise in influence of think-tanks as new sources of ideas, with many of the Conservatives' radical policies from 1979 to 1997 originating within the Adam Smith Institute, the Centre for Policy Studies, the Institute of Economic Affairs and the Social Affairs Unit. Labour has had long-standing links with the Fabian Society, but the 1990s saw the creation of a new think-tank, the Institute for Public Policy Research, which has had very close links with the party and Downing Street. There has also been a general growth in the number of think-tanks that may be more or less independent of the political parties.

Secondly there has been a major growth in the lobbying industry, which, while not on the scale of that in the USA, has raised questions about the appropriateness of some of this activity, particularly when it employs former 'insiders' from the political parties and the civil service, and about its ability to exploit relationships with government on behalf of particular clients and interests.

Finally there has been a growth in the use of direct action, initially mainly over environmental or animal rights concerns, but spreading to other issues such as the anti-capitalist demonstrations from the late 1990s. This has led Grant (2001) to suggest that 'The traditional model of pressure politics is being seriously challenged' (p. 54).

Most writers on pressure groups (for example, Grant, 1995; Coxall, 2001) point out that there are significant difficulties in attempting to assess their effectiveness in influencing policy and that there are a whole variety of factors that affect this, such as the objectives or groups, the resources available to them, the level of public support, and the external economic and political environment. However, Whiteley and Winyard (1988) outline some features that can contribute to success, including clear and realistic aims, accurate and detailed information about the impact of the system on the people whom groups seek to represent, contacts with the media, including 'responsible' publicity and the avoidance of counterproductive attacks on the character and motives of ministers, and of illegal demonstrations.

Conclusion

There are a variety of possible avenues for participation in social policy, including through organisations such as political parties and pressure groups, as voters in elections, as users of services, and, where available, other forms of citizen participation. Despite this, until recent years it is arguable that a common characteristic of social policy and the welfare state in the UK has been the very limited involvement of users or other citizens in shaping and controlling it. However, by the mid-1990s Barnes (1997), discussing community care, where there had been significant attempts to increase participation, suggested that there was considerable experience of consulting with users by the mid-1990s, but also that there was rather less evidence that user involvement had become integral to decision-making processes; on similar lines Beresford (2001) has argued that 'So far, welfare users have had minimal involvement in welfare reform despite the significance attached to such reform and the massive impact it is having' (p. 501).

Whilst the rhetoric of participation under the Conservatives was firmly rooted in the consumerist approach, Labour have also linked their approach to democratic renewal, both through reforms to sub-central government (see Chapter 5) and encouraging or requiring public bodies to consult users and the public. For example, under Best Value, local authorities, together with police and fire authorities, are required to consult about each of their services at least every five years, whilst primary care groups are also expected to increase the involvement of the public in decision making about health care. However, the Audit Commission (1999) noted that many councils felt that the results of consultations were not adequately linked to decision making and that therefore they were not as effective as they could be. In addition, many authorities found difficulties in consulting some groups, such as homeless people, travellers and ethnic minority groups.

Newman (2001) raises three key questions about the emphasis on public participation: firstly, in some instances public participation in decision making may cut across the existing institutions of representative democracy, potentially undermining them and the role of elected representatives; secondly, there are questions over who 'the people' to be consulted and involved are, including the type and extent to which notions of equality and difference are incorporated into the processes; and thirdly, new forms of consultation and participation may present new challenges to the power of the state.

It is clear from recent developments that methods of participation are continually evolving. The Labour government has shown a greater enthusiasm for referendums than any previous government, aiming in this instance for a form of direct democratic participation through the ballot box. In Scotland, it has been observed that the new Parliament has seen a significant number of public petitions presented to it (Lynch and Birrell, 2001), again a rather distinctive development for the UK. In addition, the apparent increase in direct action protests, primarily over concerns in areas other than social policy, such as support for animal rights, opposition to global capitalism, and fuel prices, perhaps suggest that, at least among some sections of the population, there is a willingness to seek new methods of making voices heard.

Ann Richardson's (1983) conclusion 'that there is no single "correct" view on participation' (p. 129), on whom it should include, and for what purposes, remains pertinent. It is also clear that some people seek to be involved whilst others do not, and that people choose very different channels for participation. Nevertheless, the combination of a grasp of social policy and a knowledge of the way in which power can be exercised and decisions made can add considerably to our understanding of the concept and practices of participation.

FURTHER READING

Coxall, B (2001) *Pressure Groups in British Politics* (Harlow: Pearson).

Croft, S and Beresford, P (1992) 'The Politics of Participation', *Critical Social Policy*, no. 35, pp. 20–44.

Independent Commission on the Future of the Voluntary Sector in England (1996) *Meeting the Challenge of Change* (London: NCVO).

Newman, J (2001) *Modernising Governance: New Labour, Policy and Society* (London: Sage).

For some case study examples see: Lupton, C, Peckham, S and Taylor, P (1998) *Managing Public Involvement in Healthcare Purchasing* (Buckingham: Open University Press).

Evaluation

8

CHAPTER OVERVIEW

Whilst the influences upon the making of social policy are widely recognised, the evaluation of social policy is under-discussed. Evaluation is an important part of the policy process and links to many of the topics in this book. This chapter discusses why there is a need for policy evaluation, methods and techniques of policy evaluation and monitoring, the problems of evaluation, and the commissioning, consumption and evaluation of evaluations. It also covers related issues and concepts such as policy transfer.

Many textbooks on the policy process have long stressed the importance of monitoring and evaluation of policies as a key part of the policy process (for example, Hogwood and Gunn, 1984; Pollitt *et al.*, 1979), particularly for judging the degree of success or failure of policies and for feeding back into the formulation and implementation of new or revised policies. If policies are seen as originating from particular decisions that are aimed at achieving particular goals, it would seem natural and appropriate that those who make those decisions, at central or local government level, would wish to determine the effects of their decisions or actions. Indeed, we know that in some instances the intentions of policies are not always achieved, for example with post-war slum clearance programmes sometimes themselves creating new problems, such as poor housing on council estates and social dislocation. This would seem particularly appropriate given some the arguments around the rational model of decision making discussed in Chapter 2, and the periodic attempts by governments to move towards some form of rational planning in social policy, perhaps evidenced most clearly historically with regard to the NHS.

Despite this, much of the assessment of policy success or failure in social policy has been impressionistic and anecdotal. In addition, in the UK much policy evaluation has stemmed from individual initiative, particularly from academics and pressure groups, rather than systematic evaluation originating with the organisations responsible for policy formulation and implementation. As a result, there are some policy areas about which a great deal is known, such as the sales of council houses and community care, whilst there are others about which little is known.

The very idea of evaluation, and related concepts such as evidence-based policy, appears to fit most closely with rational approaches to decision making; however, as discussed in Chapter 2, there are significant limitations to the utility of such models. In more incremental approaches, and those grounded in a more pluralistic process, evaluation and other forms of 'evidence' are more likely to be used as weapons by different sides in debates, with evidence being accepted when it fits with a political argument and being rejected when it does not.

The evaluation of policy inevitably involves a judgement on what has gone before or what is taking place. Systematic evaluation is likely to involve studying and identifying the target group at which the policy is aimed, the consequences of the policy both for that group and for other groups in society, and the extent to which those consequences match the policy's objectives. When rational decision making was becoming more common during the 1960s, there was an increase in attention paid to evaluation, although the emphasis tended to be upon resource allocation and expenditure levels, rather than on policy impact and evaluation. The interest in policy evaluation has continued, although it might be argued that for much of the period since 1979 evaluation took second place to the search for economies, or at least that the nature of much policy evaluation changed. This was reflected in the growing emphasis by governments on evaluation, and in particular performance measurement, frequently linked with monitoring and targets, as a management tool, rather than the evaluation of policy to determine the degree of success or failure. Arguably, the motivations behind the use of such methods were the desire to impose greater control over public sector bureaucracies, and to encourage both central and local government to recognise that their performance could be improved, with, at the same time, an emphasis on efficiency, effectiveness and economy.

Upon their return to government in 1997 Labour ostensibly placed greater emphasis upon evidence, as was apparent in the use of the terms 'evidence-based policy' and 'what works', in the more widespread use of pilot projects across a range of areas including crime prevention, education, employment and health, and through developments based upon policy transfer from other countries. However, in reflecting upon Labour's approach to social exclusion and criminal justice, and noting Labour's greater willingness to listen to messages from research, Drakeford and Vanstone (2000) regretted that this has been undermined by 'popular bandwagons' and a failure to take proper account of the social context of crime, a view which would be likely to find resonance across a range of social policy areas. In addition, Labour retained and built upon their predecessors' use of targets and performance measures, again largely as a tool for directing the implementation of policy, rather than as a measure of success. This was particularly clear in education, where tables of school performance remained a significant weapon in ministers' armouries, and in health, with the production of 'league tables' such as those purporting to measure hospital performance, although in this instance measures were also applied to central government with widespread publicity about hospital waiting lists, and media and other debates about whether the government's own targets were being met, and at what cost to other parts of the health care system.

Evaluation and monitoring

It is clearly possible to take a variety of perspectives on policy evaluation. For example, Pollitt *et al.* (1979) observe that it is possible to evaluate the quality of policy formulation, the quality and quantity of information used, the viability of a policy or set of policies, their appropriateness for the intended aims, or the policy outcome, whilst Parsons (1995) notes that evaluation has two inter-related aspects: the evaluation of policy and its constituent programmes; and the evaluation of people who work in the organisations that are responsible for implementing policy and programmes. However, the primary concern of this chapter can be related to Gerston's (1997) statement that 'Simply defined, policy evaluation assesses the effectiveness of a public policy in terms of its perceived intentions and results' (p. 120), so that policy evaluation is a judgement on what has gone before or what is taking place, and it provides feedback on what has occurred and the extent to which ends have been achieved. Crucially, evaluation is concerned with how a policy is measured against the goals it was designed to achieve, and the actual impact of the policy.

However, as outlined above, whilst the principle of evaluation as part of the policy process is widely accepted, it is also the case that so much political capital and other attention tends to be directed to agenda setting, policy formulation, and to a lesser extent policy implementation, that often basic questions such as whether a policy achieved its stated objectives, or the level of satisfaction and dissatisfaction with it and its outcomes, are neglected (Gerston, 1997).

Monitoring and evaluation can include the full gamut of social science research techniques, including both qualitative and quantitative methods such as case studies, field research, consumer surveys, ethnographic research, comparative research, experiments, primary and secondary data analysis. The use of such techniques is sometimes (although not always) part of an attempt to incorporate more of a rational approach into the policy-making process. Since 1979 there has arguably been a consistent attempt to incorporate some forms of monitoring and evaluation into parts of the social policy process. The use of performance indicators, the setting of targets, audit and inspection, quality management and efficiency scrutinies have effectively become accepted as one part of the social policy process. However, as discussed in Chapters 1 and 2, the reasons for this have arguably arisen as much from politics, ideology and the management of social policy as from a concern with the degree of success or failure of the social policies themselves.

The need for policy evaluation

In order to know whether a policy is working and the extent to which it is successful, it needs to be monitored and evaluated. Despite this, evaluation is something which is not always automatically incorporated into the social policy making process. It is often seen as something that takes place at the end of the policy-making cycle. However, this can relegate it to a minor role and thus undermine its importance and potential in the policy process (see Figure 8.1). To maximise its role and potential benefits, evaluation needs to be an integral part of the social policy process. If approached in a considered manner and fully integrated into the process, monitoring and evaluation may enable adjustments to policies, confirm that policies do work well in practice, and serve as the foundation for new polices. Easton's systems model (see Chapter 1) illustrates the potential role of evaluation in policy making, as part of the policy-making cycle which itself is a continuous process. Evaluation can provide a valuable opportunity to improve future policy-making decisions.

Figure 8.1   How can evaluation shape policy?

Above all, evaluation provides information:

- It can tell us whether a policy is working – it may expose failure of implementation strategies, under- or over-resourcing, or over-ambitious goals.
- It can provide feedback to improve future policy-making decisions (feeding into policy formulation).
- It can provide policies with credibility – without appropriate evaluation this may brought into question.
- It enables successful policies to be cited as examples of good practice and picked up and used by others.

Yet much of the emphasis on policy making goes into the formulation and implementation processes; as a result evaluation sometimes gets overlooked and questions that need to be asked may not be raised. Such questions include: to what extent did the policy meet its stated objectives and has the implementation of the policy raised other issues that need to be addressed? In the absence of policy evaluation we may have little idea whether the allocated budgets have been spent correctly, whether individuals have carried out their tasks as required, or whether rules and procedures have been applied in practice. Thus, without evaluation, the credibility of the policy and the accountability of individuals and institutions responsible for its development are brought into question.

In their study of family support in Northern Ireland, Pinkerton *et al.* (2000, fig. 8.2) highlight the importance of appropriate forms of evaluation. They identify the key question as 'How to develop family support', but also the two subsequent questions about 'What exactly is family support?' and 'How is family support best researched?' and further argue that it is crucial that the analysis of policy and the evaluation of practice are brought together. Exhibit 8.1 shows their framework for researching family support, including a feedback loop to the original questions which thus contributes further to the understanding of what family support is and the best methods for describing and analysing it.

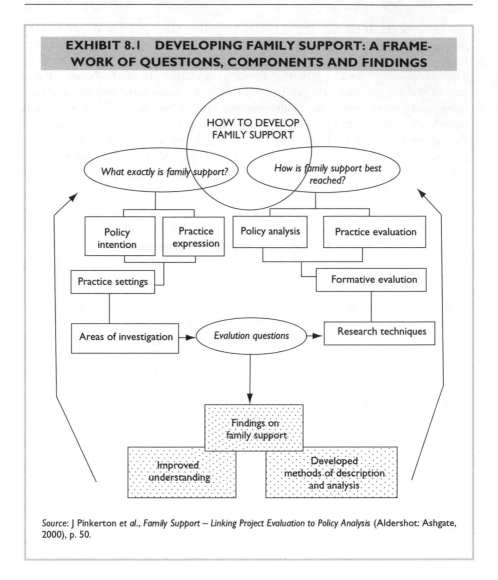

EXHIBIT 8.1   DEVELOPING FAMILY SUPPORT: A FRAME-WORK OF QUESTIONS, COMPONENTS AND FINDINGS

HOW TO DEVELOP
FAMILY SUPPORT

What exactly is family support?

How is family support best reached?

| Policy intention | Practice expression | Policy analysis | Practice evaluation |

Practice settings

Formative evaluation

Areas of investigation → Evaluation questions → Research techniques

Findings on family support

Improved understanding

Developed methods of description and analysis

Source: J Pinkerton et al., *Family Support – Linking Project Evaluation to Policy Analysis* (Aldershot: Ashgate, 2000), p. 50.

Problems in policy evaluation

Whilst the preceding section has set out strong arguments for the inclusion of monitoring and evaluation as part of the policy process, including from the developmental stage of policies, it is nevertheless important to recognise that there are a variety of potential problems and difficulties. These are outlined briefly below:

1.   Uncertainty over policy goals – the goals of policy are often diffuse, unclear or diverse. This may be because the policy area itself may be amorphous, or governments may outline what is effectively a general strategy rather than setting specific targets, as was the case with community care policy in the 1980s and 1990s. Policy makers may deliberately make policy goals obscure in an attempt to obtain the widest acceptance from the public and/or

influential groups. On other occasions the nature of policy formulation may mean that goals may not be clear, for example in incremental responses to short-term problems. In such instances there is a danger that the evaluation itself is worthless because policies' aims may be unclear or the outcomes may be too general to be of use.

2. In reality policy making often has to take into consideration many competing claims on resources. As a result the formulation and implementation of policy may be as concerned with achieving a balance between these competing claims as with ensuring effective social policy.

3. A key problem for many evaluations is the difficulty of devising a methodology which is capable of answering the research question.

4. There are significant difficulties in determining causality – in social policy (indeed in social sciences generally) it sometimes difficult to determine whether there is a cause-and-effect relationship. If action A is taken and condition B results, this does not necessarily mean that A causes B, as other actions may also have an impact; this is further complicated if the aim is to consider the extent to which a policy achieves an objective. Examples of this include the relationships between the levels of policing and crime and the form and severity of punishment and crime. Where there are a range of initiatives, as has been the case in many of Britain's most deprived areas where there may be programmes such as education action zones, employment action zones and health action zones occurring simultaneously, it will inevitably be hard to identify the effects of each.

5. Diffuse policy impacts – policy may affect groups other than those at whom the policy was directed; similarly the side-effects of policies may not be clear. The provision of benefits, such as housing benefit, will affect not only the recipients of those benefits but their families, taxpayers, and local and central government officials.

6. There are often problems around acquiring accurate and up-to-date information. For much social policy, too little is known about the range of variables. For example, we may not have full knowledge of a particular target group, such as homeless people. Similarly, take-up of some benefits can only be estimated as we do not know the full extent of the population eligible to receive them. Where a policy aims at a general improvement, for example in health education, as was the case with HIV/AIDS, the target group may again not be clear.

7. Resistance to policy evaluation – if the results of evaluations show that policies have not achieved their intended aims, then there may be negative consequences for policy makers, those responsible for implementation, and others. This might affect the current programme being implemented, the influence of individuals or groups, or their careers. Some might seek to resist evaluations or attempt to make it difficult for evaluations to proceed by, for example, making access to data difficult, possibly refusing access, or keeping incomplete records.

8. Limited time perspective – the time span of politicians, the media and the public is often short (it may only stretch as far as the next election). They thus want the results from programmes quickly, despite the fact that the

real results from educational and social research may take many years to appear. If the time dimension is not taken into account, the results may be flawed and neglect important long-term effects. The pressure for rapid feedback may also be a dilemma for evaluators. Programmes with long-term aims, such as health promotion, and that involve attempts to change behaviour, may find it difficult to illustrate real achievements over the short term, whilst pilot projects may not have sufficient time to affect the full implementation of policies.

(Adapted from Anderson, 1997).

Overall, it is important to bear in mind the two main types of issue in evaluation: firstly there are the methodological challenges; and secondly there is the fact that evaluation is an inherently political activity and there are inevitably a variety of interests and values involved in and affected by the process. Neither of these means that the evaluation of policies is necessarily a fruitless exercise, but they should be taken into account in understanding the strengths and weaknesses of evaluations.

Methods and techniques of policy evaluation

Whilst monitoring and evaluation are sometimes treated interchangeably, and may frequently be part of the same process, Hogwood and Gunn (1984) identify a clear role for monitoring in the continuous appraisal of a programme. This can help reduce programme drift, where those responsible for implementation undertake different activities from those initially envisaged, or where a programme reaches clients other than those originally intended. Monitoring can therefore help avoid failures of implementation. For effective monitoring, they note that it is necessary to have an initial specification of what a policy aims to achieve, such as the numbers and types of people it aims to serve. Monitoring therefore requires the collection of information about the extent to which goals are being met; however, it should also involve decisions about what actions should be taken if the policy is not achieving its goals.

There exist a very wide range of methods and techniques that can contribute to policy evaluation. The choice will vary with the policy to be evaluated, the timescale, budget and other factors. Rossi, Freeman and Lipsey (1999) suggest that evaluation can generally be structured around three issues: the questions the evaluation is to answer, with a clear need to identify the guiding purpose of the evaluation; the methods and procedures to be used to answer the questions; and the nature of the relationship between the evaluator and the stakeholders.

Before-and-after studies

One approach is to compare the position after a policy has been implemented with the position before. From this is may be possible to conclude whether the position of individuals or groups has altered in line with the aims of the policy. However, this has a number of problems, in particular the difficulty of disentangling the impact of one policy from the general social and economic environment, including other policies that might also affect the outcome. Such arguments were for example, sometimes applied to the 1997 Labour Government's New Deal for Young People, where the apparent success of the programme coincided with falling unemployment generally, including amongst the programme's target group, making it difficult to make a clear judgement. Essentially, it is clearly important that before-and-after studies attempt to take account of the variety of possible influences on a policy's targets.

Performance measurement/indicators

The use of performance measures was to a considerable extent encouraged or imposed by the Conservative governments from 1979 to 1997 and has been maintained by its Labour successors, so that virtually all public services including the police, prison service and libraries as well as health and social services have developed performance indicators to measure quality. Perhaps one of the most widely known examples is in education, where schools and universities have become subjected to the use of 'league tables' that are widely used as indicators of performance. However, performance measures and indicators are exactly what they say – they can provide an indication of performance and may highlight areas that need further consideration and evaluation, but they do not normally provide a full picture. They are generally underpinned by particular values and political positions so that, as Parsons (1995) notes, it is important to consider questions such as 'who sets up the criteria for measurement, how is it calculated, who asks the questions and what time period is selected for assessment' (p. 548).

One of the uses to which governments have put performance measurement is in the setting of targets, for example for school performance or hospital waiting lists, and one perhaps significant development in performance measurement under Labour was its extension to the government itself. In social policy, one example of this appeared in the Green Paper *New Ambitions for Our Country – A New Contract for Welfare* (Department of Social Security, 1998). The 'success measures' outlined in the Green Paper listed a number of targets including a reduction in the proportion of working-age people living in workless households, an increase in the proportion of lone parents, people with a long-term illness and disabled people of working age in touch with the labour market, a reduction in truancy and school exclusions and fewer people sleeping rough. These targets are wide ranging and cover many areas. Despite the fact that many of the measures are fairly general in nature and involve little or no reference to timescale, the explicit publicising of these targets may make them something on which Labour might at some stage be judged by their opponents and by the public, with the potential for them to become a political and an electoral issue. Other examples include health inequality targets for a second term and child poverty targets for 2010 and 2020.

Following Labour's introduction of the Comprehensive Spending Review, central government has seen the development of public service agreements (PSAs) which set out what the government aims to achieve with a given level of resources. Departments' performances against their PSAs are monitored by the

Treasury and fed into a Cabinet sub-committee (the Ministerial Committee on Public Services and Public Expenditure) and made public in departmental reports. Service delivery agreements have been established to set out how departments aim to achieve their PSA targets, as shown in Exhibit 8.2. However, whilst this is an interesting and noteworthy development, many of the potential criticisms of other performance indicators remain relevant for these, and care needs to be taken with their construction and interpretation (National Audit Office, 2001).

EXHIBIT 8.2   A HOME OFFICE PUBLIC SERVICE AGREEMENT AND SERVICE DELIVERY AGREEMENT

PSA target:

Objective VI: regulation of entry to, and settlement in, the UK in the interests of social stability and economic growth; the facilitation of travel by UK citizens; the support of destitute asylum seekers during consideration of their claims; and the integration of those accepted as refugees

(a) Ensure that by 2004, 75 per cent of substantive asylum applications are decided within two months

(b) Enforce the immigration laws more effectively by removing a greater proportion of failed asylum seekers

Delivery

Through the further strengthening of the Immigration and Nationality Directorate and the continued streamlining of asylum procedures and of case handling to:

- Increase the proportion of new substantive asylum applications that are decided by Immigration and Nationality Directorate within two months, to 60 per cent for the year ending March 2002; 65 per cent for the year ending March 2003; and 75 per cent for the year ending March 2004

- Maintain at 65 per cent the proportion of new after-entry applicants who are served with an initial decision within three weeks of receipt of application

Through an increase in enforcement officers and reporting centres, the effective use of the expanded detention estate, the development of readmission agreements and strategies for obtaining travel documents and extension of the programme of voluntary returns to:

> **EXHIBIT 8.2   A HOME OFFICE PUBLIC SERVICE AGREEMENT AND SERVICE DELIVERY AGREEMENT (cont'd)**
>
> - Increase the proportion of failed asylum seekers removed, by removing 30,000 failed asylum seekers in 2001/2; 33,000 in 2002/3; and 37,000 in 2003/4
>
> - Increase the number of non-asylum offenders removed, to 3600 in 2001/2; 3800 in 2002/3; and 4000 in 2003/4
>
> - Ensure a detention capacity of 2200 detention places by March 2004 (increased from 890 in June 2000)
>
> *Source:* Adapted from Home Office, *Service Delivery Agreement 2001–2004* (London: Home Office, 2000).

Audit and inspection

Whilst some areas of social policy, such as the police service through HM Inspectors of Constabulary, have long been subject to inspection, the climate of resource restraint and increasing demand for welfare services during the 1980s and 1990s was accompanied by an increased prominence of audit and inspection. This became very evident in a variety of sectors including education (schools, further education colleges and higher education institutions), health and social services, largely as a means of attempting to ensure that they are meeting service objectives and providing an efficient and effective service, offering value for money. Much of this arose from the work of the Audit Commission which was established in 1983 to ensure the auditing of local government in England and Wales and to encourage economic, efficient and effective public services. Since the mid-1990s higher education institutions have been subject to a variety of forms of quality audit. One of these, termed Subject Review (later Academic Review), undertaken by the Quality Assurance Agency for Higher Education, became widely known as 'teaching quality assessment', although this was not entirely the case. Although the methodology for this has constantly evolved it has included examination of documents (reading lists, external examiners' reports, staff/student committee meeting minutes, and so on), observation of lectures and seminars, review of curriculum content, and assessment of teaching, learning and assessment strategies as well as the provision of learning resources. All of these have notionally been measured against the institution's aims and objectives for that particular subject. Subject Review was replaced during 2003 by the 'lighter touch' Institutional Audit.

In 1985 the Social Services Inspectorate was created to set standards for and inspect parts of English and Welsh local authorities' social services provision, but the role of inspection in measuring quality received a further impetus from the requirement of the NHS and Community Care Act 1990 that they establish 'arm's length' inspection units to inspect their own and private and voluntary sector provision.

Under the Labour governments there was also arguably an extension of the purpose of audit and inspection away from making information available, including to potential consumers, and towards more clear-cut judgements, at least from the perspective of government, as to success and failure. This was clearly illustrated in education with initiatives such as Beacon Schools, which were identified as providing good quality education and high standards, and the condemnation of 'failing schools' which were deemed not to be delivering an adequate education. Similarly the system of stars given to social services departments by the Department of Health's Social Services Inspectorate in England in 2002 ranged from three stars for the 'best' departments, bringing the potential for greater freedom of operation, to zero for the 'worst' departments and the intervention of government through the use of private sector consultants. As a result it was announced by the Department of Health in May 2002 that 'performance action teams' from private sector consultants would be sent into Birmingham, Coventry, North East Lincolnshire and Walsall to help achieve significant improvements. In the health service, the Commission for Health Improvement (CHI), a non-departmental public body, was established in 2000 to monitor and improve the quality of patient care, including tackling variations between hospitals, departments within hospitals and across general practices, using a variety of methods such as reviews of clinical governance and visits to providers. In addition to routine visits the CHI is able to undertake investigations into possible service failures, as happened in July 2002 following concern over maternity services at Ashford and St Peter's NHS Trust. In local government, the introduction of Best Value (see Chapter 5) led to the Labour government extending the inspection powers of the Audit Commission, and the production of Best Value Inspection Reports (Exhibit 8.3).

EXHIBIT 8.3   SUMMARY FINDINGS OF SELECTED AUDIT COMMISSION BEST VALUE INSPECTION REPORTS

London Borough of Ealing Housing Management (July 2002)

'Fair', one star service

Average satisfaction rates amongst tenants and residents; inadequate performance in preparing empty properties for re-letting and for re-let times; weaknesses in the day-to-day repairs service; variations in performance across area offices in service delivery; a significant proportion of gas appliances in Council properties were not serviced, leaving households at risk; cleaning schedules are inadequate, leading to some heavily littered estates; performance management systems are weak; record keeping in relation to anti-social behaviour and harassment is inconsistent.

Uncertain prospects for improvement

Improvement plan will not deliver significant improvements across the borough consistently; large-scale 'pilots' mean that tenants and residents will receive differential

EXHIBIT 8.3   SUMMARY FINDINGS OF SELECTED AUDIT COMMISSION BEST VALUE INSPECTION REPORTS (cont'd)

levels of service; insufficient detail of how 'pilots' will be managed whilst delivering sustained improvements in core business areas; enormous burden of achieving 204 milestones contained within 11 key objectives, with key target dates already slipped on 30.

Recommendations

Produce a revised improvement plan with greater priority to core activities; ensure the importance of the improvement plan is understood by staff, tenants, residents and stakeholders; develop a clear strategy for rolling out pilots to bring improvements to tenants and residents; ensure involvement of tenants, residents, contractors and other stakeholders in the process; develop robust mechanisms to manage contracts, particularly in the day-to-day repairs service; ensure robust mechanisms for the servicing of gas appliances; build on the positive work to involve tenant and community groups feeding into service improvements; develop potential for housing benefit welfare officers to provide a more proactive service; ensure staff have a clear understanding of equal opportunity policies; develop a clear action plan in relation to temporary and agency staff; consider this report and work with us to produce a revised improvement plan to deliver significant improvements for tenants and residents.

Test Valley Borough Council Youth Service (November 2001)

'Good', two star service

Objectives for working with young people are clear and relate directly to corporate strategic aims and complement those of Hampshire County Council's Youth Service; strong programme of projects and initiatives which address issues facing young people, and positive feedback from young people about these; liaison and working arrangements with partner organisations are in place and work well; but key issues facing young people need to be confirmed and prioritised; the budgetary commitment of the whole Council needs to be confirmed and the impact of the contribution to projects more clearly understood; internal co-ordination needs to be strengthened.

Promising prospects for improvement

Council has a sound track record in initiating, supporting and delivering projects for youth; improvement plan identifies key proposals needed to improve internal co-ordination and performance management; Council has developed a Youth Development Group and Champions and Co-ordinators Group to improve internal focus, co-ordination and communication.

Recommendations

Ensure the Youth Strategy effectively achieves the Council's objectives and develop a linked programme of projects and initiatives; improve its performance management processes; improve external communication with partners; to ensure a clear focus in meeting the needs of young people, improve both corporate and external co-ordination.

Mordaunt (2002) also identifies a growth in the number of inspections being undertaken by inspectorates working co-operatively, perhaps arising in part from the Labour government's emphasis upon 'joined-up' government and a consequent need for the inspectorates themselves to seek to work across traditional boundaries.

However, there have been increasing criticisms of the extent of auditing and targeting (Exhibit 8.4), with some questioning the government's assumption that inspection will inevitably lead to improved services and the extent to which the centre can effectively remedy any defects that are identified by inspectors.

EXHIBIT 8.4   WHO INSPECTS HEALTH?

■ National Audit Office – reports to Parliament on how money is spent;

■ Audit Commission – certifies financial accounts;

■ Commission for Healthcare Audit and Inspection – independent, but data on clinical and management performance will be used by the Department of Health;

■ Commission for Social Services Inspection – also provides data for Department of Health;

■ National Clinical Assessment Authority – checks performance of individual doctors;

■ Health and Safety Executive – reports to Department for Work and Pensions;

■ Royal Colleges of Medicine – conduct audits of clinical performance.

'Ministers tend to think the more inspectors and targets there are the greater the improvement. Evidence is growing that both audit and targetry can be dysfunctional. Doctors, health managers and heads need space to exercise professional judgement. Attainment targets are needed but not micro-supervision'.

D Walker, 'Stand by your beds', *The Guardian*, 6 May 2002.

In April 2002 the King's Fund published a report (Appleby and Coote, 2002) which, whilst largely sympathetic to Labour's aims, suggested that the health service should have fewer and broader targets with appropriate funding to meet these.

Ashworth, Boyne and Walker (2002) sought to examine the extent to which theoretical perspectives on regulation could be identified in Wales, drawing largely on social policy examples, and concluded that there was evidence of a number of problems including 'regulatory' capture, where the regulator 'goes native' and becomes too close to the regulate, 'performance ambiguity', reflecting the difficulties of identifying the meaning and measures of organisational performance in the public sector, 'ritualistic compliance', with organisations going through the motions but with no significant alterations to behaviour, and problems with a lack of appropriate data, which thus shifts the emphasis towards soft information and opinion on the part of the regulators.

Other related analyses have also linked the growth of audit to changes in public services and the welfare state. For example, with regard to criminal justice, Carol Jones (1993) argues that the process has not only subjected agencies to an unprecedented degree of scrutiny but has also made more explicit the values underpinning the criminal justice system. However, whilst she recognises that there are potential benefits for accountability, she suggests that there have been reductions in existing forms of accountability and that there has been a shift away from notions of rational justice and the 'rule of law' towards 'managerial justice'. In a similar vein, Clarke, Gewirtz, Hughes and Humphrey (2002) have noted that the very requirement for audit is likely to have an impact upon the constructions of organisations that are likely to be audited as they seek to comply with the organisational and methodological requirements of the activity (whilst audit has also spread to areas formerly seen as professionally led, such as health and social care) whilst the practice of audit has itself broadened to include the scrutiny, evaluation and regulation of agencies involved in providing public services so that evaluative agencies are now cast by central government as effectively representatives of the public, although they themselves may not reflect the diversity of public interests.

Cost-benefit analysis

Cost-benefit analysis is a quantitative form of evaluation that sets out to identify the costs and benefits of a proposed or actual policy and to translate these into monetary values to enable comparison. Whilst most widely used in policy formulation, it is sometimes applied to existing policies. The first stage is to identify the effects of a policy and to categorise them as costs or benefits for particular groups. Then monetary values are applied to the various costs and benefits. For some goods and services this may be relatively easy, but for things such as good health or clean air, this may be difficult. At this stage it is necessary to take account of whether the effects will occur in the short or long term and to make an appropriate adjustment to estimated costs and benefits for this. Finally, the costs and benefits, direct and indirect, current and future, of the policy can then be compared and a decision made on accepting or rejecting it.

However, whilst in some respects apparently straightforward, there can be significant difficulties in the use of this approach. In particular, good quality data may be unavailable and almost impossible to gather, and for many social policies there are enormous difficulties in trying to value costs and benefits, particularly when moral and ethical questions arise. These issues were reflected in the problems encountered in trying to develop Quality Adjusted Life Years during the 1980s and 1990s as a way of enabling judgements about the value of different forms of health treatment, and potentially to provide a basis for decisions about rationing. In addition, those who bear costs, for example through income tax, may not be the same people as those who receive benefits, particularly directly, as some social policies aim to distribute benefits to the poor.

Experimentation

Burch and Wood (1990) note that effectiveness can sometimes be tested in advance through experimentation, giving the example of an experiment used in New Jersey and Pennsylvania in the USA from 1969 to 1972, which aimed to test the impact of a guaranteed annual income upon recipients' work effort. Experimentation involves the use of experimental and control groups, whereby one group receives inputs from the policy or programme whilst the other does not; both groups are also affected by all the other possible influences, making it possible to judge the impact of the policy. However, as Burch and Wood recognise, there are often very significant ethical problems, as well as practical obstacles associated with such measures. Notably, it is arguably ethically wrong to withhold potential benefits such as higher income, better education or better health care from a 'control' group. In the UK, the use of community development projects in the 1970s was effectively a form of action research that was also in some senses experimental and was compared with control areas. However, the lack of clear objectives, together with methodological problems, meant that it was difficult to draw any firm conclusions from this initiative. Despite this, Davies, Nutley and Tilley (2000) argue that the need for good quality evidence is such that there is a strong case for experimentation in some areas and that this may be particularly appropriate where a setting is relatively stable and where human intervention is likely to have a relatively small impact on the outcome.

In addition, and despite some of the difficulties outlined above, governments have continued to use the introduction of policy in limited areas as a form of piloting or experimentation, such as housing action trusts and education action zones, whilst initiatives such as Best Value in local government, elements of the New Deal, and electronically monitored curfews of 10–15-year-olds have been explicitly piloted. As Burch and Wood (1990) suggest, these indicate an approach to policy making 'which places an emphasis on "looking before you leap", but lacks the rigour needed for proper evaluation' (p. 213).

Total quality management (TQM)

As the concept of quality assurance has become more prominent in social and public services, so a number of approaches to it have become more common. These have varied widely from relatively basic attempts to assess user or customer satisfaction to the introduction of total quality management. At its best TQM should provide a very comprehensive approach to achieving quality. It demands the creation of an organisational culture that encourages quality services. It aims to promote thinking, emphasises employee involvement, can help empower workers at lower levels and can encourage integrated strategies for planning and delivering services. However, the extent and success of these approaches is dependent upon how TQM is interpreted, by whom and to what end; and frequently in practice there is little or no consensus about how it should be carried out.

An alternative approach

The approaches considered above tend to be among the most widely used. However, there are also alternative approaches such as that set out by Pfeffer and Coote (1991). They argue that, whilst these approaches do have strengths, they may ultimately fail because they do not acknowledge important distinctions between commerce and welfare as they attempt to measure and treat public welfare services in the same way as in the commercial sector. With this in mind they seek to set out a new approach, which they term 'democratic', that acknowledges the difference between commerce and welfare. They argue that such an approach needs to recognise that the main purpose of a modern welfare system is equity, not giving everyone the same but giving everyone an equal chance in life. This leads to two further goals: responsiveness to individual needs and making the public more powerful, as citizens and consumers. Whilst the goal of equity may conflict with the goals of responsiveness and empowerment, they argue that the process of defining and assuring quality can help to bridge the gap between them. How then is such an approach different from those already mentioned? The difference would appear to be in the fact that it attempts to take the best features from other approaches and to combine them in one. For example, performance indicators tend to be devised by managers, professionals and other staff; consumers do not usually have any say in them, but they would in a democratic approach. Effectively this appears to build upon the TQM view that the pursuit of quality requires a multi-faceted approach involving 'experts', managers, welfare workers and members of the public – as customers and as citizens – and to put a democratic and bottom-up slant on this.

Commissioning and using evaluations

Almost all evaluations will be both political and contestable to some extent, as all are commissioned by individuals or organisations who have may have a stake in their outcome, are undertaken by others who will also have some interest in the evaluation, and generally make some estimation of success and failure that may be used to argue for or against a policy or policies and those who instigated them. Evaluations may also feed back into the decision-making process either directly or indirectly. A significant amount of evaluation is commissioned by government, whether central, local or quasi-governmental. However, there is also a substantial amount of evaluation funded by other organisations, sometimes directly as evaluation but perhaps more often under the general guise of 'social research'. Such research can, but does not necessarily, take the form of an evaluation of a policy, but may be more concerned with either a group of policies or a part of one policy; in addition, it may not be directly designed to evaluate the stated aims or objectives, but may instead be looking at the impact of a measure on one or more groups of people. It may not therefore always fall within a strict definition of 'evaluation' but nevertheless can provide us with significant levels of information relevant to the evaluation of a policy, particularly given the relative dearth of evaluations designed into the policy process itself.

In the UK the main funders of such projects again include governments, the Economic and Social Research Council (a government-funded body responsible for funding research and training) and the major charitable foundations, such as the Joseph Rowntree Foundation, the Leverhulme Trust, the Nuffield Foundation and the Wellcome Trust, each of which may again have their own particular interests and agendas. In addition, pressure groups can undertake a considerable amount of work which sheds light upon policy implementation and which may fall under a general 'evaluation' umbrella, although again they are likely to have an underlying viewpoint. Finally, a considerable amount of unfunded work exists, including by academics and others with interests in particular issues, policies or groups.

Who evaluates?

Gerston (1997) points out that almost everyone evaluates how they are affected by policies. When taxes rise or fall, individuals make a judgement on that. Consumers of services such as health and education also consider how policy affects them. However, in terms of policy making, evaluation is often an important part of the policy process, and as such is often conducted by experts who are familiar with the issue or topic. The choice of who undertakes an evaluation can be critical, affecting not just the quality of the work but potentially also the credibility of the findings.

At its most basic, it is possible to identify two types of evaluation. Internal evaluation is undertaken within an organisation or process. This brings the advantages of familiarity with not only the main issues but also the policy environment; however, there are dangers that it may not be possible to demonstrate or achieve independence from a policy-making authority. The use of local authority inspection units to assess standards in local authority residential homes raised exactly these concerns. External evaluation is undertaken by independent organisations who nevertheless claim to have appropriate expertise. They are clearly more able to demonstrate independence, but may also be less aware of the environment in which policies operate. In the UK a significant amount of evaluation of social policies is carried out by academics, either funded by the bodies responsible for policy making and implementation or by external bodies, including charitable foundations such as the Joseph Rowntree Foundation or the Nuffield Foundation, or unfunded. Interest groups also sometimes present themselves as independent, external evaluators, and in some cases can produce high-quality work; at other times they are clearly affected by their aims and values. 'Evaluation' can therefore arguably vary from being a high-quality, objective exercise, to a much more 'political' exercise more concerned with the values that underpin policies than by any attempt to judge success or failure.

The use of evaluations

Hogwood and Gunn (1984) note that in most cases no actions appear to arise from policy evaluations, regardless of the quality of the methodology. They suggest that there are a variety of reasons for this, including that there are inevitably political judgements about acceptable levels of effectiveness; the potential limitations of the findings; the lack of fit with the decision-making timetable; organisational resistance to findings; and acceptability to those who fund, deliver or receive the outputs of the policy. This reinforces again the point that evaluations are essentially political and contestable. It also encourages us to examine the extent to which evaluations feed into policy succession (replacement by one or more new policies), maintenance (adjustments to policies) or termination (Hogwood and Peters, 1983).

Even where there is considerable governmental emphasis upon using evaluations, as with Labour's concerns with 'what works' and evidence-based policy, the translation of such ideas into practice can be problematic. Taking the example of evidence-based medicine, Harrison (1998) points out that, while the notion is apparently both rational and politically appealing, in reality the position is more complicated. He notes, for example, that there is not always agreement on the probability of a medical intervention being effective, nor on who should determine this, that evidence-based medicine is itself as much an artefact arising from social and political circumstances as from scientific or technical bases, and that whilst evidence-based medicine may be one way of rationing the provision of health services, there are others which may also have attractions.

For social policy analysts in particular, given the issues about the distribution of power and influence raised throughout this book and the discussion of participation in Chapter 7, there are also important questions about the nature and extent of the dissemination of results from evaluations and the consequent feedback into policy making.

Policy transfer

The process of policy transfer or 'lesson drawing' (Rose, 1991), whereby countries and organisations within the same country borrow ideas from each other or learn things from each other that they apply to the policy process, can be seen to be related to the evaluation process in social policy. Evaluation tells us what does and does not work. Very few problems are unique to an individual country, such as German unification, for example (Rose, 1991), so that when countries or organisations experience problems to which they need relatively 'quick' solutions, there is a clear potential benefit to looking elsewhere to see what is successful and then considering whether it can be transferred to a new environment with appropriate adaptations. The key question policy makers must ask themselves is 'Under what circumstances and to what extent would a programme now in effect elsewhere also work here?' (Rose, 1991, p. 4).

In general the stimulus for policy transfer is dissatisfaction with existing programmes or policies and a consequent demand to do something new. This may be especially true for new governments that want to make their mark and to implement policies that can be seen as distinctive from previous administrations. In the case of Labour's return to office after an 18-year gap it is possible to identify a range of policies that not only illustrate an attempt to achieve a distinctive approach from that of the previous Conservative administrations, but which are also arguably based in part on policy transfer. The transfer of control of interest rates to the Bank of England in the first few days of the 1997 government can be seen to have been copied from a variety of other countries including Germany, where the situation was perceived to have helped create low inflation and economic stability. Similarly the introduction of the New Deal can be argued to have been adapted from 'workfare' type policies in the USA. The notion of policy transfer can also sometimes have links with rational approaches to policy making through their attempts to improve the quality of the policy-making process through detailed consideration of policy options. However, in other circumstances policy transfer can grow from incrementalist approaches, perhaps particularly where policy responses are sought to respond to and cope with problems, rather than setting out to solve them.

Policy transfer is generally seen as manifesting itself at two levels: internal policy transfer and external policy transfer.

Internal policy transfer

Policy makers start this process by searching for solutions or programmes locally or internally. This might involve local government officials in search of better ways to manage customer care services looking to other local councils to see what they are doing. Also, when initiatives are particularly successful they tend to attract attention from other organisations in a similar line of work to see how the scheme works and whether it could be successfully transferred to another geographical location. Examples of such occurrences have been very wide-ranging and have included: community mental health centres, child-care schemes, school mentoring programmes, crime prevention programmes and many more. At a national level some parts of the English criminal law system have learned from Scotland. For example, Children's Panels were introduced in Scotland in the early 1970s as a more informal alternative to courts, and subsequently there have been attempts to mirror some aspects of this development to make the system in England more informal. In addition, whilst there has always been a degree of transfer between public and private sectors, the 1980s and 1990s saw a major attempt by government to realign much of the public sector to the perceived advantages of the private sector through the greater use of markets, emphasis on efficiency and effectiveness and accountability to consumers. Even within the civil service, initiatives such as the Rayner scrutiny programme, the Management Information Systems for Ministers, and the Financial Management Initiative can all be seen as attempting to take ideas from the private sector and transfer them to the public sector.

External policy transfer

As noted above, policy transfer also takes place across countries. However, in a similar fashion to internal policy transfer, where the culture and practices of different organisations may vary widely, it may be necessary to adapt a policy for it to work successfully in the new country. If such changes are minor, then they can be seen to be incremental in nature. Examples of policy transfer under the Conservatives included the privatisation of prisons, which was adapted from

New Zealand and the USA, and the electronic tagging of offenders which was developed in America during the 1980s. The creation of the Child Support Agency (CSA) drew on the American Child Support Enforcement System and to a lesser extent on the Australian CSA. Labour based various aspects of the 1998 Crime and Disorder Act on policies in the USA, with, for example, curfews being piloted in the USA and subsequently adopted in the UK. In a very different policy area, the establishment of the Food Standards Agency drew upon the experience of other countries, including the perceived failure of New Zealand's independent public health commission (Baggott, 2000). Even systems of decision making can be transferred, with the creation of an elected mayor for London being based upon models of strong mayors in the USA and some European cities.

However, it is important to recognise that policy transfer is not a one-way process. Other countries may import UK policies and adapt them to their own circumstances. For example, social housing is predominant in the Netherlands, but over recent years there has been greater attention paid to the UK model of home ownership because it is perceived as successful. In addition, it may be that one policy area is picked up and continually imported and exported between countries, gradually changing as it does so. Perhaps one of the best examples of this was the spread of privatisation within and between the UK, New Zealand and the USA in the 1980s.

Whilst policies can be and are adapted from a wide variety of countries, Rose (1991) notes that the USA is often seen as exerting a 'pull' due to its scale and novelty, whilst Sweden has also been attractive as an exemplar of a social democratic welfare state. Inevitably the countries to which governments look for examples of policy and practices are influenced by factors such as perceptions of policy or programme success and political values. Ideology and ideological battles can play a significant role, so that Dolowitz argues that:

> one of the key reasons the Conservative governments of the 1980s and 1990s turned to the United States was that they were constantly trying to instil the attitudes underpinning American social policies into the British political and social systems. Moreover, during the past twenty years governments around the world, including the current Blair government (to a certain extent) have been actively borrowing the ideological rhetoric emerging from the American New Right in relation to welfare reform. This is particularly true in terms of the New Right's ideological rhetoric in relation to 'welfare dependency'; the need to 'enforce' obligations upon 'lazy' welfare 'scroungers'; and the growing use of concepts such as 'rights and responsibilities' and 'duties' (Dolowitz, 2000, p. 23).

However, whilst governments may seek to draw upon the experiences of other countries, it is generally unrealistic to expect simply to pick up a programme that has been successful in another country and transfer it wholesale to the UK without taking into account a whole range of factors such as cultural and economic differences, the level of resources available, the potential impact(s) on the target population and whether the programme is being transferred from like to like institutions (Rose, 1991). For example, it is sometimes suggested that the UK's shortage of organ donors could be reduced through replacing the current 'opt-in' system with an 'opt-out' system along the lines that exist in several European countries. But direct comparison to demonstrate that increased levels of consent lead to increases in the number of donations and transplants may not be straightforward due to other factors, such as the number of intensive care beds required to keep the donor on life support until the transplant can be carried out, and the need for public awareness of the register of those opting out.

In addition, policy transfer can suffer precisely the same problems in formulation, implementation and monitoring and evaluation that can afflict all policies. Therefore, whilst an understanding of policy transfer can be a valuable tool in helping analyse the policy process, those who seek to undertake policy transfer also need to be aware not only of the potential benefits but also of the possible weaknesses arising from a failure to select appropriate policies and instruments (see Exhibit 8.5).

There may also be some degree of interaction between national and international contexts and influences (as, for example, Wirt and Harman (1986) argue with reference to educational reform), although attempting to analyse these relationships and to identify cause and effects is clearly a complex and challenging undertaking.

Conclusion

Evaluation has been an irregular part of the social policy process in the UK. The lack of evaluation built into policies and programmes by government and other organisations has meant that many policies and policy areas have not been evaluated; there has frequently been a reliance upon the work of others outside government, such as academics or pressure groups; and there have often been significant time and resource constraints in evaluations. This has been further complicated by the methodological and political difficulties discussed in this chapter. In introducing their book on evidence-based policy, Davies, Nutley and Tilley (2000) note that it contains 'relatively little examination of the related questions of efficiency and cost-effectiveness [and that in part this]... reflects the infancy of cost-effectiveness and cost-benefit analyses in the public sector, and the relative paucity of activity in this area' (p. 3), a view that summarises the situation for policy evaluation as a whole.

However, from the 1980s there has been a shift, at least in respect of performance measurement. The introduction of new policy instruments into welfare from 1979 onwards was an attempt by the Conservative governments to encourage public sector organisations to evaluate the way in which they operated and to improve the management and efficiency of the delivery of welfare services. Up to 1988 the emphasis was largely on 'managerialism', based on a belief that the private sector was more efficient and effective than the public sector, which was seen as too bureaucratic and inherently inefficient. A range of government initiatives were introduced over this period, drawing on private sector values, with the transfer of business performance tools into the public sector in the belief that it would help create a culture in both central and local

EXHIBIT 8.5   THE CHILD SUPPORT AGENCY – TRANSFER FROM THE USA

Why look to the USA?

■ The Thatcher government perceived the US Child Support Enforcement System (CSES), and in particular that of Wisconsin, as well developed and successful in reducing single-parent dependence on welfare benefits and instilling a sense of parental responsibility.

■ There were similar problems in the UK and the USA with child-support enforcement systems.

■ The Thatcher government shared the Reagan administration's New Right ideological perspective.

■ The Conservatives viewed the US CSES as successful in reducing the public sector borrowing requirement (PSBR), one of the government's aims for the UK.

What was transferred?

Dolowitz identifies a number of aspects including:

■ The requirement on the Child Support Agency to establish a formula for maintenance obligations;

■ The obligations on the CSA to undertake periodic review and adjustment of child-support awards;

■ The guarantee of a minimum 'protected level' of exempt income for the non-custodial parent;

■ The ability of administrators to reduce benefits for any parent refusing to co-operate in identifying the 'liable' parent unless they could prove 'good cause' for not helping;

Problems arising from transfer included:

■ A lack of attention to how the CSES operated across a range of US states and selectivity in the interpretation of information that the government did have;

■ Some of the more successful elements of the US system were not transferred;

■ Insufficient attention to the social, political and cultural differences between the USA and the UK, for example over attitudes to single parents, the ability of women to enter the labour market and the importance of work;

■ The imposition of the CSA over the pre-existing system for granting and collecting child-support maintenance, even where the couple had come to an equitable agreement within the courts, compounded by the initial failure of the formula to take account of property or capital settlements;

■ The emphasis on the reduction of the public sector borrowing requirement changed the target group to those who could make the biggest contribution, and to 'soft' targets rather than non-payers, reducing legitimacy in the eyes of the public.

Adapted from D P Dolowitz, *Policy Transfer and British Social Policy* (Buckingham: Open University Press, 2000).

government whereby efficiency, effectiveness, monitoring and evaluation would be seen as the norm. After 1988 the emphasis changed towards a style of governance based on 'the new institutional economics' through the application of markets and consumer choice (Rhodes, 1997), although concepts such as efficiency, effectiveness and economy remained central.

Under new Labour there has been a continued emphasis on performance accompanied by a more general acceptance of monitoring and evaluation which can perhaps be seen to be linked to the government's concern with 'evidence-based policy' and 'what works' (Davies, Nutley and Smith, 2000). The attitudes of both Conservative and Labour governments to performance measurement can perhaps be summed up by the National Audit Office's (2001) report *Measuring the Performance of Government Departments*, which states that:

> Performance measurement is an integral part of modern government. It stands behind the creation of targets, contracts and agreements that control service delivery. Good performance information can help Departments to develop policy, to manage their resources cost effectively, to improve Departmental and programme effectiveness and to report their performance to Parliament and the general public, so promoting accountability for public resources (National Audit Office, 2001, p. 1).

However, Moran (2001) points out that, despite real gains in the economy and in the responsiveness of public services, what he terms 'policy catastrophes', such as the poll tax, rail privatisation, the Millenium Dome and BSE, can still occur. Arguably the challenge for the future is, where appropriate, for other aspects of evaluation to be accorded a similar status as an integral part of the policy process, so that policy makers and others can be aware of whether policies are achieving their objectives, are efficient and effective and are meeting the needs of the population.

FURTHER READING

Ashworth, R, Boyne, G and Walker, R M (2002) 'Regulatory Problems in the Public Sector: Theories and Cases', *Policy and Politics*, vol. 30, pp. 195–211.

Clarke, J, Gewirtz, S, Hughes, G and Humphrey, J (2002) 'Guarding the Public Interest?', in J Clarke, S Gewirtz, and E McLaughlin (eds) *New Managerialism, New Welfare?* (London: Sage).

Dolowitz, D P (2000) *Policy Transfer and British Social Policy* (Buckingham: Open University Press, Buckingham).

Hogwood, B and Gunn, L (1984) *Policy Analysis for the Real World* (Oxford: Oxford University Press).

Rossi, P H, Freeman, H E and Lipsey, M W (1999) *Evaluation: A Systematic Approach* (Thousand Oaks, California: Sage).

For a case study evaluation see: Pinkerton, J, Higgins, K and Devine, P (2000) *Family Support – Linking Project Evaluation to Policy Analysis* (Aldershot: Ashgate).

Conclusions

9

CHAPTER OVERVIEW

This book has set out to examine the range of influences on the processes of making, implementing and formulating social policy and the exercise of power. Developments during the Conservative governments from 1979 to 1997 and under Labour since 1997 have reflected many of these influences. This chapter outlines some of the lessons that can be learnt from the examination of the policy process.

This book has introduced a variety of theories, perspectives and approaches to different aspects of the policy process as they can be applied to social policy. Some of these conflict with each other, others may serve to reinforce each other; some may be descriptive, others prescriptive. In reality their greatest value may come through offering different lenses through which, singly and jointly, we can better analyse and understand the exercise of power in the making and implementation of social policy.

As Anderson (1997) points out, 'Most policy problems, and certainly those of any magnitude, generate significant differences of view as to what is socially acceptable, economically feasible and politically acceptable. Bargaining, negotiation and compromise, not simply reliance upon the "facts", are then required to produce decisions' (p. 320). The focus on process then emphasises the ongoing and evolving nature of policy and encourages consideration of the variety of influences upon policy formulation and implementation. As was acknowledged in Chapter 1, it is not always easy to recognise the parameters of many of the concepts dealt with here, including the definitions of 'social policy' and 'policy analysis' themselves. It is also apparent that there are continual changes not only in the policies and practices that we study, but also in the tools that we can use to analyse them. For example, the influence of New Right ideas in the

1980s and 1990s on social policy was reflected not only in the policies that emerged, but also in the policy process, and in addition added new potential to our understanding of it, for example through perspectives on the operation of bureaucracies. Similarly, the debates over the value of institutional approaches and the emergence of regime theory, and over globalisation and other approaches to the changing world can also be applied to aid our comprehension of the social policy process.

Following 18 years of Conservative rule, the return of the Labour governments in 1997 and 2001 led to further change, including different emphases in policy making, such as notions of partnership and joined-up government, together with the introduction of the devolved administrations in Scotland, Wales and Northern Ireland. New developments also led to new concerns, whether it be the growth of quasi-government and questions of accountability, an increased application of markets in welfare provision and the lack of voice for the poor and powerless, or the development of performance measures and their value and implications for efficiency, effectiveness and equity. Indeed, and reflecting much of the discussion elsewhere in this book, reforms over recent years have led two seasoned observers to conclude that 'the idea and practice of public service and its users are significantly more complex than in the past' (Gray and Jenkins, 2002, p. 252) and to note three significant implications: the reassertion of the beneficial role of public service in society; that from the government's perspective 'public services is no longer closely coterminate with the public sector' (p. 251) and that the pattern of service provision is more varied and complex than previously; and that with the variety of service delivery there is equally a variety and complexity of relationships between users and services.

It is also important to recognise that governments themselves frequently pay attention to the processes of policy making, as well as the development of policies. The Conservatives' emphasis on markets during the 1980s and 1990s arose from a perspective that saw markets rather than the state as the best means of distributing goods and services, and that had major implications for many organisations responsible for making and delivering welfare policies. In terms of the tools of policy making and implementation, Labour have also made some significant changes, including devolution and emphases on partnership and democratic renewal, but at the same time there has been some further concentration of power at the centre, including the growing use of audit and inspection as tools to ensure the implementation of policy, and threats to use the private sector or other forms of takeover where public sector bodies are perceived to have 'failed', including hospitals and schools.

However, the degree of consideration paid to the policy process itself under Labour since 1997 has probably not been equalled since the Labour governments of the 1970s, which saw some attempts to introduce 'better' policy-making instruments and to operationalise 'rational' decision making in some fields. From 1997 the emphasis on 'modernisation' has been applied by Labour to some of the very mechanisms of government as well as to other parts of the state. It has been key to their attempts to improve the delivery of public services. Much of this has been outlined earlier in the book – including on devolution, local and quasi-government, for example – but it is worthy of further discussion here.

The White Paper, *Modernising Government* (Cabinet Office, 1999) set out three aims to ensure inclusive and integrated government: joined-up and strategic policy making; ensuring that users of public services, rather than providers, are the focus; and delivering high quality and efficient public services. Related to these there were also commitments to use new technology to meet the needs of citizens and business, and a commitment to value public service. These have then had an impact on the government's approaches to policy making, with emphases on joined-up government, evidence-based policy and such like. For example, the National Audit Office (2001) report on the performance of government departments for 2000/1 noted that 'Significant outcomes cannot always be achieved by organisations working alone: partnerships with other Departments and agencies are often essential' (p. 22) and that 'The existence of different formats of [performance] measures enables Departments to match the measure closely to policy objectives and their context' (p. 28) so that 'Well-designed outcome objectives and targets can assist and encourage departments to work in partnership with others to deliver outcomes' (p. 6). The Conservatives' development of performance measurement has therefore been utilised to attempt to drive forward partnership and co-operation in policy making and implementation, including initiatives at central and sub-central government levels.

In addition, the Cabinet Office's Strategic Policy Making Team (1999) produced a report on *Professional Policy Making for the Twenty First Century* as a follow-up to the White Paper on *Modernising Government* (Exhibit 9.1). This recognised the shortcomings of idealised models of the policy process and set out instead to produce a 'descriptive model' of policy making that was acceptable to policy makers.

The document identified a small number of policy areas as 'exemplary', including the New Deal for Lone Parents and the New Deal for Disabled People, identifying as a common feature that these were being run on project management lines, and therefore suggesting that some of the disciplines associated with such an approach can help in the policy process. New mechanisms, such as public service agreements and service delivery agreements (see Chapter 8) have been introduced to attempt to identify specific government departments as responsible for the achievement of policy goals, but they are also intended to encourage co-operation and co-ordination through recognising the role of other departments. For example, the Home Office's target for 2001–04 of reducing the proportion of under-25-year-olds reporting the use of Class A drugs was shared with the Department for Education and Employment and the Department of Health (National Audit Office, 2001).

In line with the stress on 'modernisation', Labour have also identified 'e-government' as an area which can alter the relationship between citizens and government, for example through allowing online access to information services 24 hours a day, seven days a week, and is committed to having all government services available electronically (primarily via the Internet but also through telephone call centres, digital television or other means) by 2005. However, the potential for using this to remodel the power relationship between citizens and the state has been much less discussed by the government, and at the same time there remain significant questions about equality of access through such means for different social groups.

EXHIBIT 9.1   THE CABINET OFFICE STRATEGIC POLICY MAKING TEAM'S DESCRIPTIVE MODEL OF POLICY MAKING

A series of high level 'features' which, if adhered to, should produce fully effective policies:

Three 'themes' – vision, effectiveness and continuous improvement;

Nine core 'competencies':

1. Forward looking – takes a long-term view of the likely impact of policy;

2. Outward looking – takes account of factors in the national, European and international situation and communicates policy effectively;

3. Innovative and creative – questions established ways of dealing with things and encourages new ideas; open to comments and suggestions from others;

4. Using evidence – uses best available evidence from a wide range of sources and involves key stakeholders from an early stage;

5. Inclusive – takes account of the impact on the needs of all those directly or indirectly affected by the policy;

6. Joined up – looks beyond institutional boundaries to the Government's strategic objectives; establishes the ethical and legal base for policy;

7. Evaluates – builds systematic evaluation of early outcomes into the policy process

8. Reviews – keeps established policy under review to ensure it continues to deal with the problems it was designed to tackle, taking account of associated effects elsewhere;

9. Learns lessons – learns from experience of what works and what does not.

Source: Cabinet Office Strategic Policy Making Team, *Professional Policy Making for the Twenty First Century* (London: Cabinet Office, 1999).

One of the other key strands of Labour's approach has been reform of the public sector, with an emphasis on user-led services, with the centre setting national priorities and frameworks for accountability and inspection, and a variety of providers giving choice to users.

All of these elements are important for social policy, in part because developments in education, health and the personal social services seem likely to lie at the centre of such reform with continued setting of standards and targets and involvement of the private sector as some of the government's tools for achieving reforms, and also because major social policy concerns, such as crime and criminal justice, child poverty, inequalities in health, and urban decay and regeneration, are complex challenges which do not lie within the remit of and cannot effectively be tackled by any one department of government.

Some of the developments under Labour have been discussed elsewhere in this book. Many have been considered by other writers (for example, see Newman, 2001; Powell, 1999; Rao, 2000). Newman (2001) relates some of the ideas discussed in this book, and Labour's approach to governance and modernisation, to the Third Way, and suggests that notions of gender, ethnicity, sexuality and nationhood did not sit easily with the government's attempts to build new forms and systems of governance. Similarly, the tension between Labour's apparent desire for some devolution of power to sub-central government but the continued emphasis on central control was a theme of the 1997 to 2001 government. Stewart's view of the main weakness of the White Paper, *Modernising Government* (Cabinet Office, 1999), that it is based upon the underlying assumption of a top-down approach without the recognition that this could be balanced by a bottom-up approach, and that 'Special attention could be paid to the role of community planning, of new forms of public involvement and of diversity as a basis for organisational learning' (Stewart, 1999, p. 12), finds a strong resonance across the social policy process.

Wherever there is a struggle for resources that do not exist in quantities sufficient for those who need or wish for them, there will be dispute. Similarly, there will be disagreements about the values which underlie the distribution of goods and services. These are often particularly apparent in social policy. Much of the study of the policy process is therefore based in a consideration of the interaction between issues, actors, institutions and society.

In a complex society and political system the policy process is also likely to be complicated and untidy. There are a wide range of actors and other influences upon the policy process. In addition, arguably, political authority and power are fragmented, involving not only central and sub-central government, but quasi-government, the media, business, pressure groups and more. The increased usage of the concept of social exclusion, encouraging a focus on the ways in which people are prevented from fully participating in society, potentially aids the acceptance of a policy process approach within social policy.

For analysts of social policy there are a variety of ideas, including democracy, equity, empowerment and participation that should underpin the entire policy process. Social policy should be concerned to improve people's welfare in the broadest sense, including their participation in the decision-making processes. The implication of this is that there should be greater democratic control over the institutions and organisations that make decisions and provide services, and a greater attention devoted to processes for bottom-up policy making, accountability and evaluation. The concept of 'citizenship' should extend from debates over 'rights' and 'responsibilities' to a concern with participation and involvement at all levels of decision making. The imbalances in power outlined in many places in this book must be addressed to ensure a more open, democratic and accountable development of social policy.

Bibliography

Alcock, P, Erskine, A and May, M (eds) (2003) *The Student's Companion to Social Policy* (Oxford: Blackwell).

Anderson, J E (1997) *Public Policymaking: An Introduction* (Boston: Houghton Mifflin).

Annesley, C (2001) 'New Labour and Welfare', in S Ludlam and M J Smith (eds) *New Labour in Government* (London: Macmillan).

Appleby, J and Coote, A (2002) *Five Year Health Check: A Review of Health Policy, 1997–2002* (London: King's Fund).

Arnold, P, Bochel, H, Brodhurst, S and Page, D (1993) *Community Care: The Housing Dimension* (York: Joseph Rowntree Foundation).

Arnstein, S (1969) 'A Ladder of Citizen Participation', *Journal of the American Institute of Planners*, vol. 35, pp. 216–24.

Ashworth, R, Boyne, G and Walker, R M (2002) 'Regulatory Problems in the Public Sector: Theories and Cases', *Policy and Politics*, vol. 30, pp. 195–211.

Atkinson, R (2000) 'Narratives of Policy: The Construction of Urban Problems and Urban Policy in the Official Discourse of British Government 1968–1998', *Critical Social Policy*, vol. 20, pp. 211–32.

Audit Commission (1999) *Listen Up! Effective Community Consultation* (London: Stationery Office).

Bachrach, P and Baratz, M (1963) 'Decisions and Nondecisions: An Analytical Framework', *American Political Science Review*, vol. 57, pp. 641–51.

Bachrach, P and Baratz, M (1970) *Power and Poverty, Theory and Practice* (New York: Oxford University Press).

Baggott, R (1995) *Pressure Groups Today* (Manchester: Manchester University Press).

Baggott, R (2000) *Public Health: Policy and Politics* (Basingstoke: Palgrave).

Bains, M (Chairman) (1972) *The New Local Authorities: Management and Structure* (London: HMSO).

Baldock, J, Manning, N, Miller, S and Vickerstaff, S (eds) (1999) *Social Policy* (Oxford: Oxford University Press).

Barnes, M (1997) *Care, Communities and Citizens* (Harlow: Longman).

Barrett, S and Fudge, C (1981) *Policy and Action* (London: Methuen).

Baumgartner, G and Jones, B (1993) *Agendas and Instability in American Politics* (Chicago: University of Chicago Press).

Beresford, P (2001) 'Service Users, Social Policy and the Future of Welfare', *Critical Social Policy*, vol. 21, pp. 494–512.

Beresford, P and Croft, C (1993) *Citizen Involvement: A Practical Guide for Change* (London: Macmillan).

Beveridge, W (1953) *Power and Influence* (London: Hodder and Stoughton).

Billis, D (1984) *Welfare Bureaucracies: Their Design and Change in Response to Social Problems* (London: Heinemann).

Birch, A H (1993) *The Concepts and Theories of Modern Democracy* (London: Routledge).

Bochel, H M (1992) *Parliament and Welfare Policy* (Aldershot: Dartmouth).

Boddy, M and Fudge, C (eds) (1984) *Local Socialism* (London: Macmillan).

Bottomore, T (1966) *Elites and Society* (Harmondsworth: Penguin).

Brown, M (1999) 'Reconceptualizing Public and Private in Urban Regime Theory: Governance in AIDS Politics', *International Journal of Urban and Regional Research*, vol. 23, pp. 70–87.

Brown, R G S (1971) *The Administrative Process in Britain* (London: Methuen).

Buchanan, J (1986) *Liberty, Market and State: Political Economy in the 1980s* (Brighton: Wheatsheaf).

Budge, I, Crewe, I, McKay, D and Newton, K (2001) *The New British Politics* (Harlow: Pearson).

Burch, M and Wood, B (1990) *Public Policy in Britain* (Oxford: Blackwell).

Butcher, T (2002) *Delivering Welfare* (Buckingham: Open University Press).

Cabinet Office (1996) *government.direct* (London: Stationery Office).

Cabinet Office (1998a) *Public Bodies 1998* (London: Stationery Office).

Cabinet Office (1998b) *Quangos: Opening the Doors* (London: Cabinet Office).

Cabinet Office (1999) *Modernising Government* (London: Stationery Office).

Cabinet Office (2001) *Public Bodies 2001* (London: Stationery Office).

Cabinet Office Strategic Policy Making Team (1999) *Professional Policy Making for the Twenty First Century* (London: Cabinet Office).

Cahill, M (1994) *The New Social Policy* (Oxford: Blackwell).

Cawson, A (1982) *Corporatism and Welfare* (London: Heinemann).

Cawson, A and Saunders, P (1983) 'Corporatism, Competitive Politics and Class Struggle' in R King (ed.) *Capital and Politics* (London: Routledge and Kegan Paul).

Challis, L, Fuller, S, Henwood, M, Klein, R, Plowden, W, Webb, A, Whittingham, P and Wistow, G (1988) *Joint Approaches to Social Policy: Rationality and Practice* (Cambridge: Cambridge University Press).

Chandler, J A (1996) *Local Government Today* (Manchester: Manchester University Press).

Chester, N (1979) 'Fringe Bodies, Quangos and All That', *Public Administration*, vol. 57, no. 1, pp. 51–4.

Clarke, J, Gewirtz, S, Hughes, G and Humphrey, J (2002) 'Guarding the Public Interest?', in J Clarke, S Gewirtz, and E McLaughlin (eds) *New Managerialism, New Welfare?* (London: Sage).

Clarke, J, Gewirtz, S and McLaughlin, E (2002a) 'Reinventing the Welfare State' in J Clarke, S Gewirtz and E McLaughlin (eds) *New Managerialism, New Welfare?* (London: Sage).

Clarke, J, Gewirtz, S and McLaughlin, E (eds) (2002b) *New Managerialism, New Welfare?* (London: Sage).

Cobb, R W and Elder, C E (1972) *Participation in American Politics: The Dynamics of Agenda-Building* (Baltimore, MD: Johns Hopkins University Press).

Cochrane, A (1993) *Whatever Happened to Local Government?* (Buckingham: Open University Press).

Colomer, J (2001) *Political Institutions: Democracy and Social Choice* (Oxford: Oxford University Press).

Commission on Public Private Partnerships (2001) *Building Better Partnerships* (London: Institute for Public Policy Research).

Committee on Standards in Public Life (1995) *First Report* (London: Stationery Office).

Committee on Standards in Public Life (1996) *Local Public Spending Bodies* (London: Stationery Office).

Constitution Unit (1996) *Regional Government in England* (London: Constitution Unit).

Cooper, L, Coote, A, Davies, D and Jackson, C (1995) *Voices Off: Tackling the Democratic Deficit in Health* (London: Institute for Public Policy Research).

Coxall, B (2001) *Pressure Groups in British Politics* (Harlow: Pearson).

Coxall, B and Robins, L (1989) *Contemporary British Politics: An Introduction* (London: Macmillan).

Crenson, M A (1971) *The Unpolitics of Air Pollution: A Study of Non-Decision Making in the Cities* (Baltimore, MD: Johns Hopkins University Press).

Croft, S and Beresford, P (1992) 'The Politics of Participation', *Critical Social Policy*, no. 35, pp. 20–44.

Dahl, R A (1957) 'The Concept of Power', *Behavioural Science*, vol. 2, pp. 201–5.

Dahl, R A (1961) *Who Governs? Democracy and Power in an American City* (New Haven, CT: Yale University Press).

Dahl, R A (1985) *A Preface to Economic Democracy* (Cambridge: Polity).

Dahl, R A (1986) 'Rethinking *Who Governs?* New Haven Revisited' in R J Waste (ed.) *Community Power Directions for Future Research* (Newbury Park, CA: Sage).

Dahlerup, D (1988) 'From a Small to a Large Minority', *Scandinavian Political Studies*, vol. 11, pp. 275–98.

Davies, H T O, Nutley, S M and Tilley, N (2000) 'Debates on the Role of Experimentation' in H T O Davies, S M Nutley and P C Smith (eds) *What Works? Evidence-Based Policy and Practice in Public Services* (Bristol: Policy).

Davies, H T O, Nutley, S M and Smith, P C (eds) (2000) *What Works? Evidence-Based Policy and Practice in Public Services* (Bristol: Policy).

Davies, J S (2001) *Partnerships and Regimes: The Politics of Urban Regeneration in the UK* (Aldershot: Ashgate).

Deakin, N (2000) *'Putting Narrow-Mindedness Out of Countenance': The UK Voluntary Sector in the New Millennium*, Centre for Civil Society Working Paper no. 4 (London: LSE).

Deakin, N and Parry, R (2000) *The Treasury and Social Policy* (Basingstoke: Macmillan).

Deakin, N and Wright, A (1990) 'Introduction' in N Deakin and A Wright (eds) *Consuming Public Services* (London: Routledge).

Department for Education and Employment (2000) *The Role of the Local Education Authority in School Education* (London: DfEE).

Department of the Environment, Transport and the Regions (1998) *Modern Local Government: In Touch with the People* (London: Stationery Office).

Department of Health (1997) *The New NHS* (London: Stationery Office).

Department of Health (1998) *Modernising Social Services: Promoting Independence, Improving Protection, Raising Standards* (London: Stationery Office).

Department of Health (2000) *The NHS Plan: A Plan for Investment, a Plan for Reform* (London: Stationery Office).

Department of Social Security (1998) *New Ambitions for Our Country: A New Contract for Welfare* (London: Stationery Office).

Department for Transport, Local Government and the Regions (2001) *Strong Local Leadership: Quality Public Services* (London: Stationery Office).

Department for Transport, Local Government and the Regions (2002) *Your Region, Your Choice: Revitalising the English Regions* (London: Stationery Office).

Doig, A (1979) 'The Machinery of Government and the Growth of Governmental Bodies', *Public Administration*, vol. 15, pp. 209–31.

Dolowitz, D P (2000) *Policy Transfer and British Social Policy* (Buckingham: Open University Press).

Donnison, D (1982) *The Politics of Poverty* (Oxford: Martin Robertson).

Downs, A (1957) *An Economic Theory of Democracy* (New York: Harper and Row).

Downs, A (1972) 'Up and Down with Ecology: The Issue Attention Cycle', *Public Interest*, vol. 28, pp. 38–50.

Drakeford, M and Vanstone, M (2000) 'Social Exclusion and the Politics of Criminal Justice: A Tale of Two Administrations', *Howard Journal*, vol. 39, pp. 369–81.

Dror, Y (1964) 'Muddling Through – Science or Inertia?', *Public Administration Review*, vol. 24, pp. 153–7.

Dror, Y (1989) *Public Policymaking Reexamined* (New Brunswick, NJ: Transaction).

Duncan, S (2002) 'Policy Discourses on "Reconciling Work and Life" in the EU', *Social Policy and Society*, vol. 1, pp. 305–14.

Dunleavy, P (1986) 'Explaining the Privatization Boom: Public Choice versus Radical Approaches', *Public Administration*, vol. 64, pp. 13–34.

Dunleavy, P (1991) *Democracy, Bureaucracy and Public Choice: Economic Explanations in Political Science* (Hemel Hempstead: Harvester Wheatsheaf).

Dunsire, A (1999) 'Then and Now: Public Administration, 1953–1999', *Political Studies*, vol. 47, pp. 360–78.

Dye, T R (1984) *Understanding Public Policy* (Englewood Cliffs, NJ: Prentice Hall).

Easton, D (1953) *The Political System* (New York: Alfred A Knopf).

Easton, D (1965) *A Framework for Political Analysis* (Englewood Cliffs, NJ: Prentice Hall).

Education and Skills Select Committee (2002) *Third Report – Individual Learning Accounts* (London: House of Commons).

Elkin, S (1987) *City and Regime in the American Republic* (Chicago: University of Chicago Press).

Elmore, R (1980) 'Backward Mapping: Implementation Research and Policy Decisions', *Political Science Quarterly*, vol. 94, pp. 601–16.

Engels, F (1981) *The Origins of the Family, Private Property and the State* (London: Lawrence and Wishart).

Esping-Andersen, G (ed.) (1996) *Welfare States in Transition: National Adaptations in Global Economies* (London: Sage).

Etzioni, A (1967) 'Mixed Scanning: A "Third" Approach to Decision Making', *Public Administration Review*, vol. 27, pp. 385–92.

Evans, R (2001) 'Disobedient Servants', *The Guardian*, 8 May.

Farnham, D and Horton, S (1996a) 'Managing Private and Public Organisations', in D Farnham and S Horton (eds) *Managing the New Public Services* (London: Macmillan).

Farnham, D and Horton, S (1996b) (eds) *Managing the New Public Services* (London: Macmillan).

Field, F (1982) *Poverty and Politics: The Inside Story of the CPAG Campaigns in the 1970s* (London: Heinemann).

Finer, S (1997) *The History of Government* (Oxford: Oxford University Press).

Flinders, M (2001) 'Mechanisms of Judicial Accountability in British Central Government', *Parliamentary Affairs*, vol. 54, pp. 54–71.

Flinders, M (2002) 'Governance in Whitehall', *Public Administration*, vol. 80, pp. 51–75.

Flynn, N (1993) *Public Sector Management* (Hemel Hempstead: Harvester Wheatsheaf).

Foster, C D and Plowden, F J (1996) *The State Under Stress* (Buckingham: Open University Press).

Fulton Committee (1968) *The Civil Service, Vol. 1, Report of the Committee 1966–68* (London: HMSO).

Gerston, L N (1997) *Public Policy Making: Process and Principles* (New York: M E Sharpe).

Giddens, A (1998) *The Third Way: The Renewal of Social Democracy* (Cambridge: Polity).

Gleeson, D and Shain, F (1999) 'By Appointment: Governance, Markets and Managerialism in Further Education', *British Educational Research Journal*, vol. 25, pp. 545–61.

Grant, W (1995) *Pressure Groups, Politics and Democracy in Britain* (Hemel Hempstead: Harvester Wheatsheaf).

Grant, W (2001) 'Pressure Politics: From "Insider" Politics to Direct Action?', *Parliamentary Affairs*, vol. 54, pp. 337–48.

Gray, A and Jenkins, B (2002) 'Government and Administration: Reasserting Public Services and their Consumers', *Parliamentary Affairs*, vol. 55, pp. 235–53.

Gray, C (1994) *Government Beyond the Centre: Sub-National Politics in Britain* (London: Macmillan).

Greenwood, J and Wilson, D (1989) *Public Administration in Britain Today* (London: Routledge).

Greenwood, J, Pyper, R and Wilson, D (2002) *New Public Administration in Britain* (Basingstoke: Palgrave Macmillan).

Greer, A and Hoggett, A (2000) 'Contemporary Governance and Local Public Spending Bodies', *Public Administration*, vol. 78, pp. 513–29.

Griffith, J A G (1997) *The Politics of the Judiciary* (London: Fontana).

Guardian, The, 23 May 1999; 22 Feb. 2002; 27 Apr. 2002.

Gunn, L (1978) 'Why is Implementation so Difficult?', *Management Services in Government*, vol. 33, pp. 169–76.

Hall, W and Weir, S (1996) *The Untouchables: Power and Accountability in the Quango State* (London: Democratic Audit/Scarman Trust).

Ham, C (1999) *Health Policy in Britain* (Basingstoke: Macmillan).

Ham, C and Hill, M (1984) *The Policy Process in the Modern Capitalist State* (Brighton: Wheatsheaf).

Ham, C and Hill, M (1993) *The Policy Process in the Modern Capitalist State* (2nd edn, Hemel Hempstead: Harvester Wheatsheaf).

Hampton, W (1991) *Local Government and Urban Politics* (Harlow: Longman).

Harrison, S, Hunter, D J and Pollitt, C (1990) *The Dynamics of British Health Policy* (London: Unwin Hyman).

Harrison, S (1998) 'The Politics of Evidence-Based Medicine in the United Kingdom', *Policy and Politics*, vol. 26, pp. 15–31.

Heclo, H (1972) 'Review Article: Policy Analysis', *British Journal of Political Science*, vol. 2, pp. 83–108.

Heywood, A (1997) *Politics* (London: Macmillan).

Hill, M (ed.) (1993) *The Policy Process: A Reader* (Hemel Hempstead: Harvester).

Hill, M (1997a) *The Policy Process in the Modern State* (Hemel Hempstead: Prentice Hall).

Hill, M (ed.) (1997b) *The Policy Process: A Reader* (Hemel Hempstead: Prentice Hall).

Hill, M and Bramley, G (1986) *Analysing Social Policy* (Oxford: Blackwell).

Hill, M and Hupe, P (2002) *Implementing Public Policy* (Sage: London).

Hinton, N and Hyde, M (1981) 'The Voluntary Sector in a Remodelled Welfare State' in C Jones and J Stevenson (eds) *The Yearbook of Social Policy in Britain 1980–81* (Harlow: Longman).

Hirschman, A O (1970) *Exit, Voice and Loyalty: Responses to Decline in Firms, Organisations and States* (Cambridge, MA: Harvard University Press).

Hirst, P (1995) 'Quangos and Democratic Government', *Parliamentary Affairs*, vol. 48, pp. 341–59.

Hirst, P and Thompson, G (1995) 'Globalization and the Future of the Nation State', *Economy and Society*, vol. 24, pp. 408–42.

Hirst, P and Thompson, G (1996) *Globalization in Question* (Cambridge: Polity).

HM Treasury (1979) *The Government's Expenditure Plans 1980–81* (London: HMSO).

Hogwood, B (1995) 'The 'Growth' of Quangos' in F F Ridley and D Wilson (eds) *The Quango Debate* (Oxford: Oxford University Press).

Hogwood, B and Gunn, L (1984) *Policy Analysis for the Real World* (Oxford: Oxford University Press).

Hogwood, B and Peters, B G (1983) *Policy Dynamics* (Brighton: Wheatsheaf).

Home Office (1998) *Compact on Relations between Government and the Voluntary and Community Sector in England* (London: Stationery Office).

Home Office (2000) *Service Delivery Agreement 2001–2004* (London: Home Office).

Home Office (2002) *Active Communities: Initial Findings from the 2001 Home Office Citizenship Survey* (London: Home Office).

Hood, C C (1976) *The Limits of Administration* (London: Wiley).

Hood, C C (1991) 'A Public Management for All Seasons?' *Public Administration*, vol. 69, pp. 3–19.

Horton, S and Farnham D (eds) (1999) *Public Management in Britain* (Basingstoke: Macmillan).

Hudson, B (1997) 'Michael Lipsky and Street-Level Bureaucracy: A Neglected Perspective' in M Hill (ed.) *The Policy Process: A Reader* (Hemel Hempstead: Prentice Hall).

Hudson, B and Henwood, M (2002) 'The NHS and Social Care: The Final Countdown?', *Policy and Politics*, vol. 30, pp. 153–66.

Ibbs, R (1988) *Improving Management in Government: The Next Steps: Report to the Prime Minister* (London: HMSO).

ICFVSE (Independent Commission on the Future of the Voluntary Sector in England) (1996) *Meeting the Challenge of Change* (London: National Council for Voluntary Organisations).

James, O (2001) 'Evaluating Executive Agencies in UK Government', *Public Policy and Administration*, vol. 16, pp. 24–52.

Jessop, B (1988) *Conservative Regimes and the Transition to Post-Fordism: The Cases of Britain and West Germany*, Essex Papers in Government no. 47 (Colchester: University of Essex).

Jessop, B (1990) *State Theory: Putting Capitalist States in their Place* (Cambridge: Polity).

Jones, B, Kavanagh, D, Moran, M and Norton, P (2001) *Politics UK* (Harlow: Longman).

Jones, C (1993) 'Auditing Criminal Justice', *British Journal of Criminology*, vol. 33, pp. 275–90.

Jones, K and Bird, K (2000) 'Partnership in Education Action Zones', *British Educational Research Journal*, vol. 26, pp. 491–506.

Jordan, B (1998) *The New Politics of Welfare* (London: Sage).

Jordan, W (1985) *The State: Authority and Autonomy* (Oxford: Basil Blackwell).

Judge, D (1995) 'Pluralism' in D Judge, G Stoker and H Wolman (eds) *Theories of Urban Politics* (London: Sage).

Judge, D, Stoker, G and Wolman, H (eds) (1995) *Theories of Urban Politics* (London: Sage).

King, R (ed.) (1983) *Capital and Politics* (London: Routledge and Kegan Paul).

Kingdon, J (1984) *Agendas, Alternatives and Public Policy* (Boston: Little, Brown).

Labour Party (1997) *New Labour: Because Britain Deserves Better* (London: Labour Party).

Leach, S (1996) 'The Local Government Review: An Inter-Organisational Perspective' in I Hampsher-Monk and J Stanyer (eds) *Contemporary Political Studies 1996*, Proceedings of the Political Studies Association Annual Conference, vol. 1, pp. 198–209.

Lee, S (2000) 'New Labour, New Centralism: The Centralisation of Policy and the Devolution of Administration in England and its Regions', *Public Policy and Administration*, vol. 15, pp. 96–109.

Levin, P (1997) *Making Social Policy* (Buckingham: Open University Press).

Lindblom, C E (1959) 'The Science of "Muddling Through"', *Public Administration Review*, vol. 19, pp. 78–88.

Lindblom, C E (1965) *The Intelligence of Democracy* (New York: Free Press).

Lindblom, C E and Woodhouse, E J (1993) *The Policy-Making Process* (Englewood Cliffs, NJ: Prentice Hall).

Ling, T (2000) 'Unpacking Partnership: Health Care' in J Clarke, S Gewirtz and E McLaughlin (eds) *New Managerialism, New Welfare?* (London: Sage).

Lipsky, M (1976) 'Towards a Theory of Street-Level Bureaucracy' in W D Hawley *et al.*, *Theoretical Perspectives on Urban Policy* (Englewood Cliffs, NJ: Prentice Hall).

Lipsky, M (1980) *Street-Level Bureaucracy: Dilemmas of the Individual in Public Services* (New York: Russell Sage Foundation).

Lister, R (1990) *The Exclusive Society* (London: Child Poverty Action Group).

Lister, R (1998), 'Fighting Social Exclusion... With One Hand Tied Behind Our Back', *New Economy*, vol. 5, pp. 14–18.

Local Government Association (2000) *Local Leadership, Local Progress – A Survey of Local Authorities on Political Management and Probity* (London: LGA).

Loney, M, Boswell, D and Clarke, J (eds) (1983) *Social Policy and Social Welfare* (Milton Keynes: Open University Press).

Lowell Field, H and Higley, J (1980) *Elitism* (London: Routledge and Kegan Paul).

Lowndes, V, Stoker, G, Pratchett, L, Wilson, D, Leach, S and Wingfield, M (1998) *Enhancing Public Participation in Local Government* (London: DETR).

Ludlam, S and Smith, M J (2001) *New Labour in Government* (London: Macmillan).

Lukes, S (1974) *Power: A Radical View* (London: Macmillan).

Lupton, C, Peckham, S and Taylor, P (1998) *Managing Public Involvement in Health-care Purchasing* (Buckingham: Open University Press).

Lynch, P and Birrell, S (2001) 'Grievances Galore', *The Guardian*, 7 May 2001.

McDonald, R (2002) 'Street-Level Bureaucrats? Heart Disease, Health Economics and Policy in a Primary Care Group', *Health and Social Care in the Community*, vol. 10, pp. 129–35.

MacGregor, S (1981) *The Politics of Poverty* (London: Longman).

McLelland, S (2002) 'Health Policy in Wales – Distinctive or Derivative?' *Social Policy and Society*, vol. 1, pp. 325–33.

Majone, G (1989) *Evidence, Argument and Persuasion in the Policy Process* (New Haven, CT: Yale University Press).

Marshall, T H (1975) *Social Policy* (London: Hutchinson).

May, M (2003) and Bochel, C (2003) 'Careers and Social Policy Graduates' in P Alcock, A Erskine and M May (eds) *The Student's Companion to Social Policy* (Oxford: Blackwell).

Mazey, S (1998) 'The European Union and Women's Rights: From the Europeaniza-tion of National Agendas to the Nationalization of a European Agenda', *Journal of European Public Policy*, vol. 5, pp. 131–52.

Meisel, J H (1958) *The Myth of the Ruling Class* (Ann Arbor, MI: University of Michigan Press).

Michels, P (1915) *Political Parties: A Sociological Study of the Oligarchical Tendencies of Modern Democracy* (London: Constable).

Middlemass, K (1979) *Politics in Industrial Society* (London: Andre Deutsch).

Miliband, R (1969) *The State in Capitalist Society* (London: Weidenfield and Nicholson).

Miliband, R (1974) 'The Politics of Poverty' in D Wedderburn (ed.) *Poverty, Inequality and Class Structure* (Cambridge: Cambridge University Press).

Ministry of Housing and Local Government (1970) *Reform of Local Government in England* (London: HMSO).

Moran, M (2001) 'Not Steering but Drowning: Policy Catastrophes and the Regulatory State', *Political Quarterly*, vol. 72, pp. 415–27.

Mordaunt, E (2002) 'The Emergence of Multi-Inspectorate Inspections: "Going it Alone is Not an Option"', *Public Administration*, vol. 78, pp. 751–69.

National Audit Office (2001) *Measuring the Performance of Government Departments: Report by the Comptroller and Auditor General* (London: Stationery Office).

Newman, J (2001) *Modernising Governance: New Labour, Policy and Society* (London: Sage).

Newton, K (1976) *Second City Politics* (Oxford: Clarendon).

Niskanen, W (1971) *Bureaucracy and Representative Government* (Chicago: Aldine-Atherton).

Niskanen, W (1973) *Bureaucracy: Servant or Master?* (London: Institute of Economic Affairs).

Norton, P (2001) 'The House of Commons' in B Jones *et al.*, *Politics UK* (Hemel Hempstead: Pearson).

Office of the Commissioner for Public Appointments (2002) *Seventh Report 2001–2002* (London: Cabinet Office).

Olsen, M (1968) *The Logic of Collective Action* (Cambridge, MA: Harvard University Press).

Parry, G, Moyser, G and Day, N (1992) *Political Participation and Democracy in Britain* (Cambridge: Cambridge University Press).

Parry, R (1999) 'Quangos and the Structure of the Public Sector in Scotland', *Scottish Affairs*, no. 29, pp. 12–27.

Parry, R (2002) 'Delivery Structures and Policy Development in Post-Devolution Scotland', *Social Policy and Society*, vol. 1, pp. 315–24.

Parsons, W (1995) *Public Policy: An Introduction to the Theory and Practice of Policy Analysis* (Aldershot: Edward Elgar).

Parton, N (1991) *Governing the Family: Child Care, Child Protection and the State* (London: Macmillan).

Pemberton, H (2000) 'Policy Networks and Policy Learning: UK Economic Policy in the 1960s and 1970s', *Public Administration*, vol. 78, pp. 771–92.

Perlman, M (1976) 'The Economic Theory of Bureaucracy' in G Tullock (ed.) *The Vote Motive* (London: Institute of Economic Affairs).

Peters, B G (1997) 'Shouldn't Row, Can't Steer: What's a Government to Do?' *Public Policy and Administration*, Special Issue: Understanding Governance, vol. 12, pp. 51–61.

Peters, B G (1999) *Institutional Theory in Political Science: The New Institutionalism* (London: Pinter).

Pettigrew, A, Ferlie, E and McKee, L (1992) *Shaping Strategic Change: Making Change in Large Organisations – The Case of the National Health Service* (London: Sage).

Pfeffer, N and Coote, A (1991) *Is Quality Good for You?* (London: Institute for Public Policy Research).

Pilkington, C (1999) *The Civil Service in Britain Today* (Manchester: Manchester University Press).

Pinkerton, J, Higgins, K and Devine, P (2000) *Family Support – Linking Project Evaluation to Policy Analysis* (Aldershot: Ashgate).

Pliatzky, L (1980) *Report on Non-Departmental Public Bodies* (London: HMSO).

Pollitt, C (1990) *Managerialism and the New Public Services* (Oxford: Blackwell).

Pollitt, C, Lewis, L, Negro, J and Patten, J (1979) *Public Policy in Theory and Practice* (Sevenoaks: Hodder and Stoughton/Open University Press).

Pollitt, C, Birchall, J and Putnam, K (1997) *Opting-Out and the Experience of Self-Management in Education, Housing and Health Care*, Local Governance Programme Working Paper no. 2 (Swindon: Economic and Social Research Council).

Poulantzas, N (1973) *Political Power and Social Classes* (London: New Left).

Powell, M (ed.) (1999) *New Labour: New Welfare State?* (Bristol: Policy).

Prachett, L (2002) 'Local Government', *Parliamentary Affairs*, vol. 55, pp. 331–46.

Pressman, J and Wildavsky, A (1973) *Implementation* (Berkeley, CA: University of California Press).

Public Accounts Committee (1994) *The Proper Conduct of Public Business* (London: HMSO).

Public Accounts Committee (2002) *The New Deal for Young People* (London: Stationery Office).

Pyper, R and Robins, L (eds) (1995) *Governing in the UK in the 1990s* (London: Macmillan).

Ranson, S and Stewart, J (1994) *Management for the Public Domain* (London: Macmillan).

Rao, N (2000) *Reviving Local Democracy: New Labour, New Politics?* (Bristol: Policy).

Raynsford, N (1986) 'The 1977 Housing (Homeless Persons) Act' in *Policy Change in Britain: Three Case Studies* (London: Royal Institute for Public Administration).

Redcliffe-Maude, Lord (Chairman) (1969) *Royal Commission on Local Government in England, 1966–1969*, vol. I report (London: HMSO).

Rhodes, R A W (1981) *Control and Power in Central–Local Government Relations* (London: Gower).

Rhodes, R A W (ed.) (1991) *The New Public Management*, Special Issue of *Public Administration*, vol. 69 (Spring).

Rhodes, R A W (1997) *Understanding Governance: Policy Networks, Governance, Reflexivity and Accountability* (Buckingham: Open University Press).

Rhodes, R A W (2000) 'New Labour's Civil Service: Summing-up Joining-up', *Political Quarterly*, vol. 71, pp. 151–66.

Rhodes, R A W and Dunleavy, P (eds) (1995) *Prime Minister, Cabinet and Core Executive* (London: Macmillan).

Rhodes, R A W and Marsh, D (eds) (1992) *Policy Networks in British Government* (Oxford: Clarendon).

Richards, D and Smith, M (2002) *Governance and Public Policy in the UK* (Oxford: Oxford University Press).

Richardson, A (1983) *Participation* (London: Routledge and Kegan Paul).

Richardson, J J and Jordan, A G (1979) *Governing Under Pressure: The Policy Process in a Post-Parliamentary Democracy* (Oxford: Martin Robertson).

Ridley, F F and Wilson, D (eds) (1995) *The Quango Debate* (Oxford: Oxford University Press).

Roller, E and Sloat, A (2002) 'The Impact of Europeanisation on Regional Governance: A Study of Catalonia and Scotland', *Public Policy and Administration*, vol. 17, pp. 68–86.

Rose, R (1991) 'What is Lesson-Drawing?', *Journal of Public Policy*, vol. 11, pp. 3–30.

Rose, R (2001) *The Prime Minister in a Shrinking World* (Cambridge: Polity).

Rossi, P H, Freeman, H E and Lipsey, M W (1999) *Evaluation: A Systematic Approach* (Thousand Oaks, CA: Sage).

Rust, V and Blakemore, K (1990) 'Educational Reform in Norway and in England and Wales: A Corporatist Interpretation', *Comparative Education Review*, vol. 34, pp. 500–22.

Sabatier, P (1998) 'The Advocacy Coalition Framework: Revisions and Relevance for Europe', *Journal of European Public Policy*, vol. 5, pp. 98–130.

Sabatier, P and Jenkins-Smith, H (eds) (1993) *Policy Change and Learning* (Boulder, CO: Westview).

Saggar, S (1991) *Race and Public Policy* (Aldershot: Avebury).

Salmon, H (1995) 'Community, Communitarianism and Local Government', *Local Government Policy Making*, vol. 22, pp. 3–12.

Salter, B and Tapper, T (2000) 'The Politics of Governance in Higher Education: the Case of Quality Assurance', *Political Studies*, vol. 48, pp. 66–87.

Saunders, P (1979) *Urban Politics: A Sociological Interpretation* (London: Hutchinson).

Saunders, P (1981) *Social Theory and the Urban Question* (London: Hutchinson).

Saunders, P (1984) 'Rethinking Local Politics' in M Boddy and C Fudge (eds) *Local Socialism* (London: Macmillan).

Schmitter, P and Lehmbruch, G (eds) (1979) *Trends Towards Corporatist Intermediation* (Beverly Hills, CA: Sage).

Schumpeter, J A (1974) *Capitalism, Socialism and Democracy* (London: Allen and Unwin).

Scott, J (2001) *Power* (Cambridge: Polity).

Scottish Executive Central Research Unit (2000) *Assessment of Innovative Approaches to Testing Community Opinion* (Edinburgh: Scottish Executive).

Scottish Office (1997) *Scotland's Parliament* (London: Stationery Office).

Science and Technology Select Committee (2002) *Fourth Report – Developments in Human Genetics and Embryology* (London: House of Commons).

Seebohm Committee (1968) *Report of the Committee on Local Authority and Allied Personal Social Services* (London: HMSO).

Silcock, R (2001) 'What is e-Government?', *Parliamentary Affairs*, vol. 54, pp. 88–101.

Simon, H (1957 [1945]) *Administrative Behaviour* (New York: Free Press).

Simon, H (1960) *The New Science of Management Decision* (Englewood Cliffs, NJ: Prentice Hall).

Skelcher, C (1998) *The Appointed State: Quasi-Governmental Organisations and Democracy* (Buckingham: Open University Press).

Smith, M J (1999) *The Core Executive in Britain* (London: Macmillan).

Social Exclusion Unit (1998) *Bringing Britain Together: A National Strategy for Neighbourhood Renewal* (London: Cabinet Office).

Stewart, J (1995) 'Appointed Boards and Local Government', in F F Ridley and D Wilson (eds) *The Quango Debate* (Oxford: Oxford University Press).

Stewart, J (1999) 'Modernising Government Considered', *Local Governance*, vol. 25, pp. 3–12.

Stewart, J (2000a) *The Nature of British Local Government* (London: Macmillan).

Stewart, J (2000b) 'Beacon Councils', *Local Governance*, vol. 26, pp. 205–9.

Stewart, J and Stoker, G (1995a) 'Fifteen Years of Local Government Restructuring, 1979–1994: An Evaluation' in J Stewart and G Stoker (eds) *Local Government in the 1990s* (London: Macmillan).

Stewart, J and Stoker, G (eds) (1995b) *Local Government in the 1990s* (London: Macmillan).

Stoker, G (1989) 'Creating a Local Government for a Post-Fordist Society: The Thatcher Project' in G Stoker and J Stewart (eds) *The Future of Local Government* (London: Macmillan).

Stoker, G (1991) *The Politics of Local Government* (London: Macmillan).

Stoker, G (1995) 'Regime Theory and Urban Politics' in D Judge, G Stoker and H Wolman (eds) *Theories of Urban Politics* (London: Sage).

Stoker, G (2000a) 'Introduction' in G Stoker (ed.) *The New Politics of British Local Governance* (London: Macmillan).

Stoker, G (ed.) (2000b) *The New Politics of British Local Governance* (London: Macmillan).

Stone, C (1989) *Regime Politics: Governing Atlanta, 1946–1988* (Lawrence, KS: University Press of Kansas).

Stone, C (2001) 'The Atlanta Experience Re-examined: The Link between Agenda and Regime Change', *International Journal of Urban and Regional Research*, vol. 25, pp. 20–34.

Straw, J (2000) 'Human Rights and Personal Responsibility – a New Citizenship for a New Millenium', speech given at St Paul's Cathedral, London, 2 October (London: Home Office).

Taylor, I (2000) 'Local Government under New Labour: Enabling or Enabled?', *Local Governance*, vol. 26, pp. 39–46.

Tomlinson, M (2002) *Inquiry into A-Level Standards* (London: Department for Education and Skills).

Townsend, P (1979) *Poverty in the United Kingdom* (Harmondsworth: Penguin).

Trowler, P (1998) *Education Policy* (Eastbourne: Gildredge).

Tullock, G (ed.) (1976) *The Vote Motive* (London: Institute of Economic Affairs).

Tullock, G (1988) *Wealth, Poverty and Politics* (London: Blackwell).

Tullock, G (1993) 'The Economic Theory of Bureaucracy' in M Hill (ed.) *The Policy Process: A Reader* (Hemel Hempstead: Harvester Wheatsheaf).

Walker, A (1983) 'Social Policy, Administration and the Construction of Welfare' in M Loney, D Boswell and J Clarke (eds) *Social Policy and Social Welfare* (Milton Keynes: Open University Press).

Walker, D (2002) 'Stand by your Beds', *Guardian*, 6 May.

Wann, M (1995) *Building Social Capital: Self Help in a Twenty-First Century Welfare State* (London: Institute for Public Policy Research).

Wassof, F and Hill, M (2002) 'Family Policy in Scotland', *Social Policy and Society*, vol. 1, pp. 171–82.

Weir, S and Hall, W (1994) *EGO TRIP: Extra Governmental Organisations in the United Kingdom and their Accountability* (London: Charter 88 Trust).

Whelan, R (ed.) (1999) *Involuntary Action: How Voluntary is the 'Voluntary' Sector?* (London: Institute of Economic Affairs).

Whiteley, P and Winyard, S (1984) 'The Origins of the "New Poverty Lobby"', *Political Studies*, vol. 32, pp. 32–54.

Whiteley, P and Winyard, S (1988) 'The Poverty Lobby in British Politics', *Parliamentary Affairs*, vol. 41, pp. 195–208.

Williams, F (1989) *Social Policy: A Critical Introduction* (Cambridge: Polity).

Wilson, D (1995) 'Elected Local Government and Central–Local Relations' in R Pyper and L Robins (eds) *Governing in the UK in the 1990s* (Basingstoke: Macmillan).

Wilson, D and Game, C (1998) *Local Government in the United Kingdom* (London: Macmillan).

Wilson, D and Game, C (2002) *Local Government in the United Kingdom* (London: Macmillan).

Wirt, F and Harman, G (eds) *Education, the Recession and the World Village* (Philadelphia, PA: Falmer).

Wistow, G (1992) 'The Health Service Policy Community' in R A W Rhodes and D Marsh (eds) *Policy Networks in British Government* (Oxford: Clarendon).

Woodhouse, D (1998) 'The Judiciary in the 1990s: Guardian of the Welfare State?' *Policy and Politics*, vol. 26, pp. 457–70.

Wright, A (1994) 'The Quango Quagmire', *Guardian*, 23 May.

Wright Mills, C (1956) *The Power Elite* (New York: Oxford University Press).

Wyatt, M (2002) 'Partnership in Health and Social Care: The Implications of Government Guidance in the 1990s in England, with Particular Reference to Voluntary Organisations', *Policy and Politics*, vol. 30, pp. 167–82.

Index